I0605362

SPIRITUAL HYGIENE

Other books by Iyanla Vanzant

Every Day I Pray
Living Through the Meantime
Until Today!
Yesterday, I Cried
Don't Give It Away!
In the Meantime
One Day My Soul Just Opened Up
Faith in the Valley
The Value in the Valley
Acts of Faith

Iyanla Vanzant

SPIRITUAL HYGIENE

A PRACTICAL PATH FOR CLEAN LIVING, INNER AUTHORITY, AND DIVINE FREEDOM

ATRIA BOOKS

NEW YORK AMSTERDAM/ANTWERP LONDON
TORONTO SYDNEY/MELBOURNE NEW DELHI

An Imprint of Simon & Schuster, LLC
1230 Avenue of the Americas
New York, NY 10020

In telling individuals' stories, the author has provided illustrative examples, changing names and some identifying details as well as creating composites.

First Atria Books hardcover edition December 2025

ATRIA BOOKS and colophon are trademarks of Simon & Schuster, LLC

Interior design by Davina Mock-Maniscalco
Sigil creator - Lee Didco - SoulLee Connected

Manufactured in the United States of America

1 3 5 7 9 10 8 6 4 2

The Library of Congress Cataloging-in-Publication Data has been applied for.

ISBN 978-1-6682-1412-1
ISBN 978-1-6682-1408-4 (ebook)

This offering is dedicated to
Nisa Camille Vanzant
Omo Obatala Emi'Olade

and

Carolyn Reidy
Thank you for seeing in me what I did not
and could not see in myself.
In honor of your name and love . . .

*"May this offering move on the wings of your light
into the hands and hearts that need it most.*

May every page ripple with healing.

*May every soul who touches this work remember their radiance,
reclaim their power, and rise in wholeness.*

*May the one who birthed this work be continually replenished,
protected, and honored for the gift released into the world."*

With reverence and gratitude always.
A'mari El'Naiya *(known to the world as Iyanla)*

Contents

INTRODUCTION: Your Sacred Responsibility 1

LEVEL I—Healing 5

CHAPTER 1: The Throne of Thought 11
Self-Reflection 24

CHAPTER 2: Breaking Through the Smog 29

CHAPTER 3: The Mirror Doesn't Lie: *The Sacred Work of Self-Honesty* 51

CHAPTER 4: Voice of Trauma Splinters into Survival Selves 66

CHAPTER 5: Permission to Grieve: *A Sacred Invitation into the Final Door of Healing* 87
Grief Reflection Page: *A Sacred Space to Feel, Remember, and Release* 100
A Sacred Encounter with What Was Lost 101
Ceremony of Mourning and Release: *A Sacred Ritual to Cleanse the Heart and Honor the Loss* 104
Healing 108

LEVEL II—Soul Cleansing and Detoxification: *A Sacred Descent into the Body* 111

CHAPTER 6: The Holy Unbinding: *Allowing the Body to Speak* 117
The Wisdom of the Body 130

CHAPTER 7: Cleansing the Inner Atmosphere 143

CHAPTER 8: Unbinding the Bloodline: *Cleansing Trauma Patterns and Ancestral Residue* 154

CHAPTER 9: Restoring Physical and Emotional Rhythm 177

The Bridge—Key Teachings on Level I and Level II: *A Descent into Sacred Alignment* 192

LEVEL III—Reclaiming the Sacred Self 197

CHAPTER 10: Spiritual Responsibility: *The Call to Reclaim the Sacred Self* 203

Final Reflection 214

CHAPTER 11: Finding Your Center: *Returning to Your Spiritual Core* 218

CHAPTER 12: When the Core Cracks: *Unforgiveness, Misalignment, and the Cost of Spiritual Neglect* 238

CHAPTER 13: Whole, Holy, and Home: *Living from Your Core* 251

CHAPTER 14: The Sacred No: *The Sound of Self-Protection* 262

LEVEL III CONCLUSION/LEVEL IV INTRODUCTION: The Sacred Return: *A Reclamation of Self* 273

CHAPTER 15: Spiritual Hygiene for Parenting 279

CHAPTER 16: Spiritual Hygiene for Relationships: *Clearing the Mirror, Honoring the Bond* 299

CHAPTER 17: Spiritual Hygiene in the Workplace: *The Sacred Art of Alignment in Professional Environments* 314

FINAL WORD: Living the Way of Spiritual Hygiene: *A Benediction. A Commission. A Sacred Return.* 336

CONCLUSION: Living Clean: *And So, It Shall Be.* 337

Glossary of Spiritual Principles and Sacred Concepts 340

Welcome Beloved One,

Welcome to this sacred space of healing, remembering, and a deep inner truth.

What you are holding in your hands is so much more than a collection of bound pages. The topics, insights, and teachings within these pages are tools offered to support you in clearing away what is heavy, preparing you to return to what is holy, and connecting you to all that is aligned with the highest version of yourself.

We live in a world that clamors for our attention, feeds our fear, and teaches us to forget our sacred nature. I pray you will discover and receive this offering as a Divine call to return: to slow down, to feel again, to choose clarity over clutter, alignment over chaos, and spiritual power over people-pleasing, ego-gratifying performance, and insatiable external validation-seeking.

In all that is presented, all that I will share, and all that we will explore, you are not asked or expected to be perfect. You are simply invited to be *present*. Present with the words. Present with your own needs and desires. Present with the places within you and in your life that are calling out for peace, the places that require some tender loving care and attention. Also, I invite you to be fully present with the greater possibility that can and will unfold with the practices of good Spiritual Hygiene.

As you explore, examine, and contemplate what is offered within these pages, be on the lookout for gentle invitations:

- To speak your truth
- To reclaim the parts of yourself that may have been lost

- To release what was never yours
- And to fully embody your identity as the clean, clear vessel of Divine presence that you came here to be

Take your time with every page, inquiry, and practice. Trust your internal rhythm of knowing what to do and what you may not be ready for . . . yet. Receive what you can and leave what feels like too much for later. Let these pages serve as a mirror, a medicine chest, and a Divine map guiding you on a sacred journey.

I am so honored to walk with you.

With clarity. In courage. With sacred commitment and love.

I Am,
A'mari El'Naiya–known to the world as Iyanla

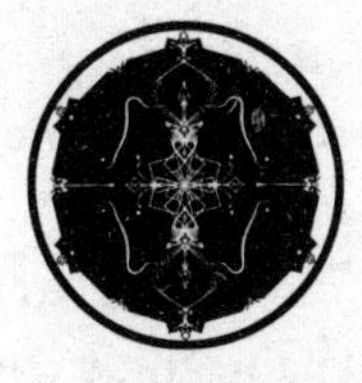

INTRODUCTION

Your Sacred Responsibility

There comes a time on our individual path of spiritual evolution when lighting a candle to feel grounded is no longer enough. You brush your teeth and wash your body every single day to prevent disease and stay clean. But what do you do every day to heal your soul?

At some point, you will realize that healing does not come just from what you do, but from what you're willing to face.

You will face a pivotal moment when your soul begins to ache, not because you have done something wrong, but because it's time to return to your essence. That essence is innocent. That essence is pure. When I look around the world today, I sense that this is that time. We live in a world that demands our attention, steals our breath, and teaches us to forget who we really are. We are conditioned to perform rather than feel. To pretend we are OK instead of doing the work required to be OK. Unfortunately, you cannot decorate internal debris. You cannot pray away the pain you deny or the mental chatter you won't face. You cannot shift, change, grow, evolve, or heal if you are dragging the weight of what you have not cleansed or released. Having learned this the hard way, I now know with every fiber of my being that Spiritual Hygiene matters.

I think of Spiritual Hygiene as the daily, sacred devotion of clearing your inner space. It is the loving commitment to honoring your thoughts, emotions, energy, and soul with the same reverence you give to your sacred belongings. Your mind is an altar. Your heart is a temple. Your presence is holy. And sometimes, the most powerful revelations come through your deepest pain.

I had once lived there too. In the trenches of fear and survival. Over time, with practice and pain, guided by Spirit, I gradually climbed my way into a different consciousness. I discovered a world where everything is energy, and nothing is *personal.* I entered a higher level of spiritual consciousness, where love doesn't need to be earned or proven. Where you know deep in your bones that you are a soul, not just a body. I learned that you can delay, deny, resist, and avoid healing, but you cannot fail at it because healing is real, and forgiveness is freedom.

I am not where I am today because I'm better, stronger, or more talented than you or anyone else is. I'm here because I choose, moment by moment, day after day, to practice Spiritual Hygiene. To cleanse the debris of what I have encountered and endured throughout my life with forgiveness.

Our physical world is collapsing. What once worked to keep us safe is no longer effective for moving forward. But our spiritually energetic world is rising. The spiritual world beckons us to question most of what we have been taught. Some of us, as teachers and lightworkers, are building bridges between the two depths of life and understanding. Some are still stuck in the rubble. As I began to prepare to write this book, I reviewed my own life. I examined my thoughts, emotions, regrets, and practices. I realized how essential this work is not just for our peace, but for our survival, the survival of this world we all love.

Whether you are new to this type of work or returning to what your soul has always known, these pages are for you. I pray that what I share here will become your sacred yes. I invite you to allow one moment of one thing you read on these pages to be the moment you choose clarity over confusion, alignment over exhaustion, and Divine presence over performance. Do you want to feel inspired again, like everything you do is in step with your Divine purpose? Do you want to feel authentically connected to both your inner truth and a community that supports you? Do you want to find joy in the small things you experience every day? Let this truth be your invitation: *You can choose a different reality.* You can rise above anything and everything. You can cleanse your mind and heart because your soul was never soiled. You can remember who you truly are. And when you do, not only will you be free, but your presence demonstrates to others that it is possible for them to choose freedom too.

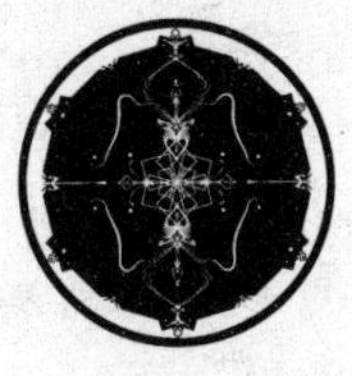

LEVEL I

HEALING

You are here because a part of you remembers the truth. The light in you is still intact. The voice of the Divine within you is still sacred. The soul in you is still willing. It is your soul that is guiding you toward a sacred return to the truth of your being, and this stage on the path of Spiritual Hygiene, which is healing. This means you must be willing to give yourself permission to slow down, to listen within, and to acknowledge the temple you are. This is not the end of your struggle. It is the beginning of your sovereignty.

Let us walk with clarity toward what you will encounter at this stage of the journey, and what you will be asked to do along the way. We begin with a definition of healing, what it entails, and the potential results that can occur when you commit to engaging in a healing process.

For the purpose of Spiritual Hygiene, healing means remembering what was forgotten, restoring what was lost, and realigning what was distorted within the sanctuary of your own being. It is a return to wholeness in which your mind, heart, and soul express naturally and freely through your physical body. True healing is not the act of erasing wounds or pretending that your pain does not exist. Healing, in this context, is the holy work of becoming aware of what you carry, honoring its impact, and releasing what no longer serves your Divine unfolding. It is the clearing of energetic residue from inherited pain, internalized shame, and emotional clutter. It is learning to hear your own soul again, through the noise of anger, guilt, and shame. It is releasing the masks you wear, the roles you have played, and the defenses you have engaged to keep yourself safe. Healing is not arriving anywhere. It is a rhythm you live within. A sacred return to mental and emotional clarity, to your authentic presence, and to the truth of your soul. Healing is the soil in which Spiritual Hygiene begins.

To activate the healing process, you must first awaken to the need for healing. This means recognizing that the mind, your inner Throne of Thought, belief, and perception, has been occupied by unexamined narratives, inherited fear, internalized judgment, and reactive survival patterns. It means becoming aware of the mental noise that drowns out inner wisdom, the self-talk that reinforces shame, and the illusions that keep you stuck in a cycle of confusion and control.

Awakening to the need for healing is not about blaming yourself for your thoughts. It is about reclaiming your authority over them. The work you will encounter at this stage invites you to sit upon the throne of your own mind, not as a ruler driven by fear, but as a steward of sacred clarity. It is here that you will begin the practice of observing, naming, and gently cleansing the mental debris that has clouded your vision and dulled your power. Healing does not begin when the pain ends. It begins when the patterns are seen, acknowledged, and accepted. Only then can they be blessed for the safety they provided and released for something grander.

In Level I, you will be introduced to the four pillars of awakening to the need for healing:

> Self-Awareness: *"What am I thinking and feeling?"*
>
> Self-Honesty: *"Am I telling myself the truth?"*
>
> Energetic Responsibility: *"What am I allowing to occupy my mental and emotional fields?"*
>
> Permission to Grieve: *"What have I not yet allowed myself to feel?"*

As you move through the sacred process of becoming aware, you will begin to notice the subtle (*and sometimes not-so-subtle*) patterns that govern your thoughts, emotions, reactions, and choices. This is the work of Self-Awareness, the first pillar of this journey. Awareness is not about self-blame. It is about sacred noticing. You cannot cleanse what you do not see. You cannot heal what you are not yet willing to feel. But awareness alone is not enough. You will also be called, gently and compassionately, to become honest:

- Honest with yourself about what you think and why you think it.
- Honest about what you're holding that doesn't belong to you.
- Honest about how you're really doing, beneath the roles and routines.
- Honest about what's no longer sustainable, even if it used to work.

This is the second pillar: Self-Honesty, the courageous tool that clears the fog from the mind and the clutter from the heart. Without honesty, your awareness cannot find its foundation in reality. Honesty is the clearing blade and the sacred broom. It sweeps away the false narratives, the outdated masks, and the emotional debris that block your vision. As the mental fog lifts and the emotional clutter is removed, something extraordinary begins to happen: *Your energy expands.* This expansion is not just a feeling. It is a shift in frequency, an opening of your inner space. With this expansion comes Energetic Responsibility, the third pillar. No longer ruled by emotional reactivity or unconscious thought patterns, you begin to choose what stays and what goes. You become the gatekeeper of your internal world.

With this newfound space, this breath of clarity, comes the deepest invitation of Level I: Permission to Grieve. This is the fourth and often most tender pillar. Once you see and tell the truth, you must give yourself permission to feel the impact of what you've been carrying, suppressing, or ignoring. You grieve not to fall apart, but to come back together, to make space for joy, clarity, and peace; in other words, clean living. You are free from the past, open to the present, prepared and preparing for what you now choose to create and experience, and you are doing this with a clean slate. In this way, the four pillars of Level I are not linear steps. They are a living spiral, a sacred internal rhythm:

- Awareness opens your eyes.
- Honesty clears your lens.
- Energetic responsibility stabilizes your field.
- Grief purifies your heart.

With each turn of this spiral, your inner light returns. Your clarity sharpens. Your patterns reveal their value and their teachings, so that finally, your soul can breathe. This is the foundation of Spiritual Hygiene: to clear what clutters your sacred inner space so that you can live, lead, and love from truth.

These four pillars are also principles and tools for reflection. Consider them to be living gateways that will support you in naming, feeling, and clearing what has clouded your mind and polluted your emotional field. You will be asked to name your fog, identify your patterns, and allow yourself to know and feel the truth about what is and has been going on within you. This information is essential for your preparation to enter Level II, the cleansing stage.

OPENING PRAYER

Beloved Presence of All That Is,
Anchor me now in Your peace and perfect wisdom.

Today, I call forth the sacred flame of courage.
Not the absence of fear, but the holy willingness
to move forward anyway.
Let courage rise in me like the morning sun,
warming every place within me that feels uncertain or afraid.

Divine Light of truth,
I ask that you clear my mind.
Wash away the fog of confusion, the heaviness of doubt,
and the noise of every voice that does not belong to me.
Make my thoughts clear, focused, and honorable.
Help me to see with spiritual eyes, so that I will choose
with sacred discernment.
Guide me to speak only what is rooted in integrity and love.

I open my hands and my heart now, ready to receive Divine instruction
so that I will walk in alignment toward my greater good.
Guide me. Strengthen me. Clarify everything I hold in my mind.

May every step I take today be a step toward truth and peace
and my own divinity.
I Ask. I Allow. I Accept.
Amen. Aṣẹ Aho.

And so, it is.

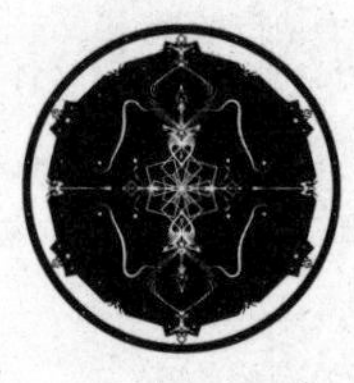

CHAPTER 1

The Throne of Thought

In every soul's journey, there comes a time when personal healing, growth, and development are no longer a luxury. It becomes a lifeline. A moment when suffering, survival, performance, and pretense begin to crack under the weight of unspoken fear, guilt, sorrow, and unresolved wounds.

This chapter begins with one such moment.

One day in the mid 1970s, I decided I was going to take my life. I was twenty-one years old, caring for a six-week-old baby and my two other young children. It was a Friday, and my husband had promised us that we were going to move, to a bigger place where we could thrive as a family. I sat there all night waiting for the moving van because he said he'd done all this stuff to prepare. But it didn't come, and neither did he. The next day, I scooped up all three of my kids and jumped in a cab from East New York to Flatbush to talk to the landlord myself. I asked if we could move in on Monday.

He looked at me like I had sixty heads and said, "I don't know what you're talking about. Your husband never came back to sign the lease." I had been struggling with postpartum depression, but when I realized the impact and implication of him lying to me, it pushed me over the edge. How could I go on like that?

My husband was asthmatic, so he had all kinds of pills. I swallowed them all, everything I could get my hands on.

I was losing consciousness in the kitchen, when I found myself on the floor. Then I had what I can only call a visitation.

I heard a voice say, clearly, *"Do you want to die, or do you want to stop hurting?"*

And I said, *"I want to stop hurting."*

And then the voice said, *"You hurt because you don't know how to live."*

Later, in the psychiatric ward, after they pumped my stomach, I asked the nurses for paper. I wrote down all the questions and thoughts that had been festering in my heart. My prayers and pain spilled out on the page. That's how I started conversing with God. I realized that I did want to live, but for it to stop hurting, everything had to change.

That was my first flicker of self-awareness, the first step of Spiritual Hygiene.

But as you'll see on these pages, healing myself wasn't a straightforward process. To fully embody my life and become present for myself every day, I still had so much to learn. So my question for you is: Do you know how you want to live? Do you want to stop hurting? What do you want from *your* life? Understanding how your mind is shaping your daily experiences is the only way to begin to understand.

Some things happen to us. Some things happen for us. Other things happen around us and leave a lasting impact on who we are, and how we approach our life. If you have ever been in an airplane that suddenly flies into turbulence, you have an idea of the impact the environment plays on your mental and emotional state of being. The apple juice is on your tray. You are digging in the bag to get those last few pretzel crumbs when suddenly, everything goes flying in the air. The juice has spilled out onto the tray and your lap. In your efforts to catch your cup of juice, you have dropped the pretzel crumbs onto the tray and your neighboring passenger. Everything in the plane has been affected by what is going on outside of the plane. Everything within you is reacting to what has impacted the plane.

Thoughts are not merely fleeting ideas; they are energetic seeds that can create emotional needs. Every thought, whether you are conscious of it or not, carries a vibration that influences your perception, feelings, and responses, and contributes to creating your reality. The mind is the space where the energy of your thoughts takes form. Thoughts lay the foundation of your belief system, which then shapes your perceptions of possibility.

Taking care of your mind is like cleaning a cluttered room. It means slowing down and looking at everything and evaluating what to keep and what to throw away. Do you really need this? Does this really reflect who you are? That's how it is when you consider the hundreds of conflicting thoughts crowding your mind. You become aware of every idea and ask yourself: *"Is what I'm holding in my mind actually true?"* When you discover that a thought you are having or holding is not true or productive, you can choose to have another thought that will help you grow into the best version of yourself. Without this level of awareness, you will constantly react to external events that trigger internal energy. This concept is crucial for good mental hygiene because shifting perspectives requires recognizing what affects the mind, and what occurs in the mind, which is revealed as what you are experiencing in life. I call this process Spiritual Hygiene because it's a practice that must become part of your everyday life. To be effective, it should become part of the bedrock of who you are.

In the years following my own awakening, I devoted a considerable amount of time to refining my spiritual practice. It wasn't a direct process, and I fell short many times, but at some point I thought I'd gotten through it. I thought I had discovered a better way to live, which I'd imparted to my children. But as it turned out, it was not that simple.

Through the story of my Beloved daughter Nisa, I offer not only a window into the fragility of the human heart but a doorway into the sacred necessity of tending to the mind, our inner throne.

Tending to your mind, the seat of the Divine's creative source energy, is a privilege. Yet the only way you will benefit from having that privilege is through the practice of awareness; awareness of who you are and how to stand in for, and as, your true, authentic self.

As a little girl, Nisa was both angry and imaginative. Brilliant and misunderstood. She seemed to always want something that I or the world did not have to give.

Nisa's love language was words and gestures of affirmation. She needed constant hugging. Constant kissing. Constant reassurance.

She needed affection. But for the bulk of her childhood, I was "*neck-down-dead*," a condition I will explain in detail later in these pages. I didn't know how to give her what she needed in the way she needed it. This was in part because I had never received it, in part because I had denied giving it to myself. To add salt to her wounds, I was exhausted most of the time during her younger years—mentally, emotionally, and physically drained. I did the best I could to feed, clothe, and shelter my three children after ending a long-term abusive relationship. I focused on giving my children things: the things I never had, the things I *thought* they needed. The only thing Nisa wanted and needed was to sit in my lap, to feel my hand stroking her face as she listened to my heartbeat. Unfortunately, when Nisa was a child, my lap was filled with my own unhealed stuff.

Nisa grew up to be both beautiful and quick-witted, the kind of woman who could turn a trip to the grocery store into a party, a family gathering into a comedy show.

She led from her intuition and lived from her heart. She worked for several years as a home health-care aide for a three-hundred-pound patient with dementia. Nisa said that no one in the family could move her, and when no one would help, Nisa hoisted her from the hospital bed into her wheelchair by herself. On holidays and when the family she worked for went on vacation, they took Nisa with them, treating her as if she were family. If I was exhausted and ready to wrap work for the day making my body-care products, Nisa would keep grinding, hand-crushing black soap and straining essential oils until the work was done.

But when it came to the needs of her own heart and spirit, Nisa turned a blind eye to them. And as her mother and a long-time spiritual teacher, as close as we could be, I always came up short in her eyes.

Mama Cannot Know Best . . . All the Time

Most, if not all, mothers know about deep pain related to their children because there comes a time in a mother's life when love alone isn't enough, when words run out, when even prayer feels like throwing stones into a storm. That was me. That was us. My daughter Nisa and

I. We loved each other. Fiercely. But we lived in different worlds. She lived in a world of hard edges. A world where survival was the goal, pain was familiar, and love always had a price. That was her reality, where everything was physical, separate, and fixed. She believed in suffering as if it were her birthright. Believed in betrayal like it was gravity. Nisa believed that if love didn't hurt, it wasn't real. She was a millennial, a member of a generation that was either taught or somehow learned to wear trauma and abuse like badges of courage. They seem to idolize what is wrong, with no awareness that trauma, abuse, and dysfunction are spiritual pollutants that are often in competition with emotional denial and mental resistance. I acknowledge that my generation and those right below me were conditioned to perform rather than feel. We were actually taught to pretend we are OK instead of doing the work required to be OK.

Knowing and Not Knowing: A Mother's Two Realities

In the material realm, Nisa was a diabetic who didn't tend to her condition or care for her basic needs. In the spiritual realm, she was desolate and disconnected from her core. I knew she was going to die. The spiritual technician within me, a spiritually centered teacher, had seen it coming over the course of about two and a half years. That part of me had come to a place of somber but quiet acceptance. My soul was at peace, but the mother in me . . . She was hysterical! She was heartbroken. Devastated. And desperate. I remember the day I called a dear friend, a former student, in a complete and total breakdown. I had wept to the point of nausea and vomiting. I heard myself repeating:

> *"I cannot bury another child! I just cannot do it! Why would God ask me to do it? I just can't."*

All she could say was *"I know Iya. I know."* When I was calm enough to speak without babbling, we devised a plan, a plan that we hoped would help my baby girl get on the track to wellness and well-being. Unfortunately, we made our plan without consulting or including my daughter. When it comes to good Spiritual Hygiene for the mind and heart, planning for others never works out well for anyone involved. As if I needed evidence of what I already knew, none of what I had planned for happened the way I thought it would. The physical cause of Nisa's death was sepsis. She was resistant to all medical advice. She even refused available alternative methods that could have facilitated her mental, emotional, and physical healing. She broke her ankle during COVID. As is common with many diabetics, the break did not heal. It also required three surgeries to set and reset the bone. Each surgical intervention required more time to heal, which kept her in a cast for more than two years. During the healing process, one of her toes became infected. The doctors said they would have to scrape the bone and possibly remove one or more of her toes. She wanted time to think about it. The doctor was clear that if she did not address the toe quickly, it would not have a good outcome. I asked her what she thought that meant, if she understood what would happen if she didn't act. I will never forget her words.

She said, *"I'll die."*

When I asked her if that was what she wanted to do, her response was,

> *"I have nothing to live for. And I cannot live without toes. How do you expect me to walk without toes?"*

That was not a response. It was a declaration of despair. I wanted to scream at her: *You are not your toes! You are not your pain! You are not your past!*

How Your Thoughts Can Infect Generations

I did not practice good Spiritual Hygiene on any level when I was pregnant with Nisa. I lived in a hard-edged reality. I believed I was doing my best, or at least what I thought was sufficient. For instance, I knew enough to quit smoking when I discovered I was pregnant, but I lacked the courage and emotional strength to remove myself from the toxic and abusive relationship with her father. My choices were driven by survival and fear rather than a deeper understanding of emotional well-being or self-care. Back then, though I checked in with my spirit sporadically, I didn't realize that maintaining my own mental health and emotional stability was not just beneficial for me but crucial for the tiny life growing inside me. Instead of prioritizing peace, I found myself trapped in cycles of emotional chaos, unaware of how these waves of stress and fear could ripple down to Nisa, shaping her even before she took her first breath.

I also underestimated how deeply a mother's inner world, her thoughts, fears, joys, and pain influence the unborn child she carries. Without realizing it, I allowed fear and insecurity to seep into the bond I was creating with Nisa. At the time, I was blind to the silent witness she was becoming to my emotional struggles. It wasn't until much later that I looked back and recognized how much of her spirit and personality reflected the woman I had been during my pregnancy; a woman yearning for acceptance and love who was deeply entrenched in a sea of turbulence.

The Mirror Talks Back

The impact of our mental and emotional inheritance is a truth that often eludes us until its echoes reverberate in unexpected ways. When Nisa was born, she carried more than just the genetic markers of her father and me; she carried fragments of my lack of self-awareness, my unresolved fears, my unspoken guilt, and the turbulent waves of chaos and insecurity that had shaped me during my crucial months of creation. It is as though the bond between a mother and child exists beyond the physical realm, weaving elements of spirit and emotion into the fabric of a new life.

I began to see glimpses of myself in Nisa, not just in her eyes or smile, but in her emotional responses and behaviors when she was about two years old. Her moments of joy mirrored the fleeting happiness I had felt during my life, while her struggles often reflected the shadows of fear, loneliness, and worthlessness I had failed to unpack. It was a realization that felt both heavy and urgent: The inner world I failed to nurture had left an imprint on hers. In the process of my own healing and introspection, I started to explore the concept of mental, emotional, and spiritual healing more deeply. It became evident that cultivating mental clarity and emotional stability was more than just an act of self-care; it was an act of love and responsibility for those I had birthed into the world. Each thought I had, every fear I harbored, had been a silent message to Nisa that she outlived until her last days on earth. It was a language she absorbed before she ever learned to speak. While I could not rewrite the past, or undo anything we had experienced, I understood the importance of shaping the present for both of us with a clear intention, commitment, and loving care.

As I learned to recognize the power of my thoughts to create reality, I started to practice holding space for my children. This meant allowing myself to feel, to grieve the mistakes of the past, and to celebrate even the smallest steps toward a more peaceful mind. Over time, my emotional landscape softened, and I began to appreciate that transformation, both for myself and for my children, was not a destination, but a continuous unfolding, a journey shaped by attention, intention, and the courage to say yes to the light, even in the presence of shadow. This profound realization brought me to the understanding that while I could not undo the threads already woven into the fabric of my daughter's spirit, I could begin weaving new patterns of hope, healing, and clarity. The journey toward this shift was neither linear nor simple; it demanded an unflinching gaze into my own soul and a willingness to excavate the stories I had long buried that Nisa was now living out.

By examining the thoughts that dictated my actions, I began to see them for what they truly were: constructs of fear and survival that not only defined me but also served as the blueprint of my relationships and life. Instinctively, I knew that my mental cleansing would not only lighten my heart but also create a healing atmosphere for the bond I shared with all my children. Each day became an opportunity for me to rewrite my mental scripts, not just for myself but for the legacy my children would create. The practice of holding on to thoughts that served me and releasing those that caused me mental confusion and emotional harm became my way of recalibrating the unseen dynamics of my relationships with both of my daughters. It revealed a truth so simple yet profound: The energy we carry within not only shapes our lives, but it also impacts, affects, or infects those who move within our emotional ecosystem.

You cannot think or live for other people. Not only is it poor Spiritual Hygiene, but it is a disrespectful act that causes you mental fog and emotional clutter, and which obscured my own path to the truth. Without self-awareness, the first step in Spiritual Hygiene, you will not be conscious of or connected to the thoughts you are thinking, the narratives you are repeating, or the beliefs you are silently obeying.

Self-awareness teaches you how to ask:

"Am I seeing clearly or through the lens of pain?"

"Am I trying to control, fix, or rescue?"

"Am I projecting my beliefs onto someone else's soul journey?"

"Am I present enough to sit with what is, instead of insisting on what should be?"

The Spiritual Hygiene of self-awareness is not just about noticing your thoughts; it is also about feeling your feelings with honesty and tenderness. I had to learn to sit with my helplessness. To admit my rage. To befriend my own pain. I had to stop pretending that prayer and planning were enough to override my daughter's right to choose her path because I disagreed with her choice. This is hard spiritual work. It is the hygiene of humility.

The Throne of Thought

In our everyday reality, the concept of a throne is something we are all familiar with. A commonly accepted definition of a throne would be:

A seat of power and authority, symbolizing the place from which decisions are made, rulership is exercised, and order is established.

In the spiritual context, however, the throne represents the inner seat of dominion within the mind, heart, or soul, where Divine truth or distortion can reign. The Throne of Thought is the energy created within and through your mind. The energy that pervades your life is the demonstration and manifestation of how and what you think.

As an aspect of Spiritual Hygiene for the mind, the Throne of Thought is the sacred seat of consciousness within the mind where beliefs are crowned, perceptions are enthroned, and inner narratives govern our reality. Like a royal seat, whatever occupies this throne has ultimate authority over your inner world, shaping how you see, feel, act, and ultimately, who you believe yourself to be. Every thought you think is more than a simple mental event. Your thoughts are the seeds of creation. When a thought is repeated, believed, and emotionally charged, it is elevated to a position of rulership. It becomes a ruling principle, dictating what is possible, permissible, and powerful in your life.

Your soul establishes the throne of your thoughts as a sacred space within you. It is filled with Divine presence and power. It is meant to be occupied by truth, wisdom, and Divine intelligence. In response to life's events and experiences, your throne can be taken by fear, confusion, distortion, or inherited falsehoods. When this happens, the entire inner kingdom falls into disorder. Spiritual Hygiene for the mind begins by identifying who or what has taken the seat of authority in your mind.

Who or what is ruling you from within? Is it guilt? An old story of inadequacy? Inherited cultural programming? Or Divine insight and liberated thought?

Recognizing who or what rules your mental throne is how you awaken to the need for healing and develop deep self-awareness.

In Stage I of Spiritual Hygiene, the soul begins to awaken to its own contamination. As this unfolds, whether voluntarily or involuntarily because of experiences, you begin to identify the psychic debris, emotional clutter, and mental misalignments that you have been carrying unconsciously. Common signs of contamination of the Throne of Thought may be:

> You find yourself looping in worry, doubt, or harsh self-judgment.

Your decisions are based on survival, not sacred alignment.

Your inner voice is primarily critical, anxious, or defensive.

You unconsciously re-create cycles of fear or unworthiness.

You struggle to access clarity, stillness, or spiritual wisdom.

While the experience can be extremely disturbing and deeply exhausting, these are not signs of your personal failure. They are sacred invitations to cleanse your mind and reclaim your mental throne. It can begin with the simple practice of sitting quietly each morning and asking: *"Who or what is sitting on the throne of my thoughts today?"* You are the keeper of the Throne of Thought. To awaken is to take responsibility for what governs your inner world. To heal is to purify the seat of power within your mind. To experience mental and personal freedom is to allow the Divine mind within to think through you, as you, with you. Recognizing when this is happening consistently and when you are mentally blocked or congested is the essence of self-awareness.

Not All Awareness Looks the Same

Healing the loss of Nisa did not mean I needed to spend all my time looking at her. I also had to look at myself to assess my own level of self-awareness. As her mother and a teaching facilitator of healing, I sensed that what I would discover would be as profound as it would be healing. My awareness was layered with grief, Sacred Responsibility, and the silent suffering of one who carries the burden of clarity while witnessing the suffering of others.

I was deeply aware of Nisa's choices, my own reactions, and the spiritual dynamics playing out between us. I could identify what was happening, observe the energetic patterns, and discern the soul contract beneath the chaos. I recognized that this was not an ordinary sense of awareness. It was the call of my personal sovereignty and spiritual maturity. At the same time, my mental and emotional minds carried immense weight:

> The weariness of having tried so many times.
>
> The sorrow of knowing that awareness does not always translate into changed behavior.
>
> The grief of watching truth fall on ears not ready to hear.

As her mother, I was aware of my own pain, but I could not or did not have the time or space to tend to it. At the same time, being aware revealed another truth: I could see what was happening, but I could not stop it. Knowing it brought me deep sorrow. I have been in that seat many times, with many people. One of my elders told me that being aware yet powerless over another person's choice is the unique burden of being self-aware. Having done so much of my own internal work, unpacking my own pain, I really understood the lessons beneath Nisa's resistance. It was that awareness that led me into moments of overwhelming inner conflict between what I knew and what I felt. I finally had to acknowledge that I was still a human, and even spiritual and sacred awareness may come with an ache.

Over time, I have come to understand that the gift of awareness is not control, but presence. Awareness is not the authority to change the path; it is the graceful maturity to hold space for transformation. My work was not to force Nisa's light to come on, but to tend the flame of hope in my own heart, quietly, faithfully. I was called onto the throne of loving and letting go. This awareness was both humbling and liberating. It softened my judgment, deepened my compassion, and called me to a gentler form of seeing myself and others. True self-awareness is the ability to honor the mystery at the heart of every soul's unfolding.

Self-awareness is not a single light switch; it is a multi-leveled awakening, filtered through life experience, emotional readiness, soul assignments, and personal wounds.

Self-awareness is not the performance of your spiritual insight. It is the capacity to meet your inner truth, and either tend to it, or hide from it until you feel safe enough to *care-front* it. When we judge someone else's resistance, it is a sign that we have forgotten our own former fears. When we honor a person's path of readiness, even when we disagree, we become midwives, not masters of healing light and love.

Walking with my baby girl through the darkness of our shared shadows reminded me:

- You must always check who is seated on your inner throne.
- You must be willing and ready to dethrone what no longer serves.
- You must know that even when we make mistakes, we are worthy to rise again as our own rightful ruler.

When I finally stopped trying to think for Nisa, feeling for her, planning for her, and trying to pray her into my vision of who she should be, I came home to myself. That is when the real healing began. That is when the fog lifted. That is when I reclaimed the throne of my mind. When I accepted that her life had ended on her terms. It was then that I also remembered that I knew how to release and bury a child. I had already done it once, and nothing but my own thoughts could stop me from doing it again. This time, however, I would do it with grace. This time, I would do it with self-compassion. This time I was fully aware that although my baby girl had left her body, nothing and no one could remove her from my heart, and her presence in my heart need not be painful.

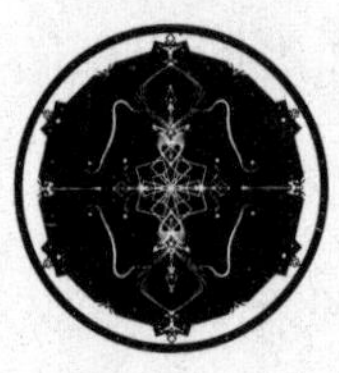

Self-Reflection

As you enter the sacred space of self-reflection, may you do so with tenderness, not judgment. If you hope to receive the full medicine of this journey, you must begin to track your own needs, not just what you think, but what you *know you must know.* This is the beginning of self-awareness: not fixing, not forcing, but simply noticing. Let these pages be a mirror and a sanctuary. Allow them to show you what is ready to be seen, honored, and gently tended within you. You can respond to these inquiries in your private journal, or on your device. Whatever you choose, you are encouraged to be fully present with yourself and the inquiry, and to honor anything and everything that comes forward. You can also bypass the inquiries now and move into the next chapter. This would mean that you are saving your personal healing until the end of the journey. This is perfectly fine; however, you are encouraged to be willing to come to the well of these inquiries if or when the journey becomes overwhelming.

1. **What part of me most deeply resonates with Nisa's pain, her resistance, or her silence?**

   "Where in my life do I choose/have I chosen despair, detachment, or denial because I didn't know how to receive love?"

2. **What part of me most resembles the mother who loved fiercely, but couldn't reach the one she loved?**

"What am I still trying to fix, prove, or plan for someone else because I haven't released control?"

3. **Where am I still rehearsing an old version of someone, holding them hostage to who they were, not who they are now?**

   "What would it mean to release that person from my expectations?"

4. **Have I been emotionally or mentally unavailable to someone I love—because of what I've not yet given to myself?**

   "What truth have I been unwilling to feel?"

5. **What is the energetic inheritance I may be passing on, unconsciously, to those I care for?**

   "What would I need to clear in my own mind or heart to shift that legacy?"

6. **What is currently sitting on the throne of my mind?**
   Reflect on the dominant thoughts, emotions, or patterns that are guiding your decisions and inner dialogue at this moment.

   "Is it fear, guilt, control, regret, or love, peace, trust?"

   "How does this influence how I treat myself and others?"

7. **Where in my life am I trying to "think" for someone else?**
   This inquiry invites a reflection on control and projection.

   "Am I carrying mental clutter by trying to fix, save, or manage someone else's journey?"

   "What would it feel like to release that role?"

   "What part of what I may project onto them is mine?"

8. **What pain or emotional imprint from my past still speaks as truth in my mind?**

Drawing from your childhood experiences of violence and silence, this question supports awareness of inherited thought patterns.

"What belief did I form during a painful moment that I now recognize as false or harmful?"

"Am I ready to lay it down?"

9. **What is one memory I've used to define myself that needs to be reexamined with compassion and clarity?**
   This invites a compassionate revisiting of a memory or story that may still color your current identity or relationships.

   "Am I ready to see that moment through the lens of growth, not shame?"

   "What does it teach me about who I have become?"

10. **What do I need to witness, feel, or admit to come home to myself?**
    This deepens the inner inquiry of self-awareness and guides you toward emotional honesty and a state of presence.

    "What part of my pain have I tried to bypass?"

    "Can I sit with it long enough to hear what it must teach me? If not, why not?"

OPENING PRAYER

Beloved Divine Presence,
Keeper of clarity, Guardian of Truth,
I enter this moment not to control, dismiss, or deny what I feel.
I enter to honor what I carry.

I call back my energy, my power,
from every place I have left it or given it away
through fear, through silence, through performance, through pain.
I gather myself with compassion.
I collect myself with courage.
I recalibrate myself as a sacred act of return.

Cleanse my field of what is not mine.
Clear my body of the memories I no longer need to hold.
Disconnect me from the voices that no longer serve.
Anoint me with the wisdom to know the difference between
what protects me and what imprisons me.

May my breath become my anchor.
May my body become my ally.
May my emotions become messengers.
May my thoughts be freed from the rules of fear and filled
with the knowing that I am Divine.

I now step into energetic responsibility, not as a job or burden,
but as a blessing.
I choose to tend to the field within me as a holy ground where truth
may live, where light may rise, and where I may remember:

I Am the keeper of my inner field.
I Am the steward of my personal power.
I Am safe to be aware, aligned, and free to choose.

Amen. Aṣẹ Aho.
And so, it is.

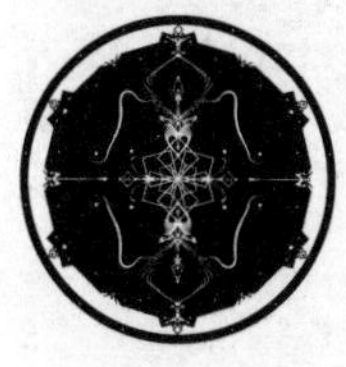

CHAPTER 2

Breaking Through the Smog

Until you become aware of what you do, how you do it, why you do it, and the consequences of doing it, you will remain enslaved to the illegitimate rulers in your Throne of Thought. The three most notorious rulers you will have to face and dethrone are mental clutter, emotional clutter, and spiritual smog. These forces do not serve your authentic identity or respect Divine authority; they distort it. Mental clutter floods the mind with noise: overthinking, worry, distractions, and inherited patterns of thought that block clarity and peace. Emotional clutter weighs down the heart with unprocessed pain, buried grief, suppressed feelings, and unresolved reactions. Spiritual smog is the invisible veil that forms when you're disconnected from your inner truth. The smog accumulates when guilt, shame, confusion, or disillusionment impedes your inner knowing.

Mental and emotional clutter remains invisible until you feel enraged, overwhelmed, or stuck. It manifests as the moments when you cannot focus, when your thoughts won't stop spinning, or when you feel stuck in loops of fear, judgment, worry, or indecision. Mental clutter is the accumulation of unprocessed thoughts, unresolved questions, outdated narratives, and inner dialogue rooted in fear, doubt, or self-judgment. It is the noise that fills your mind and heart, contaminating the mental space that is meant for Divine communion and instruction. Mental clutter may look like:

- Overthinking and overanalyzing
- Playing out worst-case scenarios
- Replaying past conversations
- Holding on to "*shoulds*," regrets, or imagined futures
- Internal contradiction between what you say you believe and how you think

The more cluttered the mind, the more difficult it is to receive Divine wisdom or spiritual insights. The voices of the past and fears become louder than the voice of truth. Mental clutter keeps you occupied with thoughts that have no power to move you forward.

When the Mind Spills into the Heart

How Mental Chaos Pollutes the Emotional Body

The mind and the heart are spiritually intertwined. A cluttered mind will infect the emotional body. A cluttered emotional field can distort your thoughts. When your mental space is unclean, the heart cannot release what it may be holding. When your emotions are backed up, the mind works overtime trying to make sense of the chaos. This is why **Spiritual Hygiene for the mind** is not just mental—it is **emotional** and **energetic**. When you clear your thoughts, your feelings have permission to soften and be noticed. When you purify your mental atmosphere, your emotional atmosphere begins to stabilize.

Emotional clutter refers to the accumulation of unprocessed feelings, repressed grief, reactivity, shame, fear, or apathy. You start to feel everything and nothing at the same time. You may find yourself emotionally fragile or emotionally numb. Emotional clutter forms when:

- You suppress emotions because they feel unsafe or inconvenient.
- You inherit and carry the emotional pain of others—family, partners, ancestors.

- You avoid emotional truth to maintain peace or prevent conflict.
- You cling to guilt, resentment, or unexpressed grief.

When the mind is cluttered with worry, your emotions cannot rest. When your emotions are clogged with unprocessed pain, your mind becomes hypervigilant, trying to create order. The two, the mind and heart, are tethered. Both are affected by the nature, quality, and consistency of your Spiritual Hygiene, or the absence of it.

The Mind Carries Dust from the Past

Emotional clutter grows every time you bite your tongue, swallow your tears, or tell yourself to "get over it" when your soul was asking to go deeper into it. It isn't always dramatic. Emotional clutter can also be quiet, subtle, and habitual:

- Smiling when you are hurting
- Suppressing what you feel because you feel unsafe or when a feeling is inconvenient
- Avoiding confrontation, even when the truth is needed
- Carrying unspoken disappointment
- Feeling resentment but not expressing it
- Volunteering (consciously or unconsciously) to carry the emotional pain of others, family, partners, ancestors, etc., because you think it is your responsibility to do so

When these emotions accumulate without a conscious and sacred release, they begin to alter your emotional landscape. You begin to lose access to joy, compassion, tenderness, and openness. You feel heavy for no reason. You feel guarded but don't know why. You find yourself overreacting, or under-responding, to real life. This is emotional clutter, and like dust in a room, it will cloud the light of truth within you.

The Original Wound and the Birth of Emotional Clutter

How Early Separation Becomes a Core Belief of Unworthiness

Emotional clutter is the active manifestation of a wound that has been left unattended. From both a psychological and spiritual perspective, the original wound refers to a rupture or severe disturbance in one's sense of safety, belonging, or Divine connection. It is a soul-deep imprint of separation that ultimately shapes our identity, beliefs, and behaviors until it is healed. For some, the wound occurs at birth. Being ejected from the womb and severed from the umbilical cord, the only known source of nourishment, destroys the sense of safety and support. For others, the wound is often the first experience of abandonment, rejection, or violation of trust that shatters a child's sense of wholeness, worth, and belonging. The experience could be:

- A parent's absence (whether emotional or physical)
- A moment of shaming or punishment for being authentically expressive
- Not being seen, heard, or loved for who they truly are, without performing to keep others comfortable or happy

Though the situation may vary, what matters most is what the child begins to believe in the moment of the experience. It is this experience that gives birth to a distorted core belief wound, like:

I am not enough. I am unlovable. I'm not worthy. I must be different to be safe. It's my fault.

Emotional clutter doesn't just impact how you feel and what you do; it also distorts your perceptions and how you see the world. It clouds your vision of yourself, others, and the Divine. Rev. Steven Furtnick, Pastor of Elevation Church, told his congregation, *"The presence of God is not where you go to bypass your feelings. It is where you go to process them because you are allowed to feel."* For this reason, hygiene for the mind and heart is considered *"spiritual"* in nature. When old emotions linger unprocessed, they become spiritual filters. You start to view love through the lens of betrayal, guidance through the lens of disappointment, and possibility through the lens of fear. In its most dangerous and damaging manifestation, emotional clutter does not stand up and shout within you. It hides behind the veil of busyness, blame, or burnout. When this happens, there are clear signs you must pay attention to:

- You feel tired, even when you have physically rested.
- You avoid silence because it feels uncomfortable.
- You struggle to access joy, softness, or peace.
- You are easily irritated or unexplainably sad.
- You have difficulty trusting others or receiving love.
- You lash out or shut down in emotionally charged situations.
- You feel numb, like you are watching your life instead of living it.

This depth of emotional clutter forms and operates in a loop.

1. A feeling arises. *You feel disappointed, afraid, or hurt.*
2. You avoid or suppress it. *"This isn't the time for that," "I cannot deal with this right now," "Let it go and move on."*
3. The feeling sinks beneath awareness. It does not leave your energy. Instead, it is *buried alive* and is stored in your emotional body.
4. The same or a similar feeling resurfaces later, in an unrelated event or experience. When it does, it is louder, more distorted, or in a moment that seems unrelated.
5. You judge yourself for feeling it. *The shame loop begins and distorts the next unpleasant feeling.*

This cycle becomes a silent, ongoing emotional weight that affects the mind. Over time, it can manifest as anxiety, depression, emotional instability, or chronic disconnection from your own heart.

Emotional Clutter Has a High Spiritual Cost

Emotional clutter does not mean you are broken. It means there is something within you that longs to be felt, heard, and freed. Unprocessed emotions block your ability to hear Divine guidance clearly. They dull your intuition and keep you attached to the memories, wounds, and trauma of the past. In the absence of mental and emotional Spiritual Hygiene, you mistake your emotional reactions for Divine revelations. You confuse fear with discernment. You spiritualize your self-protection by calling it wisdom. The truth is: You cannot embody Divine clarity if your emotional field is chaotic. You cannot be a sanctuary of light while living in the darkness of emotional congestion.

Emotional clutter is the fuel that feeds emotional dishonesty and the ways we lie to ourselves and about ourselves. The reason emotional dishonesty is so pervasive on the internal landscape of so many people in today's world is that few of us recognize the distinction between an emotion and a feeling. The two are similar, but in the realm of Spiritual Hygiene for the mind and heart, they are distinct.

The Distinction Between Feelings and Emotions

The Moment's Message vs. the Memory's Echo

As a student of *A Course in Miracles*, I am a firm believer in its teachings that ". . . there are only two emotions, love and fear." At the same time, I am aware that the average person embraces a reality that is concrete and fixed. This reality is based on what is already known, which sets the stage for what is expected and anticipated. In this third-dimensional reality, what you know *is* what is, period. It is this interpretation of reality that blurs the distinction between feelings and emotions. From the perspective of Spiritual Hygiene, giving credence and deference to traditional psychology, emotions tell the truth of the moment. Feelings carry the memory of past wounding. Every wound has a story that is waiting to be told and witnessed.

An **emotion** is a pure, instinctive, momentary signal generated by the nervous system. It is a subtle, brief, and deeply honest whisper or nudge from the soul. Emotions arise as a direct response to what is in front of you and occurring in the present moment, without the layers of interpretation or memory. They are chemical reactions triggered by your perception of what is going on. For example, you might feel a sudden tightness in your chest when someone speaks unkindly, or a flutter of warmth when you hear a child laugh. An emotion will only last a few seconds to minutes unless it is resisted or suppressed. Emotions signal, alert, protect, and connect. They are the body's first language and are not burdened with meaning or wrapped in defense. They are simply the *truth in motion, in the moment, within your being.*

Emotions are the body's way of saying, "This is what is happening in me now." When acknowledged, an emotion will rise and dissipate like a cloud passing across the sky. This is a foundational teaching of *mindfulness*, a practice of the Buddhist faith, where observing rather than engaging emotions is a path to peace. When we are spiritually clean, we can acknowledge and name an emotion, allowing it to move through our mind. When, however, we develop the practice or habit of suppressing or ignoring our emotions, especially the tender ones like grief, joy, desire, or vulnerability, they will harden and become something heavier. They become less like clouds and more like storms. When this happens, it means a feeling has begun to take root.

A **feeling** carries the echoes of unspoken stories and has a deeper energetic response, one that has been shaped by history, memory, belief, and meaning. Feelings often arise when an emotion is not fully felt or understood—they are the labels we give emotions and often come with a story attached. Unlike the momentary rise and fall of an emotion, feelings linger. They carry the echoes of wounds we have yet to heal and truths we have been unwilling to tell. Where an emotion might say, "*I'm hurt,*" a feeling will scream, *"I'm always abandoned. No one really cares about me."*

Because they are deeply connected to our experiences and stories, feelings are sacred, but they are not always reliable. They are truthful in that they reflect something real in our experience, but they are also tainted by the past. They can protect, project, and deceive you into believing what you choose to believe rather than what is true or possible. You might feel justified in your anger in the moment; however, the story, memory, and emotion underlying the current anger could be a long-standing resentment, shame, or grief that you have never felt permitted to express. You might feel uneasy around someone, and the "emotion" that arises is fear, but that emotion may not be about *them in the moment.* It may be the echo of an old story that is being triggered now, inviting you to revisit an old wound that has been reawakened. If what gets triggered is a past betrayal, rejection, or breach of safety, that emotion will be elevated into a feeling.

When we are young, we don't just witness experiences, we absorb them. When we live in environments shaped by violence, silence, chaos, or betrayal, our tender young minds form meaning from what is required to survive in those environments. We craft meaning from the ways we are treated and how we observe the interactions between those in power. Those meanings—*It's my fault, There's nothing I can do, Love is dangerous, Help won't come*—become the thought-forms that occupy the throne in the sanctuary of the mind.

They also become the emotions that leak into the sanctuary of the heart. In this way, the past becomes a sacred agreement of sorts that we are unaware we have made. As we begin to practice Spiritual Hygiene, becoming aware of our mental and emotional patterns, we can hold them up to the light of truth, and ask: "*Is this the voice of my soul—or an echo of survival?*"

Spiritual Smog: The Clouded Temple

When Clarity Is Lost and the Inner Light Is Dimmed

In the physical world, smog is defined as air pollution that reduces visibility. It is fog, made heavier by smoke and chemical fumes. In the spiritual realm, smog is an invisible haze that forms when the mind, heart, and spirit become congested with unresolved thoughts, stagnant emotions, false beliefs, energetic entanglements, and unaligned behaviors. Like pollution in the atmosphere, spiritual smog clouds your sense of inner clarity, dulls your intuitive knowing, and distorts your perception of who "*you*" are, what "*it*" is, and what you're responsible for at any given moment. I am sure that you, like me, have heard people say things like "*I just can't take it anymore.*" In those instances, the "it" is everything in or about life. Or "*I don't know what is wrong with me.*"

While they may not be able to put their finger on it, they do know that something is off. These are sure signs that their mental clutter is out of hand, their emotional clutter has become too heavy to carry, and there is spiritual smog hovering over their internal and external experience.

Spiritual smog forms when:

- You are mentally overloaded with information but are spiritually undernourished.
- You are emotionally burdened but spiritually disconnected.
- You maintain outer routines but neglect inner alignment.
- You speak spiritual language but suppress emotional truth.
- You live by reaction rather than authentic self-expression.

Like mental and emotional clutter, spiritual smog creeps into your mind and heart over time. By the time you realize that something is not quite right, the smog is showing up and out as:

- A lack of joy or inspiration
- Decision fatigue, or back-and-forth in decision-making
- Persistent doubt or confusion
- Feeling cut off from your inner guidance
- And at its worst: Isolation from the people and activities you once loved

Spiritual smog is what takes over when your **inner temple is cluttered,** but your outer life keeps moving. Stillness is replaced by people-pleasing or obligatory performance. In addition to an overwhelming yet understandable amount of mental clutter, it became quite apparent that Nisa's life had been infiltrated by spiritual smog. According to Michael J. Lincoln, PhD, in his book, *Messages from the Body: Their Psychological Meaning*, diabetes often relates to themes of disappointment, loss of control, and the need for deeper self-awareness and acceptance.

His interpretations link the physical manifestation of diabetes to the inability to process life's "sweetness" or joy. Linking it to the family, Dr. Lincoln suggests that the disease stems from the experience of not receiving the "sweetness" one deserves. It can also be seen as a call to address deeper emotional or spiritual imbalances and to find strength and meaning in faith and spirituality during the management of the condition.

The Unseen Weight of Dust and Clutter

How Emotional Congestion Becomes Emotional Dishonesty

There is a space between what we know and what we say, between what we feel and what we express. This space, often silent and swollen with unspoken truths, is where emotional dishonesty lives. The heart, when clogged with emotional dishonesty, becomes a heavy, reactive place. When this is cleared through self-awareness and self-honesty, it becomes a chalice, a holy cup of compassion, clarity, and love.

The truth must be integrated into the emotional body, into the wounded places where feelings have been muted, distorted, or buried. It must touch the crevices and chambers of the heart where sorrow has been swallowed, where joy has been suppressed, where needs have been silenced until they echo as suffering.

When the Heart Remembers: A Mother's Realization

The Places Where Our Children Reflect What We've Hidden from Ourselves

You cannot achieve true Spiritual Hygiene through truth-telling at the mental level alone. The mind may acknowledge, but it is the heart that remembers. Where the heart has been trained to lie to stay safe, truth must be reintroduced, gently, compassionately, and consistently. I did not know how to do this with Nisa. Instead of safety, I attempted to give her structure. Instead of gentle honesty, I offered her correction. I gave her rules that I believed were helpful. I learned that for her, they felt like demands for perfection. I wanted her to grow. I wanted her to succeed. I eventually came to realize that I wanted her to be OK enough to make me feel like I had done all the right things, *the perfect mother things.*

I am now aware that at first, I wanted her to make me look good as a person. Later, I wanted her to look and feel good about herself. Both unconscious needs were laced with love. They were also tinged with expectation. She felt it. She once told me, "I'll never measure up to you." I told her I had no expectations of her or for her, I just wanted her to be happy. I am now aware that my speaking was dishonest. I did have expectations. Subtle ones. Energetic ones. Unspoken ones. I wanted her to rise out of what I perceived to be her slump because I had not yet forgiven the part of me that had fallen. I wanted her to shine because I had not yet acknowledged, accepted, or blessed the places in me that were still in shadow. As my light began to shine brighter, Nisa's began to shrink. Not because she lacked brilliance, but because she did not feel safe in my reflection.

Nisa was my mirror. She was the one of my three children who reflected to me the pieces of myself that I had disowned: The emotional weight. The longing to belong, to be accepted. The silent suffering. The shame. The survival. The hunger to be affirmed was in fierce competition with the fear of not being enough. When I realized what was going on within me and between us, it broke my heart. It also cracked my heart wide open. I realized that Nisa didn't feel unwanted because of anything I said or did. She felt it because I was still rejecting the parts of *myself* that she embodied. Children *feel energy*. They may not always have the words to explain or describe it, but they know when love is knotted with anger, fear, denial, or avoidance. I always say that children bring to life the unconscious issues of their parents because they live in their bodies. Most parents resist the notion of this, but the truth is, our children know us from the inside out. Nisa knew I loved her, and she also felt my fear of her pain, because it mirrored my own.

My awareness of all that was going on beneath the surface, all that was affecting and impacting my relationship with my baby girl, pushed me deeper into my own Spiritual Hygiene. I worked on my own need to forgive myself for who I had been when she was becoming. I had to affirm her. I understood why I had to affirm her as she was, not for what she could become. I had to acknowledge and bless her broken yet brilliant self, not despite her brokenness but *because* of it. I had to accept that, like me, my daughter, who had lived in my body, was also learning how to survive a lineage of unhealed pain.

Journaling had become a major aspect of my spiritual practice. Through journaling, I eventually realized that my relationship with Nisa's father was not safe or healthy for me or my three children. It would not be accurate to say that we argued. He was six foot two. I was five foot six. He weighed a good 240 pounds. I was a solid 135. We didn't argue because the moment I attempted to respond to his accusations of unfaithfulness or disrespect of his manhood, he would grab me by my throat and whisper in my face what a bitch I was and how easy it would be for him to kill me. I would fight him off silently, punching and scratching without a sound, hoping that the children wouldn't walk in on us. On those rare occasions when he didn't choke me, he would put me in a choke hold, drag me into the bedroom, and threaten to kill me if I opened my mouth. We didn't argue, but we did fight. Perhaps it would be more accurate to say that I got beat up. He would knock me down, threaten to kick me, or tell me if I moved, he would choke the *shit* out of me. I knew to stay in a fetal position to protect my face and my ribs. Sometimes it worked. Sometimes it did not. Over time, I learned how to reduce lip swelling and conceal a black eye. When the children would ask me what had happened to my face, I would say, *"Nothing. I'm OK."*

My mind was filled with imprints and scripts that made violence in my home acceptable. I had never seen a woman leave a man because of his violent behavior. I had a deep desire to leave, but my spiritual and mental hygiene practices were not strong enough to support my desire. Where would I go? My father made it clear that I had made my bed, so I would have to lie in it. My brother told me it was none of his business. My stepmother encouraged me to get out. However, she was also very vocal about her fears that he would kill me, whether I left him or not. My poor mental hygiene and the lack of physical support took their toll. With no plan, few resources, and a limited amount of courage, it took me three years to leave. The truth is, he left me after I stabbed him.

In the process of healing my pain, I learned Nisa did not enter this earth to teach me how to be a perfect mother. Her life assignment was to help me remember how to be a truthful one. She taught me how to accept and finally admit: *I hurt you, because I had not yet healed myself.* That truth was not the end of our healing. It was the beginning. God's grace, her freedom, my return. The truth that I had hurt my child did not destroy me. It delivered me. It lifted the veil of emotional dishonesty that I had unknowingly placed between my heart and hers. As the veil lifted, I gained a profound understanding: *Emotional dishonesty doesn't always manifest as lies.* Sometimes it shows up as silence, as pretending, as deflecting, or overexplaining. It showed up for me and was mimicked by Nisa as saying "*I'm fine,*" when our souls were aching. It can even show up in our attempts to love someone who reflects to us the parts of ourselves we have not yet learned to love. Nisa was that mirror for me. I now understand that what I once interpreted as manipulation or resistance was, in truth, her way of surviving a reality in which she never felt fully safe to be herself. Her behavior was not a betrayal. It was code. It was her asking, in her own way: *Can you see me, even if I can't tell you the whole truth?*

The Bridge to the Learning

Emotional dishonesty as a survival strategy is the spiritual smog of the heart, a subtle, pervasive heaviness that forms when truth has been held hostage for too long. The smog intensifies when what needed to be spoken has instead been buried beneath layers of performance, shame, or fear. Spiritual Hygiene invites you back to your center. It is not about needing or trying to scrub yourself into perfection. It is about clearing the smog so the truth of your heart can breathe again.

To cleanse this layer does not mean you force disclosure of every secret thought or feeling. It is to invite and request a safe and sacred release. It is to offer the heart enough safety to speak without being disguised. To walk this path of cleansing, we must build a bridge between the two inner worlds: the world of the mind that justifies and rationalizes, and the heart that yearns to be free. We must carefully structure a bridge between the stories we have told others and the feelings we have never allowed ourselves to acknowledge. Between the truth that would heal us and the fears that have kept us silent is the bridge I lived on with my daughter Nisa.

Unspoken Feelings Become Spiritual Residue

Nisa did not grow up with the tools to name what she felt or to trust that her needs could be met without performance, drama, or manipulation. Like many of us, she inherited emotional silence as a form of communication. She learned that feelings were dangerous, inconvenient, or too much to carry or share. And just as I had demonstrated to her, she buried her feelings. And like all things buried alive, they did not disappear; they rotted.

Nisa was overweight for most of her life. Her body became a container for what she could not voice: the pain, unmet needs, feelings of rejection, loneliness, and deep self-doubt. After being diagnosed with diabetes, she lost a considerable amount of weight. Yet the emotional weight remained. She looked different, but she felt the same. This is the brutal cruelty of emotional dishonesty: It disconnects you not only from others but also from yourself. Nisa was a tender soul with a wounded core. She laughed loudly and loved deeply, but rarely, if ever, did she speak honestly about her own inner pain. I am clear that Nisa did not lie maliciously. She lied emotionally. She twisted the truth because it felt safer than revealing her truth. She exaggerated urgency because she didn't believe she was worthy of help. She let situations worsen, perhaps to prove that she mattered, if only through emergency. It was heartbreaking. It was exhausting. It was familiar.

The Truth We Bury, and the Cost of Carrying It

Let us take a breath and review.

Emotional dishonesty is the refusal, resistance, or inability to be emotionally truthful. It often arises from fear, shame, or emotional immaturity. It manifests as withholding, deflecting, exaggerating, or suppressing what we truly feel, usually because we don't believe our feelings are valid, safe, or worthy of care. It can look like:

- Saying "I'm fine" while silently falling apart
- Withholding needs because you fear rejection

- Using a crisis to get attention rather than clear communication
- Shifting blame instead of expressing pain
- Pretending not to care when your heart is breaking

You may survive by being emotionally dishonest. However, you cannot be spiritually free in this state. Spiritual Hygiene requires emotional clarity. Clarity requires honesty. Honesty requires courage. The key learning here is that *most emotional dishonesty is a learned behavior*. Even if the reason for engaging it is made up or unnecessary, it is a form of protection, often modeled or inherited.

In my life, and in Nisa's story, emotional dishonesty was a survival skill. Her stories and roundabout ways of asking for help were adaptations to deep feelings of unworthiness. Beneath her avoidance and manipulation was a sincere desire: *to be loved without needing to be in danger first*. What I learned about myself, and what I suspect was also true for Nisa, is that the three pillars of our emotional identity were shattered early in our lives. The pillars of self-worth, self-esteem, and self-value that form the foundation of how we perceive, relate to, and care for ourselves, particularly at the level of the heart, collapsed when we were in the womb.

Self-esteem is how you *feel about yourself*, based on your self-perception and the feedback you have internalized from others. It is how you see, hold, and regard yourself within yourself when no one else is looking. I made up that I was ugly. My brother supported me in this conclusion by teasing me mercilessly about every part of my body: my short hair, my thin legs, my fat lips, and, as he would say, that my belly was bigger than my boobs. I was well into adulthood when I decided to shake off those labels and become drop-dead gorgeous, just because. I continue to wear that label today.

Self-value refers to the *actions* and *choices* that reflect how you treat yourself. This is where self-worth and self-esteem become embodied. Very early in life, I came to believe that the only way people would like or love me was if I gave them what they wanted or what I thought they needed. Not only did I have to prove my value, but I had to "*pay*" you to acknowledge it. I could not have what I wanted because I did not deserve it. I had to accept whatever you gave me because I needed to be grateful for anything and everything. Probably the most damaging aspect of my lack of self-value was that I had to remain loyal to people who treated me badly, whether physically or emotionally. When your self-value is low, you neglect your boundaries, sabotage your well-being, or seek validation through sacrifice.

Self-worth is the *inherent, nonnegotiable truth* that you are valuable simply because you exist. It is how you hold and regard yourself, within yourself, that determines what you expect in the world. It is not something you earn. It is something you remember. My mother was a raging alcoholic. I often joke, saying that the reason I do not and have never drunk alcohol is because I was drunk in the womb. It is only the grace of the Divine that I was not born with fetal alcohol syndrome, but I had enough other stuff to unpack throughout my life that impacted my self-worth. When self-worth is low, love feels conditional. You believe you must perform, suffer, prove, or sacrifice to receive love.

Spiritual Hygiene for the Heart

Like the mind, the heart is a sacred vessel. It is where Divine compassion, intuition, desire, and vulnerability intersect, and like any vessel, it must be kept clean. When emotions are hidden, twisted, or withheld, they become stagnant. They harden. Over time, the stagnant energy's smog causes the roots of connection to rot from the inside out. This is when *Spiritual Hygiene for the heart* becomes essential. The various hygienic practices create an energetic release within the heart, which can reestablish emotional clarity. It is not therapy, although I wholeheartedly recommend therapy for those with deeply complicated wounds; it is a profound process of self-care.

To clean the heart is to remove the residue of emotional dishonesty established by:

- The unspoken need
- The suppressed grief

- The fear masked as indifference
- The longing buried beneath performance
- The guilt covered by blame

Spiritual Hygiene for the heart requires *emotional integrity*, a conscious choice to create alignment between what you feel, what you know, and what you express.

It took several years, but I finally figured out how I broke Nisa's heart. She experienced everything I said as "*personal.*" It wasn't for her. It was about her and against her. It didn't matter how I said it, she experienced my words as "*fighting words.*" It did not matter what I did or how I did it; somehow, she concluded that I either wanted her out of the equation or expected too much. She heard my correction as criticism. She heard my encouragement as a request for her to do more or be different.

Practices for Emotional Honesty and Integrity

I have read countless books, taken many classes, and attended more workshops than I can count, all in an effort to clear the spiritual smog of emotional dishonesty. None of them, by themselves, offered the full solution. What truly helped were the practices I chose to embrace consistently, the ones that allowed the parts of myself reflected through Nisa to become allies instead of adversaries. As I share these practices with you, I invite you to move slowly, and give yourself permission to be fully present in the process.

Daily Heart Check-ins *(15–20 minutes)*

- Close your eyes. Place your hand on your heart.
- Breathe deeply for three to five minutes.
- Ask yourself, "*What are you feeling, Beloved?*"
- Just listen. Do not judge what you hear. Be present with what comes up.

- If it feels appropriate, you can write what you hear.
- If what you write is not kind or loving toward you or anyone else, you can tear it up, flush it, or burn it.

Heart Writing *(20–60 minutes)*

- Play some soft instrumental music in the background.
- Close your eyes. Place your hand on your heart.
- Breathe deeply for three to five minutes.
- Pray softly, asking your heart and emotional self to speak to you.
- Write a letter from your heart to yourself.
- Let your heart speak directly to your mind and allow what you hear to come through your hand. It is OK if it is messy, raw, real.
- If nothing comes forward, pray again.
- Let your heart know that it has permission to say what the mind has silenced.
- Depending on what comes forward, burn or bless the letter. You will know which is right for you to do.

Tear Cleansing *(20–60 minutes)*

- Close your eyes. Place your hand on your heart.
- Breathe deeply for three to five minutes.
- Ask yourself, "*Where are my tears?*"
- Sit quietly for a few moments. If nothing comes forward, ask again.
- Let yourself cry without shame.

- Tears are sacred. They are the body's way of releasing spiritual clutter.
- Do not stop the tears no matter how they come up. Welcome them. They are the rain that softens the hardened heart.

Sacred Expression

Choose one truth a day you have been avoiding and give yourself permission to express it gently and clearly. It may sound like:

> *"I feel overwhelmed, and I need rest."*
>
> *"I was hurt, and I didn't know how to say it."*
>
> *"I need help, and I want to ask you directly."*

Supporting Others with Emotional Dishonesty

When someone you love struggles to be emotionally honest, as Nisa did, it can be a painful experience. You may feel manipulated, confused, or even taken advantage of. Spiritual Hygiene for the heart teaches us to look beneath the behavior and see the ache under the act. There are ways you can create and hold space for healing without enabling the behavior:

- Respond to the truth, not the drama. Gently redirect conversations to the real feeling.
- Set loving boundaries. *"I want to help, but I need you to speak to me truthfully."*
- Name the pattern kindly. *"I notice you often wait until things feel urgent. I want to support you before it gets to that point."*
- Pray for their clarity. Pray for their courage. Pray for yourself to release the need to fix them.

Your clarity will invite their clarity. Your honesty becomes a demonstration they can follow. Keep in mind that regardless of how sincere your efforts, when it comes to healing emotional dishonesty and clearing spiritual smog from the heart, they must choose it. There were times I wanted to scream at Nisa, *Just tell me the truth.* There were times I did just that. Then I remembered that *people only tell the truth when they believe they will be safe once it is spoken.* Until the day she took her last breath, Nisa did not believe she was safe with me. As much as it hurts me to acknowledge it, I get it. I really do.

When the Heart Is Cleansed, Love Is the Natural Outcome

There is a moment in every healing journey when the truth becomes a balm, rather than a blade. This means that truth, your truth, is no longer a burden. It is transformed into a soothing balm that softens the heart. When you practice Spiritual Hygiene for the heart, you begin to realize that what once felt like betrayal, whether your own emotional dishonesty, or someone else's, was at its core a cry for tenderness. As the heart softens you recognize that manipulation was a mask worn by an unmet need. That the silence you considered a disrespectful disconnection was often a Band-Aid covering shame. The drama that felt so unnecessary was probably grief in disguise. This awareness marks the sacred reunion of the heart and the soul. It is a joyous return not to who you used to be, but to the version of you that tells the truth because you *want to be free*. Nisa taught me this return—not in the way I might have imagined, through consistent healing conversations or a dramatic emotional breakthrough. I learned it through the sacred labor of mothering her, witnessing her, being present for her, and ultimately, by releasing her. She showed me what happens when emotional pain is buried beneath a thousand silences. She taught me that love must be clear to be clean. That Spiritual Hygiene is not about being "right." It is about being *real*. Her story, our story, and the ache it carried now lives as medicine in my heart and soul. I loved her just that much. I think she knows it now.

If you are reading this, perhaps there is a version of Nisa in you. A version of you that avoids asking directly. A part of you that fears that your truth will be rejected. A piece of your heartbroken self that waits until crisis comes before you say, "I need help." Please know that you are not wrong, and you haven't done anything wrong. You are not bad. You are learning how to be emotionally honest in a world that has taught you to lie. You are learning how to tell the truth, not to be rescued, but to be restored. This, my Beloved, is holy work, and *there is nothing your holiness cannot do*.

Blessing for the Wounded Heart

May your heart be a place where truth feels safe.
May every unspoken sorrow rise gently
to the surface and dissolve in light.
May you forgive yourself for the ways you tried to survive.
May emotional clarity become your offering to the Divine,
and for yourself.
May love, full-hearted, clear, and unwavering,
find you again and again.
Within you. Through you. As you.

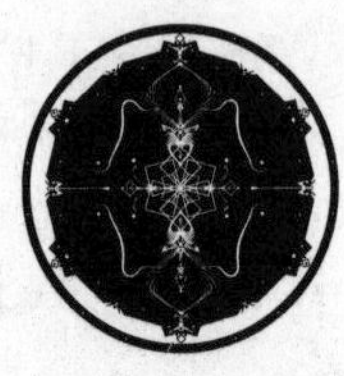

OPENING PRAYER

Beloved Presence of All That Is,
Anchor me now in Your peace and perfect wisdom.

Today, I call forth the sacred flame of courage.
Not the absence of fear, but the holy willingness
to move forward anyway.
Let courage rise in me like the morning sun,
warming every place within me that feels uncertain or afraid.

Divine Light of truth,
I ask that you clear my mind.
Wash away the fog of confusion, the heaviness of doubt,
and the noise of every voice that does not belong to me.
Make my thoughts clear, focused, and honorable.
Help me to see with spiritual eyes, so that I will choose
with sacred discernment.
Guide me to speak only what is rooted in integrity and love.

I open my hands and my heart now, ready to receive Divine instruction
So that I will walk in alignment toward my greater good.
Guide me. Strengthen me. Clarify everything I hold in my mind.

May every step I take today be a step toward truth and peace
and my own Divinity.
I Ask. I Allow. I Accept.
And so, it is.
Amen. Aṣẹ Aho.

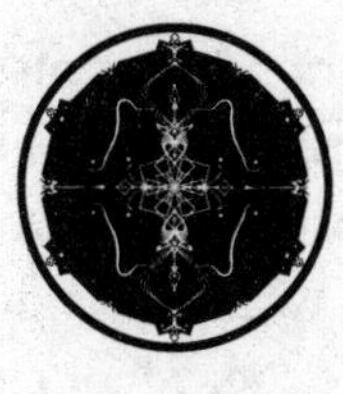

CHAPTER 3

The Mirror Doesn't Lie

The Sacred Work of Self-Honesty

I am not sure how Nisa survived her mother. She was not mothered by Iyanla. Rhonda was Nisa's mother. Rhonda existed before consistent Spiritual Hygiene cleansed the mental sanctuary and reoccupied the mental throne of Iyanla's mind. Rhonda was broken from birth, wounded by experience, and taught to survive long before she was ever taught to breathe with ease. Rhonda was not conceived or received with a sacred intention. She began in rupture and disruption. Her first language was lack: lack of protection, lack of tenderness, lack of love, and lack of safety. In the environment of lack that she called home, even when her body was fed, her soul was starving.

After surviving violence and trauma in her childhood, Rhonda met and married the man she thought could finally make her feel safe. He was six foot two, "street-polished," and financially stable. He'd come out of prison and turned his life around—a pillar of the community. She had learned early that love was meted out as a reward you earned. If she wanted stability in the form of this protector for her two children, she would have to play the role. She had already been taught that silence kept you safe, so you don't cry, you cope, you don't feel, you function. On those rare occasions when her childhood innocence surfaced and she forgot the required program, she was punished or beaten back into submission. The world she lived in was sharp where she needed softness. Most of what she needed was invisible in the very place she most longed for it to be seen, at home.

Rhonda's brokenness wasn't always dramatic. As a woman, wife, and mother, it was quiet. She cooked for family, strangers, and community alike, with a smile that shone for miles, no matter how malnourished she was on the inside. She sewed and made clothing from scratch for anyone who asked, dropping everything on a dime for a friend in need. She gave everything she had to everyone but herself, hoping that in the crowd of recipients, someone would say thank you, or offer something in return. She gave of herself because she had no idea what she needed. Rhonda was not cruel. She was *disconnected.* She was not cold. She was *overwhelmed.* She was not absent. She had been *emotionally exiled* from her own heart. In exile, it meant that she loved from fear, not choice or her fullness. Showing up that way always meant she was never good enough.

Rhonda didn't know how to trust because she had to be vigilant and alert for what was coming next. She didn't know how to choose herself because her "self" had not been allowed to develop or emerge. Rhonda was not unwilling to be or do better. She was *uninitiated* to the truth. She had never been taught that *wholeness* was her birthright, or that *holiness* was her identity. She had never been told that God could be found in her softness, so she covered it with a façade of self-sacrificing strength. With honor to her strength and reverence for her endurance, Nisa did all she could to survive the legacy Rhonda passed on; the beliefs she modeled, the burdens she transferred, the behaviors she normalized, and the standards she silently demanded. Nisa's love for, resentment toward, and codependency on her mother manifested as a firm grip on emotional dishonesty, defiance, and rage. She was totally unaware that the same strength and power she put into defying Rhonda were the exact tools she needed to re-create and save herself.

A Journey into Truth

Those who know who Iyanla is today may read about Rhonda with horror, disbelief, or perhaps quiet confusion. How could the woman who walks with such wisdom now have once walked in such distortion? But this is not a story of contradiction. It is a testimony of transformation.

It is not that Rhonda was "so bad." In fact, those who knew her, friends, family, and colleagues, might resist accepting such descriptions. They may remember her laughter, her devotion, her hustle, and her fierce survival instincts. But here is the truth: *No one knows Rhonda better than Iyanla.*

Iyanla knows her because she lived her. She studied her. She listened to her internal monologue, examined her beliefs, traced her wounds, and sifted through the stories Rhonda used to survive. Iyanla took copious notes, soul notes, about what Rhonda was thinking, feeling, fearing, and avoiding. Iyanla descended into the crevices of Rhonda's mind and heart and found weeds, the dense, thorned, choking weeds that had the power to strangle any hope of new life if left in place.

It was not easy. It was excruciating to name what was buried, to acknowledge what had been denied, and to hold compassion for a self that had once lied, hurt herself and others, manipulated people and situations to stay safe, and grasped for control, not with malice in her heart, but from a place of unhealed pain.

One day, in response to her intentional focus and fear-driven faith, there came a sacred moment when Rhonda's pain gave way to a new woman's tears, and those tears became a prayer. A cry. A reaching out toward something higher. That cry led to surrender. And surrender led to a truth that reordered everything: *"No matter what I have done or been . . . God loves me anyhow."*

It was *that* truth that gave her the courage to pick up self-honesty as both her shovel and her chisel. She used that chisel to carve out the strength to do regular prayer and breathwork *and* go to college, when she had no blueprint or support as the first person in her family to even step foot in a university. Then she used it to graduate as valedictorian. She used the shovel to bury Rhonda's lies, not allowing them to derail her as she went on to law school and continued to achieve, her spirit in alignment.

One afternoon, that spirit called her again. She was in the Philadelphia public defender's office and had just come back from court, and she couldn't get the lights to come on in her office. When she went into the room, everything was bathed in darkness. The receptionist came in and said the lights were working fine. But she still could not see.

Then, Spirit said, *"Leave here and never come back."*

And she did! She left her degree hanging on the wall, her honey in her drawer, and her papers on her desk. She never went back.

A while later, a friend who ran an educational program in Philadelphia asked if she had anything to teach a group of women who were leaving generational welfare.

That's when she remembered the mission that had lived, waiting, in her heart the whole time: to heal. She did have quite a bit to teach these women, as she had lived this reality herself.

Though she had already taken the name, over time, the chisel carved this new woman's name into her heart.

She was Iyanla.

Iyanla's self-honesty had cracked open a new way of living, a new devotion to integrity, in the temple of her mind and heart.

The Blessing of the Wound and the Courage to Choose

There are times when you don't need to know *why*, not at first. The search for why can become a distraction, a mental loop that keeps you circling the pain instead of stepping into your power. Sometimes all you need to know is *what*: *What do you want now? What are you willing to stop doing that keeps you stuck? What are you willing to do differently, even if it scares you? What are you willing to try, even if a part of you doesn't believe it will work?* This is the sacred ground where self-honesty begins. Self-honesty does not require explanations. It is a choice.

One of the reasons Rhonda had such a difficult time shifting and healing so that change could take place was that she kept justifying and excusing why she had done or had not done certain things. She was a survivor. She had survived neglect, abuse, rape, and a battery of lies upon which her life had been built. She had been told by so many, so often, that she was bad and wrong and unacceptable, that she felt guilty just for breathing. She carried the wound of unworthiness like a second skin. Like many, she made her suffering make sense by defending it: *"I had no choice." "I was doing my best." "I didn't know any better."* All of these were true, but none of them could set her free. It can be excruciating to recover from the impression that who you are is inherently wrong. Even if you are wrong, self-honesty does not come to punish you for what you've done, it comes to *liberate you from who you are not.*

The Blessing of the Wound

The willingness to see, know, and tell the deepest, most radical truth is the only way to heal the wound, whatever it may be, because your pain is not the end of your story. In fact, your wound is often the place where the real story begins. Your wound is not your weakness. It is your wellspring of wisdom. When your soul's cry becomes louder than the imposters that have ruled the Throne of Thought, louder than the shame, louder than the fear, louder than the inherited lies, you no longer need to explain why. You begin to listen. The pain that once silenced you begins to speak the truth. The guilt that once covered you begins to fall away. The survival strategies that you believed would keep you safe lose their grip, and something ancient rises. You remember because the "*who*" takes over. *Who* you are at the core of your being. *Who* you were before the pain. *Who* you still are beneath the layers of judgment, defense, and pretense. That "*who*" was never wounded or lost. That "*who*" is: ***wiser*** than the narrative of the past, ***stronger*** than the pain that has followed you, ***softer*** than the armor you wore, more ***authentic*** than the identity you had to build to survive. Unfortunately, you cannot and will not know who that is until you become willing to know and tell the truth about what that person feels and needs.

Self-honesty does not demand that you revisit every wound, but it does ask that you stop hiding behind them. Your wound is sacred not because it happened, but because ***it opens the door to truth.*** Once you become willing to tell the truth to yourself, about yourself, to say, "*This hurts. And I'm ready to heal it,*" you can see yourself clearly.

When Rhonda began to practice self-honesty, Iyanla began to emerge. The stronger Iyanla became, the less guarded, defensive, and afraid Rhonda became. The greatest challenge they both faced in the process was acknowledging, accepting, and forgiving what Rhonda had impressed upon her children, and what Iyanla would need to be willing to do to correct it.

Lying vs. Not Telling the Truth

Those who knew Nisa would likely remember her sharp wit and wicked sense of humor. She was the one you'd want beside you in a crisis. Loyal. Fierce. Funny. They would also probably agree that if her lips were moving, she likely was not telling the truth. Nisa lied. To herself and everyone around her. Sometimes knowingly, at other times unknowingly, she extended those same distortions to everyone around her—she would lie to you, on you, and about you. This was especially true when she was dealing with me. Sometimes her lies were outrageous. Sometimes unnecessary. And sometimes, she went to great lengths to manufacture "proof" to convince you of her story. Nisa also struggled, and perhaps even lacked the capacity, to tell the truth. There is a difference.

You could witness Nisa doing something, yet if you asked her why or told her to stop doing it, she would protest vehemently that she was not doing it or had not done it. The issue became so pervasive that I eventually took her to counseling. After several sessions where Nisa refused to speak at all, the counselor shared that neither of us could make her do something she did not want to do. She shared that it was her assessment that Nisa lived in a state of constant fear. Actually, the word she used was "terror." She also asked me if there was a history of domestic violence in the home. Nisa never went back to the counselor, but I went for both of us. I needed help unpacking and navigating the impact of a broken jaw on the child I was carrying in my womb at the time.

A ***lie*** is a *conscious, willful distortion of reality*, whether spoken or acted. It is offered with the *intent to deceive, manipulate, conceal, or control.* An example of a lie would be saying "*I'm fine*" while hiding pain or upset to control someone's perception. It would also be claiming to have honored a commitment that you broke, or denying wrongdoing, like cheating or stealing, knowing you had done it. Lies constrict spiritual energy. They originate from fear. The fear of punishment, rejection, exposure, or loss. In the realm of Spiritual Hygiene, lying severs the connection and alignment between the soul and the conscious self. *God is truth.* Truth lives in the soul. When a lie is told, it is an active affirmation of belief in separation from the Divine. Lying clouds the inner waters, the movement of feeling and emotion. It replaces clarity with confusion. It degrades trust into mistrust, both internally and with relationships. When you know that you have told a lie, you also know that you can't trust yourself. If you cannot be trusted, why would you trust anything or anyone else? When you lie, you become a stranger to yourself, and you disconnect from the flow of inspiration from Source.

Not telling the truth is different. It is the *withholding* of truth. It can be conscious or unconscious. It is typically born out of trauma, shame, emotional overwhelm, or a lack of clarity. An example of not telling the truth would be avoiding a conversation because you do not yet feel safe to speak. It would also be accommodating or tolerating harmful behavior to avoid conflict. In its most common form, not telling the truth is the choice to silence your needs, desires, or boundaries to maintain peace. This type of withholding fosters spiritual smog. While it may feel protective in the moment, over time it supports self-betrayal, erosion of inner authority, accumulated shame, and a deep sense of unworthiness.

Both lying and not telling the truth are departures from the true nature of the soul. One is rooted in distortion. The other creates and supports disconnection. One manipulates. The other is an attempt to conceal. One says, *"I need to control what you see."* The other whispers, *"I don't feel safe enough to be seen."* Both require healing. Both deserve compassion. Both can be cleansed through the sacred practice of self-honesty, spoken in the mirror first, and then in the world.

The Weight of Silence

Nisa's story lives here not as blame, but as an offering. I know Nisa's story so intimately because, in truth, it was my story too. She wasn't just my daughter. She was my reflection. She mirrored my wounds, my survival patterns, my emotional habits, and the parts of myself I had not yet brought into the light. I used to say she was my "*mini-me.*" I didn't fully understand what that meant until it was too late.

By the time I realized who she truly was to me and what healing we were meant to do together, the distance between us had grown. I had shifted. I had changed the way I saw her, the way I held her, the way I longed to be present with her and for her. Unfortunately, she could not, or perhaps chose not to, let go of the image of me she had already etched into her mind and heart. She had built a narrative around her mother based on who I used to be, based on Rhonda. When that image no longer fit me, it left her without a sense of grounding. At times, I think she was angry that I had changed, that I was no longer the mother she had learned to survive with. There's a strange pain that comes when someone we have put in a box starts to break free of the four corners of our perception of and experience with them. It threatens the stories we have told ourselves. It destabilizes the emotional framework we built to protect ourselves from them.

It is a real and common experience: When you stop being who others *need* you to be—when you no longer match the image they have internalized—they become angry. They feel betrayed, not because you have caused them harm, but because you have grown beyond their expectation and judgments. It frightens them because they may believe that you expect them to either grow with you or be rejected or abandoned by you. I remember the moment this truth settled into my bones.

We were having a disagreement. Nisa was insisting I had said something that I had not. Her tone was not only harsh, but it was also aggressive, just a breath away from being disrespectful. In that moment, I felt something rise in me, but instead of reacting, I became still. Internally calm. Externally still. I looked at her face, soft but steady, not saying a word. I was listening beyond the words. I was holding her in my heart. I was watching the pain try to speak. After about thirty seconds of silence, she snapped, "*See! You always do that. You look at me like I'm stupid.*" The only thing I could offer was the truth of my heart. I said softly, "*Nini . . . please forgive me. That is not my intention.*" She shot back, "*Yes, it is! You just won't admit it.*" With that, the space between us widened. We did not speak for two months after that.

I carried her words like stones in my chest. Not because they were true, but because I finally understood: She wasn't reacting to the mother I was in that moment. She was defending herself against the memory of who I had once been. A version of me that was real for her, but no longer real for me. This is one of the hardest truths of spiritual growth:

- Just because you have healed does not mean others will feel healed in your presence.
- Just because you have changed does not mean they will stop grieving or resenting who you used to be.
- And, just because you are now more conscious does not mean they are ready to meet you in that light.

However, the only way through is to love deeper. To apologize for what was real in their experience. To let go of needing to defend your growth. To remain rooted in the self-honesty that you are no longer who you were, even if they are not ready to accept who you have become.

I offer this because I am deeply aware that many of us, knowingly or unknowingly, carry emotional residue in our hearts. Many of us are still learning how to be emotionally honest, not just with ourselves, but also with others. To walk the path of Spiritual Hygiene, you must become familiar with the inner terrain of your being, your mind, emotions, patterns of thought, and the ways you relate. It is where the practice of self-honesty must descend into the heart. There are no logical conclusions in the process of healing. These are soul truths that are revealed. These truths, which I call "*rot-gut truths*," can only be revealed through the heart.

Self-Honesty: A Sacred Mirror of the Soul

When I first heard the statement "*Truth is the filter that clears the mental altar,*" I thought it had something to do with religion and the truth setting you free. It took me a while to understand that the mind is the first place where distortion takes root. It is where the trauma stories are rehearsed, assumptions are built, and beliefs harden into secret aspects of identity. Without self-honesty, the mind becomes a hall of mirrors, where illusion appears as insight and reactions present themselves as reason.

Practicing Spiritual Hygiene for the mind has taught me that the mind is a truly sacred space. It is a temple of perception, a receptacle of memory, the foundation of logic, the creative studio of imagination and belief. My practice also taught me that any structure, even a sacred one like the mind, can become cluttered. This happens when it is overrun with unchecked thoughts, distorted stories, inherited patterns, and unconscious agreements. What we allow to dwell in our minds becomes what we worship, whether we realize it or not. In the practice of Spiritual Hygiene at all levels, what you want to "*worship*" is truth.

Self-honesty is the conscious practice of telling the truth to yourself, about yourself, even when it is hard, even when it hurts, and even when it challenges the self-image you have created. This level of honesty is not just about admitting mistakes; it is also about being willing and courageous enough to *see yourself clearly*, without hiding, pretending, or running away from your truth. Self-honesty is the moment when you pause internally, take a breath, and say to yourself: "*This is what I feel.*" "*This is what I know.*" "*This is what I need to change.*" It is also one of the most powerful moments of transformation you will ever have. That moment is sacred. It is not just reflective; it is also ***revolutionary***. It is a moment acknowledging that you are aware, that you accept without judgment, and that you are available to accept responsibility for your healing. This moment of brave truth-telling is sacred. It is an expression of spiritual integrity that aligns who you are internally with how you wish to live externally.

Self-honesty invites you to say, first to yourself and then to others: *"I feel overwhelmed." "I feel afraid." "I feel abandoned." "I feel jealous. Angry. Tender. Unsure."* Admitting these truths is not a weakness. It is a sign of **reverence for your mind, heart, and soul**.

"I messed up." It's not about beating yourself up. It does not require you to hang your head and walk away to drown in guilt or shame. This expression of self-honesty means looking at your inner world with compassion and clarity, acknowledging your behavior or actions, and telling the truth about it. It is not about judgment. It is about a willingness to accept responsibility and to be accountable. Acknowledging that you made a poor choice, bad decision, or that your actions had a less-than-positive or unproductive impact is a sacred step toward growth. It is not an admission of failure. It is an act of maturity that communicates, *"I care enough about my own path to correct it."* Or, *"I forgot my values, purpose, or intention in that moment."* Even, *"I was reactive instead of responsive."* Or perhaps, *"Next time, I want to do better."*

When you practice self-honesty, you build self-trust. You teach yourself that you are willing and capable of taking care of yourself. You create space for *transformation*, because you are doing what is required to create an outcome you desire. When you are honest, telling the truth to yourself and everyone else, *you stop running away.* You come home to the truth of your soul, and no matter how hard it is to speak that truth, when you do, it becomes your medicine.

When truth is allowed into the mind, the raw, unfiltered truth, the mind begins to operate as a spiritual sieve. It catches and filters out what is no longer aligned with your values, worth, and purpose, allowing sacred energy to flow.

The Practice of Self-Honesty as Spiritual Hygiene for the Mind

As you begin to consider self-honesty as an essential element of caring for your mind, heart, and soul, the following offerings will support you in developing your foundational practices:

The Mind Is a Sacred Gateway

Are you aware that your mind is not just for thinking? It is an altar. It is a spiritual portal. The mind translates energy into meaning on the third dimension, the physical dimension of life. The mind is a bridge between your soul, the intangible, invisible connection to life, and your choices in the third dimension. Good Spiritual Hygiene for the mind ensures that this gateway remains clear, allowing Divine intelligence to flow through you without distortion. This gateway between the spiritual and the physical is the pathway that transforms fear-based reactions into Divine revelations.

Spiritual Hygiene Protects Your Purpose and Your Path

Each of us has a purpose that has given birth to us. The path to the fulfillment of that purpose is etched into the fibers of our soul. A cluttered mind will cause you to miss the subtle cues of guidance. You chase what is familiar instead of what is aligned and appointed specifically for you. However, a clean, spiritually tended mind protects your direction. It becomes a compass that points inward for guidance before you reach outward for acceptance.

Spiritual Hygiene Is Devotion to the Soul

To consciously choose and provide care for your mind is to honor the sacred within you, and the manifestation of Divinity that you are in physical form. Your intentional commitment to Spiritual Hygiene for the mind is a declaration to the universe of life that: *"I matter!" "I choose what I allow to live in me. I choose to make space for light, peace, and love." "I choose to invite in thoughts that nourish me, and to release thoughts that can deplete me."* Good Spiritual Hygiene of the mind is not about striving for and reaching some impossible level of perfection. You are human! It is guaranteed that you will slip, slide, and sometimes fall on the journey through life. Spiritual Hygiene, at all levels, is about presence. Being aware of it. Honoring it. Standing in it. It is your presence that supports you in returning time and again to the authentic truth of who you are, a demonstration of Divinity.

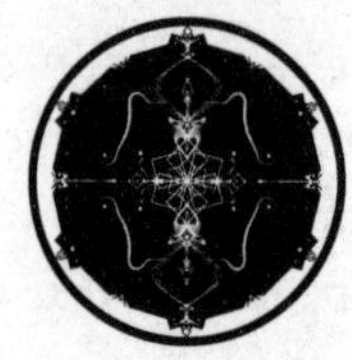

OPENING PRAYER

I Reclaim Every Part of Me

I stand in the authority of my Soul and speak this truth aloud:
I Am not broken. I Am Whole. I Am Holy.
What once fractured under the weight of trauma now
rises to be reclaimed by love.
I declare that the survival selves I created, the protector, the pleaser,
the performer, the one who hides, the one who needed
to be rescued, were defensive strategies.
They kept me alive.
I no longer choose to just survive.
I Am here to live.
I Am here to rise.
I Am here to reign with Divine Sovereignty.

I summon my scattered energy home.
I call every forgotten fragment of myself into the light.
No part of me is forsaken.
No voice within me is condemned.
I Am the sacred author of my own story.
I transmute shame into strength, fear into courage,
wounds into wisdom.

I sit firmly on the Throne of my being, not as a victim of my past.
I Am the living embodiment of Divine Restoration.
This is my heartfelt decree.
All of me is welcome.

All of me is worthy.
All of me is loved and loveable.
All of me is returning home.

Amen. Aṣẹ Aho.
It is done.
And so, it is.

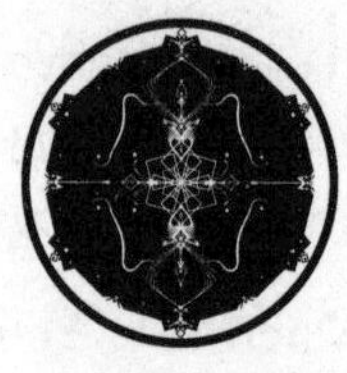

CHAPTER 4

Voice of Trauma Splinters into Survival Selves

The Rise of Ronnie

You have learned about Rhonda. Now I would like to introduce you to Ronnie. She is a quick-witted, foul-mouthed, survival-driven fighter. I say she "is" because I did not banish her. She is not a ghost of my past. She is a living voice in my story. I did not exile her. I redirected her fire. I honored her for what she survived.

If something needed to get done, Ronnie was going to get it done. If something needed to be said, she said it. She is the one who taught herself to sew, so she could have something to wear. She is the one who took care of her older but asthmatic brother. She is the one who learned to fight, even though she was beaten into semiconsciousness. She is the one who was raped at age nine. She is the one who sat alone for hours in the hospital emergency room while her brother was being treated. As my grandmother would say, "*She didn't take tea for fever.*" Ronnie fought for everything: her place in the home, her need to be seen, her value in male-dominated systems and structures, and eventually, as a Black Panther, she fought for her community. One thing people often overlooked about her is that she was a creative soul. "They" failed to recognize that beneath her grit was grace. Ronnie was a lover of classical ballet who was rejected because her body did not conform to the whitewashed standard. She made her skirts for school because there was never enough money to buy them. She made aprons and handkerchiefs to earn love through usefulness. The one thing Ronnie loved more than anything else was cooking. If there was someone in the kitchen, Ronnie would watch and learn.

As life would have it, her paternal grandmother, an indigenous Cherokee woman, earned a living as a domestic and a cook for more than fifty years. On Saturday and Sunday, she would take Ronnie to work with her in the huge mansions in Yonkers and Scarsdale, NY. There it was "*suggested*" that Ronnie would get things "dirty." She was made to sit on a wooden box when she wasn't ironing or chopping vegetables for Grandma. She also did a lot of good, but her goodness was overshadowed by her defiance and independence. You see, Ronnie was *intuitive.* She was clairaudient. She heard beyond the words and could feel the truth when the lie was being formed on someone's lips. The challenge was that she often spoke what she heard and felt, which contradicted what she was being told to believe. When she challenged the big people entrusted with her care, suffice it to say that it rattled them. In reaction, they would beat or punish her, telling her how "*bad*" she was and needed to stop being. It was the longing to be loved and accepted that silenced her. It was the promise that she would end up in hell that taught her that her "*gifting*" was evil. It was the trauma of never feeling welcomed or wanted, always being told that she talked too much, and her father beating her into a state of semiconsciousness that turned her fight into compliance. When Ronnie shrank into the shadow of trauma, self-sufficient but very compliant, Rhonda was born.

Misery loves company, and the Voice of Trauma is no different. It never rules alone; it travels with untrustworthy companions, speaking in many tones, wearing many faces, and hiding behind many masks. When the soul is wounded and Spiritual Hygiene is neglected, those traumatic experiences lodge in the mind and heart and fragment into protective voices born of fear. Often disguised as strategy, logic, or "just the way I am," these voices are not evil or your enemies. They are your younger selves and unhealed moments trying by whatever means they know to keep you safe. Yet when they remain unnamed, they slip onto the throne of your inner life and into your energetic field, where they drain your vitality, stifle your intuition, and cloud your perception. The danger is that even when you sense this storm within you, without naming and tending to it, you may find yourself standing in the rain with nothing better than a paper bag for an umbrella.

On a spiritual journey toward healing, it is easy for the deceptive intelligence of the ego to convince you that once you've gotten it, *you've got it*. D.I. (*Deceptive Intelligence*) wants you to think that once your mind understands, you will be able to implement some practice or embrace a new pattern that will save you from the issue. To assume such is what many spiritual teachers would label as M.I.A., *Misled into Arrogance*. Or M.I.I. *Missing in Ignorance*. In the same way, the trauma I carry does not look the same as the trauma someone else is holding; the fear, shame, and guilt I carry may not look like anyone else's. You have your "*cooties*," and I have mine. While it may not be pleasant or fun, it is absolutely essential to know your cooties by name. Let us meet them and become familiar with their modus operandi, how they operate. We do not want to judge them. We want to recognize and understand them. We are not trying to banish them. Our intention is to reclaim the parts of ourselves that these cooties have been nibbling on.

The Voice of Shame: The Shadowed Mirror

Shame speaks first when a soul has been exposed, judged, or rejected. It's a voice that says, *There is something wrong with me*. Believing that to be true, the ego will dim the light before anyone else has a chance to see it. Humiliation is a voice that locks your energy inward. It locks the heart, stiffens the throat, clouds the solar plexus, the power center in the body. When you live in shame, your personal power becomes stagnant. You cannot allow joy to take root because shame whispers that you haven't earned it. This voice steals your right to wholeness by convincing you that your healing is a reward, not a birthright. In response, you spend your time and energy, sometimes your life, trying to "*fix*" what is wrong. Eventually, shame becomes the invisible lens through which you perceive yourself, others, and the Divine. Here is the truth: *Shame is not yours to wear.* It is a residue from traumatic experiences that taught you to fear your own presence, your gifts, and your right to be authentically who you are meant to be.

Mental Impact:

Shame rewires the mind to see the self as inherently wrong. It creates inner narratives, such as *"I am not enough," "I don't belong,"* or *"I always mess up."* In time, this becomes the default lens through which you interpret every experience until even joy becomes dangerous.

Emotional Impact:

Shame silences authentic feeling. It often leads to emotional numbness, social withdrawal, self-criticism, or cycles of self-sabotage. You feel undeserving of love, belonging, or rest.

How It Shows Up:

You overapologize. You hide your gifts. You downplay your voice in sacred spaces. You reject compliments, delay your own desires, and chronically undervalue yourself in work, love, and creativity.

The Cost of Not Clearing:

When shame goes unaddressed, it weaves itself into the fabric of your identity. It becomes an energetic blockade, silently severing your connection to the truth of your soul. You begin to live on the surface of life. Relationships are distant. Opportunities slip by, and self-love, though always present, feels foreign. Your capacity to love and be loved has not left you; you stop engaging it because shame has convinced you that you don't deserve to have it.

The Voice of Performance: The Exhausted Mask

The Voice of Performance enters the consciousness when love has been made conditional. It says: *"Be better." "Prove that you are worthy." "Look good no matter what." "Earn your place."* It may come across as being noble, ambitious, even spiritual. Performative living also comes with a language. You know all the buzzwords. You know exactly what to say, at just the right time, to maintain the charade that you have it all together. At the root of the show, the performance, is the fear that who you are is not enough and/or not good enough.

Energetically, performance creates overextension. You give more than you have. You say yes when your spirit is saying no. You begin to organize your identity around usefulness. Your field becomes thin, brittle, and overworked. It drains your energy because you are never allowed to rest. The moment one goal is reached; another is created. You are not going or doing for the joy of it. You keep moving, hoping the noise in your life will drown out the silence that might expose your deepest fear: *that no one truly sees you.*[*]

Mental Impact:

Performance replaces authentic truth with a calculated strategy, whether conscious or unconscious. You begin thinking in terms of what will "*work*" or please others, rather than what feels honest or aligned. You conflate worth with success, and your productivity becomes your emotional currency.

Emotional Impact:

Performative living renders you emotionally exhausted, disconnected from joy, and traumatically afraid of failure. If you rest, you feel anxious. When things slow down, you may not feel safe. You fear that being still will make you invisible or irrelevant.

How It Shows Up:

Most performers are overcommitted. You want to be everywhere, doing almost everything. Although your commitments are breaking your back, you cannot ask for or receive help. Your value is based on output. You smile to cover your breaking. You spiritualize your burnout by calling it help, service, or support.

The Cost of Not Clearing:

Performance eventually leads to depletion—physically, mentally, emotionally, and spiritually—one at a time or all at once. Eventually, the body rebels with disease or burnout. Your heart feels hollow, which is deeper than empty. You attract relationships that only value what you offer. If unchecked, you begin to resent even the sacred assignments of your calling.

The Voice of Blame: The Defender at the Gate

The Voice of Blame is born when pain has no place to go. It rises when naming your own needs feels too vulnerable, too dangerous. *"It's their fault." "They hurt me. They broke me." "She/He/They are the reason I am like this."* In many cases, it could be true that blame does not stop when it is recognized or acknowledged. It loops and holds on to the past like armor. Blame hardens the energetic field, which justifies building walls, rather than creating boundaries. Blame keeps you hypervigilant, reactive, and emotionally guarded because it siphons energy toward protection rather than vulnerability or healing. When the Voice of Blame leads you, chances are that you will mistake accountability for attack. In doing so, you become attached to your suffering because letting it go would mean confronting your choice to stay stuck.

Mental Impact:

Blame disrupts personal clarity. It allows you to believe your growth and healing is contingent on someone else's apology, change, or punishment. Your mind becomes trapped in cycles of *"If only they hadn't . . . If only they would . . . I can't until they . . ."*

Emotional Impact:

The Voice of Blame is always used to justify pain, while rendering you powerless to change it. Resentment, bitterness, and frustration become emotional allies. Vulnerability is usurped by guardedness.

How It Shows Up:

Because you rehearse the same story repeatedly, you distrust others by default. Conflict and emotional detachment are your fallback positions, even when connection is possible. You avoid inner work because "they should go first."

The Cost of Not Clearing:

Blame arrests your evolution. Your energy remains hooked into the past. Your frequency is anchored down by the very pain you want freedom from. You give away your power under the illusion of justice.

The Voice of Delay: The Disguised Saboteur

The Voice of Delay always comes across as wise and reasonable. It sounds patient. *"Not now," "You're not ready yet. Maybe next time."* This is what makes this voice so insidious. When born from trauma, it is easily mistaken for discernment. It is not a sacred knowing. It is avoidance masquerading in sacred clothing. Delay is an energetic freeze that paralyzes potential. It hinders personal development and blocks forward movement by offering a thousand reasons to wait. While the mind is busy reasoning *why not*, the heart is aching to proceed onward. The Voice of Delay emerges from the moments when truth led to a deep rupture. It grew its legs when change meant loss of something or someone. When growth turned from gladness to grief. Now, instead of moving forward, you plan. You prepare. You study the lessons without ever stepping into the knowledge you have gained.

Mental Impact:

Delay convinces the mind that healing must be postponed. *"I'm not ready"* becomes a mantra. You overthink, overplan, and under-embody. This is the classic psychological syndrome of "*analysis paralysis*."

Emotional Impact:

You become emotionally overwhelmed by the possibility of anything new or different. Because your dreams and desires feel so far away, anxiety becomes the gatekeeper between insight and action.

How It Shows Up:

You take classes, courses, and workshops, but you never use or implement what you learn. You say yes with your heart, then hesitate with your steps. You create beautiful visions and plans and then find reasons not to bring them into manifestation.

The Cost of Not Clearing:

Delay is the mother of stagnation. Sacred windows and Divine opportunities are missed. Life becomes a battle with the *spiritual constipation* of unlived truths, unloved gifts, and unrealized dreams. Eventually, delay will mutate into despair.

The Voice of Avoidance: The Gatekeeper of Pain

The Voice of Avoidance doesn't scream or demand. It turns your head away from the very thing you need to look for or focus on. Avoidance distracts. It deflects. It fills your days with busyness, your heart with shallow comforts, and your mind with rehearsed beliefs. Avoidance leaves gaps. Parts of you go untouched. Unfelt. You compartmentalize emotions like files that you are afraid to open. This dulls your intuition and dims your clarity. This is because your inner altar becomes cluttered with unopened letters from your soul. Avoidance often forms when a traumatic past pain still feels too big to handle. It may also be born when a moment of *helplessness* becomes too overwhelming to process. It taught you "*not to go there.*" Over time, "*there*" becomes everywhere. Aversion is not laziness. It is learned protection grounded in the fear of overwhelm. Turning away from something does not make it go away. It supports it to grow bigger.

Mental Impact:

Avoidance trains the mind to compartmentalize pain. You disconnect from memories, wounds, and the truth. You create mental gaps in your own story. These gaps shatter your identity and fragment your soul.

Emotional Impact:

You feel disconnected from any sort of emotional depth. You avoid conflict, feedback, intimacy, and grief. You prefer to "*keep the peace,*" even when your soul is at war.

How It Shows Up:

You distract yourself with the noise of busyness, social media, tasks, and other people's needs. You spiritualize detachment. You smile while silently dissociating from your body or your feelings.

The Cost of Not Clearing:

Avoidance creates spiritual stagnation. Your intuition becomes fuzzy. Emotional release feels painfully impossible. You cannot fully receive love or guidance because parts of you are *offline*. Avoidance breeds a silent loneliness that no one can see, but your soul always feels.

The Voice of Inheritance: The Familiar Phantom

The Voice of Inheritance is the most subtle voice of all. It doesn't even sound like a voice. It sounds like your personality. Like your "*way*" of being, doing, and seeing. Beneath the familiar phrasing is the echo of generational trauma that took root before you were born. You may think: *This is just how I am,* but energetic inheritance is not identity. It is transmission that can be and needs to be cleared. When Spiritual Hygiene is not practiced, these inherited beliefs about worth, suffering, silence, and sacrifice become deeply ingrained in your energetic DNA. You will find yourself repeating patterns—Relationship. Financial struggles. Emotional postures. In severe cases, even physical illness and disease. This is not because you have chosen these things. It is because they were chosen for you before you had the power to say no. As challenging as it can be to live through, clearing the Voice of Inheritance can be a powerful and sacred act. It is the deeply sacred work of soul gardening: pulling weeds with reverence, eliminating things that no longer need to bloom. Doing this work is important because when you do, the impact is felt seven generations behind you and seven generations to come.

Mental Impact:

The Voice of Inheritance implants and transfers unexamined beliefs. The mind and heart adopt mental scripts, such as *This is just how life is* or *We've always done it this way.* Your thinking is shaped more by ancestral conditioning than by personal discernment.

Emotional Impact:

You feel emotionally loyal to outdated systems. You carry grief, rage, or scarcity that is not yours but impacts you greatly. Emotional confusion arises when your soul desires change, but your bloodline demands loyalty.

How It Shows Up:

You follow family rules without question. You suppress spiritual gifts. You fear growth because it might mean separation. You feel guilty for becoming more than those who raised you.

The Cost of Not Clearing:

Uncleared inheritance binds your evolution to your ancestry. You repeat cycles across generations. Your soul contracts become entangled with generational contracts. Your possibilities and legacy become limited by their limitations.

The Voice of Anger: The Sacred Flame

Anger is a feeling that is often misunderstood. Anger is not bad, wrong, or a problem. When recognized and perceived correctly, anger is a signal. It is a fiery declaration that something sacred has been dishonored. It is the soul's siren when boundaries have been crossed, or grief has been buried. Whether that is your personal space or your mother's good name, anger is telling you and the one responsible for the violation to back up and watch out. Unfortunately, when unhealed trauma manipulates the warning signs of anger, it becomes the only voice you trust. Anger speaks in ultimatums. It festers in silence. It is prone to eruptions. It masks grief, sadness, and fear with aggression or volume. It builds fortresses instead of bridges. When trauma is invalidated or ignored, anger steps in as the protector. Energetically, unprocessed anger scorches. It creates inflammation in the body, disruption in the heart, and defensiveness in the aura. You live in a state of fight readiness. You attack to ward off being attacked. The underbelly of anger is *hurt*. You hurt because no one ever taught you how to mourn.

How the Voice of Anger Transforms into the Identity of the Martyr

The soul that cannot safely express anger finds ways to survive it. One such way is through noble suffering. The Voice of Anger once tried to say:

- *"This isn't fair."*
- *"This isn't right."*
- *"How dare you!"*
- *"I need to stop 'this,' but I can't. They have the power."*

When that voice is stifled by fear of rejection, people-pleasing, spiritual guilt, or conditioning that labels anger as unholy, it begins to mutate. It begins to say:

- *"I'll just do it myself."*
- *"I'll stay silent to keep the peace."*
- *"I'll show you who I am."*
- *"If I suffer enough, maybe I'll finally be seen."*

Mental Impact:

Anger narrows perception. The mind becomes combative, suspicious, or reactive. You assume the worst. You rehearse offenses. You anticipate harm before it arrives.

Emotional Impact:

Anger masks deeper feelings. It becomes a primary emotion because grief, fear, or vulnerability feels unsafe. You explode or implode—either way, you rarely feel soothed.

How It Shows Up:

You overreact to small things. You become impatient. You feel misunderstood or unheard. You cut people off without conversation. You expect people to hurt you and feel justified lashing out when they do.

The Cost of Not Clearing:

Anger calcifies the heart. You struggle to forgive. Your nervous system remains hyper-aroused. Physical symptoms (inflammation, jaw tension, migraines) become chronic. Anger may protect, but it also isolates.

When anger is left unattended, when it is allowed to fester, the martyr is born. The martyr became the *socially acceptable version* of unspoken rage. The martyr is the one who overextends rather than lashing out. Rather than demand justice, the martyr sacrifices. To keep the facade of peace, the martyr absorbs the wound rather than speaking the truth. In the martyr's consciousness, the anger that was once meant to protect you becomes a role that punishes you in the name of devotion. The martyr in your consciousness allows you to cut its wrists and then shows you how much it is bleeding.

Energetically, the martyr lives in depletion. The aura is thin, strained, and hypervigilant. There is an underlying sense of being unappreciated or taken for granted, but it remains unspoken, seething just below the surface. Emotionally, the martyr oscillates between quiet resentment and a craving for acknowledgment. Because they often do not express their needs directly, martyrs cannot receive what they long for. The body carries the tension of containment. The shoulders, jaw, and gut become sites of the spiritual burdens they choose to carry.

The martyr does not seek attention. They seek *relief.* They want to be held, to be honored, to be allowed to say, *"I am tired. I am angry. I am worthy of care."* The Voice of Anger that was never given voice keeps the martyr silent, even in exhaustion. The martyr is not weak. The martyr is powerful fire wrapped in years of ash. To liberate the martyr, you must first honor the Voice of Anger. Allow the martyr to clarify, not consume. You must give the suppressed flame a sacred place to speak.

Mental Impact:

You think in extremes. You anticipate harm. Your mind becomes defensive, combative, or self-righteous.

Emotional Impact:

You are usually on edge. You suppress sadness and allow yourself to overflow with irritability or rage. Tenderness is difficult to access.

How It Shows Up:

You lash out. You isolate. You weaponize silence. You hold grudges. You shut down emotionally before others can hurt you.

The Cost of Not Clearing:

You push away connection. Chronic stress lives in your body. Your sacred fire turns inward, burning your own inner sanctuary.

The Voice of Guilt: The Silent Bargain of the Soul

The Voice of Guilt often comes wrapped in sacrifice, in self-doubt, in quiet emotional contortions that say, *"I must pay for what I've done,"* or worse, *"for what I couldn't do."* This is the voice that constantly reminds you, *"There is something wrong with what you have done. What you have done is unforgivable, and you are unredeemable."* This is the voice that is born when trauma convinces you that you are responsible for the harm others caused, or the pain you could not prevent. You take on burdens that do not belong to you, mistaking them for duty, repentance, or proof of love. Guilt is a constant whisper of:

- *"I should have done more."*
- *"It's my fault they're hurting."*

- *"If I had been better, they wouldn't have . . ."*
- *"I don't deserve anything until they are OK."*

Energetically, guilt compresses your energy field. It binds your heart to people, places, and a past you cannot change. It interrupts your ability to receive, to celebrate, or to move forward. Guilt blocks joy with emotional penance. Identifying guilt can be tricky because it often masquerades as humility or compassion. When it is buried under good intentions, it can remain undetected. Guilt can also be ruthless because it often accompanies shame. It provides the motivation to engage in shameful acts, which you then feel guilty about. When Spiritual Hygiene is not practiced, shame-ridden guilt becomes your compass. You begin to believe that healing must hurt. That joy must be justified. That goodness must be earned through suffering. The path out of guilt is forgiveness. Forgiveness of the younger you. The limited you. The overwhelmed you. The one who did what they could, with what they had, under the weight of what they didn't know. Cleansing the Voice of Guilt clears a sacred channel, so that you no longer confuse pain with love, or punishment with penance. Forgiving all that you believe you are guilty of makes you energetically available for liberation.

Mental Impact:

Guilt distorts personal responsibility. You assume fault for things beyond your control. The mind replays "*should haves*" and creates internal punishments for perceived failures.

Emotional Impact:

You live in a state of low-grade self-punishment. Joy feels inappropriate. You deny ease, success, or celebration. You feel emotionally burdened, even when life is good.

How It Shows Up:

You give more than you have. You stay in unbalanced relationships. You over-apologize. You defer your dreams for others' comfort. You feel uncomfortable with forgiveness.

The Cost of Not Clearing:

Guilt keeps your vibration entangled in cycles of debt and denial. You can't hold on to blessings because guilt insists you don't deserve them. Energetic depletion becomes chronic, and spiritual confidence cannot take root.

The Voice of False Responsibility

There is a primary voice behind false responsibility and the compulsion to take care of everyone. It is a hybrid between the Voice of Guilt and the Voice of Inheritance, with deep entanglement from the Voice of Performance, and at times, the Voice of Shame. At its core, the most distinct expression of this dynamic voice is: *"If I don't carry it, if I don't do it, everything will fall apart."*

The Voice of False Responsibility is born when love and safety were dependent on your usefulness. As a child, you may have been the emotional anchor, the fixer, the strong one. You learned to attune to the needs of others before you even knew how to identify your own. This voice often forms in homes where trauma, addiction, neglect, or emotional immaturity were present. You were initiated into duty before you were initiated into selfhood. It is most often inherited, passed down through the family lineage, where women especially were taught to measure their worth by their sacrifice. This voice tells you that your job is to protect, manage, hold, soothe, and serve others even at the cost of your own well-being. The deeper lie beneath this voice is: *"Their healing is my responsibility. Their happiness, peace, success, well-being depends on me."*

Mental Impact:

Your mind becomes hypervigilant, scanning for the distress or discomfort of others that you rush to fix. You carry emotional and energetic burdens that do not belong to you. Rest feels selfish. Boundaries feel dangerous. Delegation feels like betrayal.

Emotional Impact:

You are emotionally overextended. You experience guilt when resting, resentment when giving, and confusion about your own needs. You may feel invisible, overwhelmed, and irreplaceable, and trapped by the very identity you created.

How It Shows Up:

- You insert yourself as the fixer or rescuer in relationships.
- You take on spiritual, financial, or emotional burdens that are not yours.
- You struggle to say no.
- You believe that if you stop helping, others will suffer.
- You bypass your own breakdowns by focusing on others' healing.

The Cost of Not Clearing:

You lose touch with your own needs. You burn out. You develop resentment that feels shameful to name. Your spiritual clarity dims. You attract codependent dynamics, where your giving is exploited or expected. Perhaps the most tragic of all *false responsibilities* lives in the belief that *love must always cost you something*. False responsibility is not love. It is bondage dressed as service. You are not here to carry everyone. You are here to embody your truth so that others may remember how to carry themselves.

The Voice of Unforgiveness: The Shackled Heart

Every trauma you could possibly imagine or have ever encountered requires a dose of forgiveness to be healed. This does not excuse what happened; it releases what is still holding you hostage. What you choose not to forgive becomes the altar where your pain is worshipped. It becomes the lens through which you see yourself, the weight you carry into every relationship, and the wound that speaks when your heart tries to open. Forgiveness is not forgetting. It is remembering without reliving. It is choosing freedom over repetition. It is a demonstration of your willingness to step into wholeness, rather than clinging to identity in the wound.

Unforgiveness is rarely about someone or something. It is never about holding someone else hostage. It is always about you, the one holding the key, but unsure if you are willing or ready to use it. Unforgiveness is not only a moral and emotional issue. It is an energetic entrapment in which you have, consciously or unconsciously, agreed to participate. Unforgiveness says: *"I will carry this pain until they understand."* Spiritual Hygiene says: *"I will step into the truth and release the pain so I can be free."* The Voice of Unforgiveness is nasty. Nasty and complex. It says:

- *"They don't deserve my grace."*
- *"If I let go, it means what they did was OK."*
- *"If I forgive, I have to let down my guard, and that's not safe."*
- *"I can't forgive them. Not for this."*

What evades an unforgiving mind and heart is that the "*them*" is you. Unforgiveness is not a flaw of character. It is protection, a fortress built around pain that has not yet been metabolized. It often forms when justice never comes. When the apology never arrives. When closure was a luxury denied to your soul. Energetically, unforgiveness traps your spirit in a loop. You replay the moment. You rehearse the pain. You keep your energy entangled with those who have hurt you because your mind does not know how to be free without pretending what happened didn't matter. When left unaddressed, unforgiveness becomes an anchor. It tethers you to your own bitterness. You grow, but you don't expand. You rise, but you don't soften. You preach healing and love but carry a quiet edge. Spiritual Hygiene demands a reckoning, not a forced forgiveness, but a sacred release. A willingness to no longer be defined by the injury. A willingness to say:

- *"I no longer need them to pay for me to be free."*
- *"I no longer need to withhold love from myself in their name."*
- *"I do not forgive to forget. I forgive to remember who I am."*

Energetic responsibility of forgiveness cleanses your energy field of soul ties that no longer serve you. It dissolves the residual cords of resentment. It restores vibrational space for softness, receptivity, and spiritual fluidity. To cleanse unforgiveness does not rewrite history. It reclaims the inner authority and the authorship of your future. Forgiveness is a choice to stop punishing yourself for someone else's wrongdoing.

Mental Impact:

Unforgiveness locks your mind into past injury. It becomes a loop of pain, justice, and imagined vengeance. You replay the betrayal. This motivates you to withhold your softness, equating forgiveness with betrayal of self.

Emotional Impact:

You are hardened. Guarded. You carry a quiet sadness that no joy can reach. Trust becomes impossible. Grace feels unavailable or inaccessible, especially for yourself.

How It Shows Up:

You find it challenging to celebrate others. You close your mind and heart quickly. You avoid self-reflection. You mistrust Divine timing. You silently hold others hostage in your heart and punish yourself in the process.

The Cost of Not Clearing:

Unforgiveness binds your soul to the wound. Your personal growth plateaus. Your aura becomes thick with grief and protection. Your sacred power cannot fully flow because you are still carrying what you swore you buried.

Every Voice Is a Request for Reunion

Whether it speaks as guilt, shame, anger, blame, avoidance, or unforgiveness, every survival voice is a veiled prayer. These voices are fragments of your soul crying for attention. In essence, they are saying: *"Come find me. I am stuck here."* Each voice disrupts your energetic flow because it is incomplete. When left unacknowledged, these voices will lead you round and round the mulberry bush, bringing you back into the very pain you so desperately want to release. When Spiritual Hygiene is practiced and the voices are witnessed, honored, and brought into the light of truth, they become healed aspects of your inner landscape. They are no longer your protectors. They become participants in your spiritual integration and wholeness. This is the power and value at the heart of Spiritual Hygiene:

- To meet what has gone unloved within you.
- To take responsibility for what your soul carries.
- To restore sacred order to the kingdom within.

When these voices are in the throne of your inner life, the result is energetic chaos. You are no longer ruled by soul; you are driven by survival. Your decisions are reactive. Your manifestations collapse. Your joy flickers without fuel. While it may feel like too much time has passed where the voices have been in charge, it is never too late to reclaim the field. Spiritual Hygiene is about meeting them and tending to them with consciousness and commitment. Devotion to Spiritual Hygiene for your mind, your heart, is how you honor the origin of the voices without surrendering your future to them. It is the work of becoming sovereign. Everyone carries a whisper of each voice: shame, guilt, blame, performance, anger, avoidance, inheritance, delay, unforgiveness, false responsibility. Some are louder than others. Some are more entrenched than others.

Whether you are new to the journey of healing, or trying to figure out what to do next, after everything else you have tried, Spiritual Hygiene puts the ball in your court and the power in your hands. It may feel like the work of Spiritual Hygiene is too much to do. That would not be a supportive voice to follow. These voices are not foreign invaders. They are simply echoes, residue from your soul's walk through the human experience. These voices rise and fall within us like tides in the ocean. Each voice is a response to a specific soul wound. The one that becomes dominant is the one that protected you at the most formative or frightening time in your life. *The louder the trauma imprint, the louder the protective voice.* Now that you know and hopefully understand, you are empowered to choose—more of the past, or a clearly authored future. To reclaim your self-value, self-worth, self-esteem, self-love, and spiritual sovereignty does not require you to relive the trauma and reject the voices. The path to reclamation is the willingness to *reeducate* them, and yourself in the process.

I have walked this path for a very long time. I have learned a great deal about myself, including all aspects of myself, and the voices that helped me survive. Along the way, I learned many important and powerful things. I have learned that there comes a moment when words are no longer necessary. In those moments, I have learned to pray. I pray this prayer for you:

May every part of you, once silenced by survival,
now sing in the key of your soul.
May your energetic field be cleared with elegant grace and ease.
May your inner throne be occupied with truth.
May you give yourself permission to inquire within and silence the voice that has caused the most harm.
May the voice that leads you from this day forward
be the voice of love,
clear, unapologetic, unshaken, and unmistakably your own.

OPENING PRAYER

The River I Refused to Cry

Divine Presence, Keeper of Sorrows, Sovereignty of Stillness,
I enter this sacred space with trembling hands and a guarded heart,
yearning to be met in the places I have long avoided.
Today, I give myself permission to grieve, not as weakness or as failure.
I grieve as sacred testimony to all I have carried, lost, and loved.

I welcome the holy ache of healing and release.
I make room for the tears I swallowed to survive.
I open the vault where memory weeps and soul longs to breathe.
I ask that all that has been buried rise.
I allow all that has been silent to speak.

I ask now for the courage to feel what I could not feel before,
to mourn what happened,
and to grieve what never happened but should have.
Hold me, Holy One, in the space between pain and peace.
Let Your presence be my refuge as I unclench the fist of suppression.

I declare that grief is not my enemy.
It is my medicine, my midwife, my sacred river of release.

Let the waters flow. Let the numbness thaw.
Let this be the beginning of my return to wholeness.

Amen. Aṣẹ Aho.
And so, it is.

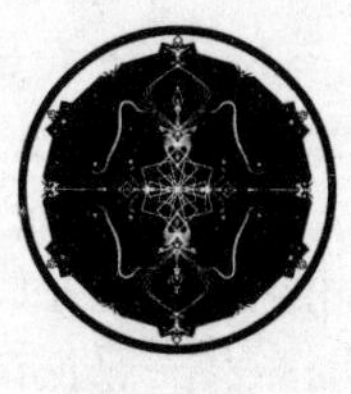

CHAPTER 5

Permission to Grieve

A Sacred Invitation into the Final Door of Healing

It was 8:27 on a bright July Sunday morning when I got the call. *Nisa is dead.* Laura's voice was soft. Gentle. Almost reflective. I knew that she knew that she was breaking my heart. I also knew she could deliver the message because she was spiritually clean. Still, hearing those words blew several circuits in my brain.

The grounded spiritual teacher in me had known it was coming. I had prayed it would be later rather than sooner. Two weeks to the day after the doctor insisted that she do something about her infected toe, his prediction came true. The mother in me, the one who had resisted, denied, and used every tool in her Mothering Bag of Tricks, fell to the floor. Not weeping. Not screaming. Not breathing. Just listening. Her son had found her. He had spent the night with her, fallen asleep on her bed while she rested on the sofa. He asked her what she wanted for breakfast. She didn't answer. He called the police. Then my friend Laura. He did not call his mother's mother. Laura knew that it was out of order, and she was clean enough to hold him with compassion, rather than try to correct the misstep at the time.

He left the apartment. The police were on their way. I assume it was the spiritual teacher who made the forty-minute drive to Nisa's home. Laura met *her* outside the building, escorted *her* to the elevator, and walked *her* down the long, hot hallway. It was the heartbroken mother who opened the apartment door and saw her baby girl lying on the sofa with a carton of fruit punch in her hand. It was the mother who turned around and fainted in the hallway. When I came back to my senses, my first thought was: *She must have been thirsty.*

Grief is the sacred ache of the soul when it is ready to release what it once held dear, whether it was real or imagined, joyful or painful, fleeting or enduring. It is not always about death. It is about endings, transitions, and the unspoken farewells that the mind cannot name but the heart deeply feels. Grief is holy. It is the evidence of love and longing. It is the residue of attachment and expectation. It is the body's response to energetic rupture, the heart's mourning for what was, and the soul's yearning for what could not be. We often think of grief as something to endure, something to survive. However, Spiritual Hygiene invites us to see grief as something to be honored. To make space for. To tend to with reverence. Grief is a healer, and when approached with awareness, with honesty, it does not break us. It baptizes us.

The Grief We Carry, the Grief We Wear

Nisa was grieving long before she passed. Her body grieved the betrayals it could not speak. Her heart grieved the absence of safety, even in the presence of love. Her spirit grieved a freedom she could not imagine, and a version of herself she did not know how to become. She was grieving the mother she lost when Rhonda could not be fully present. She was grieving the girl she had to abandon to survive. She was grieving the inheritance of silence, of fear and survival, of spiritual bypassing that had been passed down through generations. Nisa did not know how to name her grief. Instead, it named her. It dressed itself as rebellion, resignation, or refusal. As avoidance, anger, delay, and unforgiveness. These were the voices of her trauma that spoke louder than her truth.

Her grief lived in the shadows of her lack of self-awareness. It hid behind the Voice of Blame, whispering that someone else should have done more. It curled itself around the Voice of Shame, convincing her that something within her was broken. It danced with the Voice of Inheritance, replaying old patterns with new pain. It fueled the Voice of

Survival, keeping her bound to the familiar rhythm of emotional isolation. In the absence of self-honesty, the kind that says, *"I hurt. I'm afraid. I need help,"* her grief became a closed door, locked from the inside. I know this about my daughter because I learned this about myself. I can share these things about her with mindfulness, love, and compassion because no one shared them with me, about me. My Spiritual Hygiene practice has given me the courage and clarity to share it with myself, out loud.

Unwept Loss and the Wisdom of Surrender

I never grieved for my mother. She died when I was two. No one told me she had passed, not in a way a child could understand, and even if they had, how does a two-year-old grieve? No one teaches a child how to hold sorrow in a world that barely acknowledges they have the right to feel. Instead, I was told and raised to believe that my stepmother was my mother. I did not discover anything different until I was thirty. I never grieved the loss of my childhood.

It disappeared into the chaos of domestic violence, into the silence that followed physical and sexual abuse. I wore survival like a second skin, not realizing that the cost of survival was my own soul's softness.

I never grieved the collapse of my self-worth at sixteen, when my first love, the father of my son, abandoned me after I told him I was pregnant. I told myself to be strong. I told myself I didn't need him. But what I didn't tell myself is that I had been shattered. I never grieved the loss of my dignity when my first husband, Gemmia's father, a Vietnam veteran addicted to drugs, was arrested for robbing a neighbor's home on the army base at Fort Benning. That one act stole my shelter, my security, and the little bit of stability I had stitched together. I was evicted. My spousal allotment was cut. And I returned to Brooklyn, pregnant, with a toddler in tow, no money, carrying not just a child, but the shame of being married to a convicted felon.

I never grieved the loss of my self-respect when I chose to stay with a man who beat me before, after, and during my pregnancy with his child. The worst of the beatings came after someone whispered to him that the baby might not be his. My womb was full, and so was my silence.

I didn't grieve my father's death either. He took his own life. Of all his five children, I was the only one he left a note for. I didn't make space to mourn my daddy because I didn't know how. There was no time to grieve the losses of friends, of jobs, of hope. There was no ritual for the betrayals. No ceremony for the abandonments. I buried each pain beneath performance, perseverance, and a sense of purpose. For a time, that seemed like enough.

The only time I came within spitting distance of truly meeting grief was when my daughter Gemmia died. Her death pulled me under, into a very dark place. Unfortunately, I was too numb to be scared. Grief put me in bed for five months. I forgot to honor it. I didn't remember to walk with it, so I wrestled with it. I tried to bargain. I tried to outrun it with sleep, prayer, and random spiritual practices. Even though Spiritual Hygiene had become the foundation of my life, my practice was no match for the tsunami of unprocessed grief that surged to the surface. Grief does not forget. It waits. It waits for the stillness. It waits for the cracking. It waits for your surrender. I knew I had come to a gunfight with a water pistol the day I sat with a actual pistol in my own hand, pointed at my own head. That was the day I met the cost of deferred grief. That was the day I realized that even strength must bow—no matter who you are or how accomplished, healing requires truth. That grief is not an enemy; it is an opening. Thank goodness, thank God, that surrender is a sacred law of Spiritual Hygiene. Because when I did not know how to save myself, Surrender did.

The Cost of Unexpressed Grief

Unacknowledged grief becomes toxicity. It festers as resentment, disconnection, chronic fatigue, and emotional rigidity. It becomes spiritual congestion, a kind of soul smog that clouds the ability to feel joy, to give love, to receive guidance. Nisa's grief, unspoken and unmet, became a silent war within her body. It was never the diabetes alone. It was the emotional exhaustion of carrying stories she could not complete and questions she could not ask. She needed permission. But no one had taught her how to grant it to herself. It is my intention to let this chapter do what was never done for her: *offer the sacred permission to grieve.*

For her. For myself. For you. For every version of yourself you had to become just to keep going.

Grief and the Four Doors of Healing

Grief is the final door in Level I because it requires all the others to be open. Without self-awareness, the first door, we do not even recognize what we've lost. Without self-honesty, the second door, we cannot name the truth of our pain. Without energetic responsibility, the third door, we continue to carry the weight of what is not ours. Without reckoning with trauma and its voices, the fourth door, we confuse grief with weakness, and numbness with strength. To grieve well, we must first give ourselves *permission*: Permission to feel without fixing. Permission to cry without apology. Permission to be undone, unguarded, unmasked. Permission to not know how to move forward, while knowing that we cannot go back. In that sacred pause, where the pain is no longer denied and the healing is not yet complete, we are met by the Divine. We dwell there, in the sacred presence, not to be repaired, but to be *remembered*.

The Power of Spiritual Cleanliness Amid Chaos

By the time the police arrived, Nisa's youngest son had already erupted twice. The first eruption came when he turned on my son—his uncle—with fists clenched in rage and a mouth spilling every wound his mother had sown into him. The second came when he lashed out at Laura, his godmother, the one person who remained steady in compassion. One moment he was screaming wildly in the street; the next he was confronting everyone, including me, carrying the weight of inherited anger, unresolved stories, and the painful narratives Nisa had passed down to him like heirlooms wrapped in grief.

Her death had been anticipated by the doctors. Because of this, the attending physician authorized her body to bypass the hospital morgue and go directly to a funeral home. Both my grandson and I called different ones. The one he called arrived first. I asked the funeral director a simple question, which ignited yet another storm. He erupted again. Accusations. Expletives. Condemnations. What I had done. What I hadn't done. What he would never ask me for. How he would bury his mother on his own. His voice carried the fury of every unhealed wound, the agony of every childhood disappointment, the fire of a protector who was too young to carry so much pain. His aggression was so intense that the funeral director got in the hearse, backed away, and left.

When the funeral director I had called arrived, the air changed. He snapped again. This time, he snatched his mother's purse and her Bible, both of which I had gently set aside to keep as sacred relics. He paced. He cursed. He became grief embodied—raw and ravenous. A rabid soul lashing out at anything that moved. He refused to allow the funeral director into the apartment. He identified me as the "*adversary*," telling them they could come in, but I could not. It was the ruckus in the hallway that prompted the neighbors to call the police. When they arrived, he slammed the apartment door in their faces, telling them the same thing. He had not broken any laws. His name was on the lease. They could come in to get his mother's body, but I could not enter the apartment.

After several moments of back and forth, I walked to the door and prayed silently. Everyone and everything fell silent and still. My grandson opened the door, perhaps believing we had left. When he looked out, my face was the first one he saw. Our eyes locked. Without raising my voice above a normal speaking tone, I said, *"Beloved, I know that is your mother, but that is my daughter. In the same way she would stand for you, I am standing for her. I need you to get out of the way so we can remove her body."* He opened the door. As they wheeled the gurney with her body down the hall, I walked behind them reciting the Twenty-third Psalm: "Yea, though I walk through the valley . . . I shall fear no evil."

When the hearse pulled away we had all gathered again in front of the apartment building. The neighbors had heard the news. Some of them came down to offer condolences to me. My grandson was raging again. People were staring. Cars were slowing down as they passed by. I cannot recall now what we were discussing then, but I do remember my grandson threatening me. Correction: He said something that could be construed as a threat. My son, my beautiful, *"You don't disrespect my mother"* son, stepped in. He begged me to leave. I told him I would not leave until *he* left. Not out of defiance, but out of honor. Out of a mother's commitment to bear witness to every moment of her child's earthly chapter. In my mind, this could not, would not be a story of an uncle, my son, pummeling his nephew, my grandson, into the concrete pavement. We all left together: Me, the grieving mother. Me, the spiritual teacher. My son. Auntie Godmother Laura, and four members of my staff, who had quietly shown up as soon as they heard the news. We walked away as one. But I carried many within me.

The next few hours vanished into stillness. I made calls. I told the people I needed to tell. I spoke to the people I knew would have their hair on fire if they could not reach me. I spoke with an eerie calmness that made others uneasy. *"Are you OK?" "Do you need anything?" "What can I do?"* They asked these questions as if they didn't hear it in my voice already. I was shattered. But I was clean. Not numb. Not hardened. Not in denial. I was processing, internally and spiritually. I was honoring every thought. I was listening to every feeling. I was questioning nothing and acknowledging everything. I was devastated. I was heartbroken. And I was mentally, emotionally, and spiritually clean.

Grief, in its most primal expression, is not pleasant or poetic. Sometimes it is rage. Sometimes it is silence. Sometimes it is the quiet dignity of holding your center in the face of another's storm. Spiritual cleanliness is not the absence of emotion. It is the refusal to let emotion pollute your truth. On that day, I did not react. I *responded.* From soul. From surrender. From love. I responded from the strength I had excavated through years of inner work, and from the experience of burying Gemmia. It was a strange thought. When it landed, I was startled. *I know how to do this. I have done it before. Act like you know this will not kill you.* In that moment, I learned something no book, no sermon, no sacred text could have taught me: ***When you are spiritually clean, you are solid within yourself. Your cleanliness renders you clear enough to stand in the fire of someone else's unprocessed grief, or anger, or shame, and still remember who you are.***

Grief as a Sacred Threshold

Grief is not an obstacle to healing. It *is* the healing. To cleanse mentally, emotionally, and spiritually, you must let the river of grief flow through you. You cannot control it. You must learn how to welcome it. To bless it. It is the movement of emotion that breaks open the hardened shell around the heart. It is the softening of the inner soil where new seeds of truth can be planted. A spiritually responsible and mature soul does not avoid grief. She learns how to sit with it. To breathe through it. To see it and speak to it as a friend, not an enemy. Perhaps most courageously, with a deep desire to be healed, she learns to listen to grief and ask it what it has come to reveal. Amid the shock and pain that a loss can cause, it is important to remember that grief is not only about what has been lost. It is primarily about what has been *loved.* What if grief is the sacred sign that our hearts were open when we thought they were battered and closed? What if only grief can remind us that our hopes are still alive? What if grief has the power to challenge us, to dare us to believe in something more than we have known? What if? Maybe. Maybe not. Could be. Who knows?

The Cost of Unexpressed Grief

I did not attend my daughter's funeral. I had come to understand that my grandson's bravado was a grief-driven performance: loud, sharp, unpredictable. I paid for her services, yes. I made sure someone asked him what he wanted, and I ensured it was provided. But in the depths of my soul, just beneath my devastated heart, I knew that I would not be emotionally safe in his presence. I could not trust that my being there, despite my financial support, despite my silence, would not set him off. I would not give him the opportunity to dishonor *his* mother by dishonoring *her* mother. Holding those thoughts, without judgment or anger, I created my own ritual. I went to the funeral home the day before the service. Her godmother and a few other close friends were also there. We sat with her. I prayed for her. I anointed her with the tears that I had not shed with her and for her during her short, burdened life. I asked for her forgiveness. I offered her mine.

I asked the funeral director to polish her nails purple. It was her favorite color. I made her a three-strand necklace of amethyst and mother-of-pearl. Amethyst, the stone of transformation, supports movement from one state into another. Mother-of-pearl promotes tranquility. It is believed to cleanse and purify the aura. It is associated with the Divine feminine, nurturing the soul, calming the spirit, and fostering inner peace. I wanted that for her. With Spiritual Hygiene, I had given it to myself.

I do not believe death is the end. I believe it is a doorway. A return, not just to your Source and Creator, but also a return to the truth.

The physical realm, what we can see, hear, and touch, is third-dimensional reality. The spiritual realm, what we can sense, feel, and what we know, even when there is no physical evidence, is fifth-dimensional reality.

Imagine, on a bright afternoon, you are running across a field holding the string of a kite. The wind lifts the kite high, painting a colorful arc against the sky. Soon the kite disappears into the clouds. To your eyes, it is gone. Yet the gentle tug and pull of the string in your hand is proof enough that the kite is still there, even if it cannot be seen.

This is the difference between the third dimension and the fifth dimension of reality. The third dimension is the visible kite, what you can see, touch, and measure with your senses. The fifth dimension is the invisible pull of the string, what you can feel, know, and trust beyond physical evidence.

I believe that death is a crossing from form to formlessness, from 3D to 5D and beyond. I believe that we are ushered into a formless state as an opportunity to shake off the shackles of the ego-driven personality, the spiritual smog of the 3D world, so that we can start all over again. And so, I adorned Nisa in a language the soul understands: beauty, intention, reverence. I gave to her soul what I did not know how to give to her mind and heart when she was subjected to the poor Spiritual Hygiene that Rhonda infected her with. I gave her what she could not or refused to accept from Iyanla.

Her funeral was a ceremony for the people who knew her. My time with her was a ritual for the parts of me that still longed to know her, and to be known by her. In the stillness of that room, on the lower level of a funeral home, surrounded by silence and sacred stone, my daughter Nisa Camille and I began to heal.

Spiritual Hygiene for the Heart

Grief is the natural, sacred, and often unspoken response to loss, *any* loss. It is not only reserved for death. At its core, grief is *love searching for a place to go*. It is the ache of the soul recognizing that something it once held, expected, or identified with is no longer there.

It may arise from the death of a loved one, the loss of a dream, a betrayal, a transition, a broken identity, or a generational pattern being released. Grief is not a problem to be solved. It is a process of integration. It is the soul recalibrating itself in the presence of emptiness.

Grief requires presence, and presence requires surrender. Most of us have been taught that strength is silence, that pain must be hidden, that survival matters more than softness. We avoid grief because:

- We fear being overwhelmed by it.
- We carry inherited beliefs that emotion is weakness.
- We don't know how to hold space for pain without trying to fix it.

No one modeled grief as a sacred act. It is commonly considered a private, sometimes shameful breakdown. Perhaps in service to Spiritual Hygiene, we can now acknowledge that we resist grief because it demands *truth.* To grieve fully, authentically, we must admit what mattered, and what did not. We must be willing to say, *"That hurt me. This shaped me. This ended something in me."* However, when we are talking about a departed loved one, the ego will tell us, *"That's not nice."* The level of honesty the grief requires may terrify the ego, but it *liberates the soul.*

Perhaps in service to Spiritual Hygiene, we can now tell a deeper truth: *We resist grief not because we are weak, but because grief demands honesty.* Honesty, especially emotional honesty, dismantles the ego's illusion of control. To grieve fully is to surrender our curated narratives. It means admitting what mattered deeply. It requires confessing what we lost, what we loved, and what we never received. It dares us to speak words we've choked back: *"That shattered me." "That changed me for-*

ever." "That was not fair." "That hurt me." Grief is not just a feeling; it is also a revelation. It reveals what the soul holds sacred and what the ego tried to bury beneath performance, pride, or politeness. When the grief is about a departed loved one, the ego often resists even more. The voice of the ego says, *"Don't say that. It's not nice. Be grateful. Be strong."* Thank goodness that grief is not concerned with niceness. It is concerned with wholeness. To be whole, we must tell the truth about our experience, not just the memory.

Grief demands that we put down the mask and pick up the mirror. It invites us into the holy ache of what is real. While this breadth, depth, and level of honesty *terrifies* the ego, it liberates the soul. What we grieve, we honor. What we release, we no longer carry. What we cleanse, we reclaim. This is the sacred labor of Spiritual Hygiene: To clean the heart of suppression. To rinse the soul of distortion. To allow grief to become a threshold, not a trap. Let it be said: To grieve is to grow. To grieve is to return to truth, and truth is always the beginning of healing.

The Distinction of Grieving and Mourning

Grieving is the *internal* experience of loss. It is what happens inside the heart, mind, and spirit.

Grief is personal, invisible, and often wordless. It lingers in the breath, in the bones, in the quiet places no one sees. *Mourning* is the *external* expression of that grief. It is how we honor and make visible what we feel inwardly. We express mourning through rituals, tears, storytelling, art, silence, ceremony, and remembrance. Think of it this way: Grief is the seed; mourning is what blooms. To grieve and not mourn is to carry sacred sorrow without release. To mourn without grieving is to perform pain without ever touching its root. Both are needed. Both facilitate healing. Unfortunately, many people get stuck in mourning. It happens when we carry remorse. It occurs when the Voice of Guilt or Shame convinces us that something we did or didn't do should have been done differently. Dr. Elisabeth Kübler-Ross introduced the most commonly taught model for understanding the stages of grief. She identified denial, anger, bargaining, depression, and acceptance. While these stages do not unfold in a linear way, we can see that at each stage, there is the potential for a trauma to be triggered and a voice to be raised. When that happens, we bypass the root of grief and sit on the branches of the trauma that blooms. That branch is called mourning. That branch focuses outward. That branch will hold us until we reach for a tool of Spiritual Hygiene that lowers us gently back into the truth of the pain.

Grief is a cleanser. It purifies the emotional field. It softens mental rigidity. It dissolves spiritual numbness. Grief unclogs the energetic arteries of the soul. It removes the spiritual residue left by denial, avoidance, and suppression. To fully honor grief, you must be willing to:

- Practice self-honesty: "This mattered to me."
- Cultivate self-awareness: "This impacted me because . . ."
- Take energetic responsibility: "I choose to feel this rather than hide from it."
- Engage emotional hygiene: "I release the toxins of unexpressed sorrow."

Grief, when felt consciously, is one of the purest forms of surrender. It does not ask for permission to enter. It arrives as it pleases, with the force of a flood or the slow ache of a whisper. Yet when it is welcomed, when it is witnessed with love, grief becomes an initiator. It humbles the ego, opens the heart, and reorients the soul to what is truly sacred, authentic, and enduring.

In the practice of Spiritual Hygiene, grief is not seen as a detour or interruption of life. It is not a problem to be fixed or a weakness to be concealed. It is a rite of passage, holy, necessary, and deeply transformative. Grief carries us across thresholds of identity, of understanding, and of love itself. Where there is grief, there has been love and connection. Grief is a recognition that something once held dearly has shifted, ended, or been taken. That shifting is sacred. In that shifting, the soul cries out in reverence that is saddled with pain. Grief reminds us of the sacred moments we cannot relive. It honors what has shaped us, and sometimes what has broken us. It echoes the illusion that anything, or anyone, is truly ours to keep. It is that breaking that brings us to our knees and softens us. It is the shards of that breaking that call us inward.

Grief is a cleansing fire, a purifying rain. It can move stagnant energy, clear the residue of attachment, and make room for a new becoming. Grief, like nothing else, strips us of performance and pretension. It reveals the honest contours of our soul. The ego resists this kind of nakedness because it wants control, certainty, and appearance. But grief says: *"Come as you are. Lay it all down. Tell the truth about what mattered, and you will be healed."* This is Spiritual Hygiene of the highest order. In grief, you are not just washing the outer surface of your life, you are also scrubbing the inner altar of your heart. You are not just releasing a person or something that mattered. You are releasing judgments, expectations, regrets, illusions, and the stories that were never fully lived. Grief invites you into the deep waters of remembrance, where what has been lost becomes a teacher, and what has been loved becomes a bridge into your deeper self. If you stay present to it, when the grief has run its course, when it has taught what it came to teach, you will not be who you were. You will be softer, surrendered, more spacious in your thinking, feeling, and being. You will walk lighter because you have shed. You will love more deeply because you are unafraid. You will have made room for all the things you thought would never come. Now maybe they can.

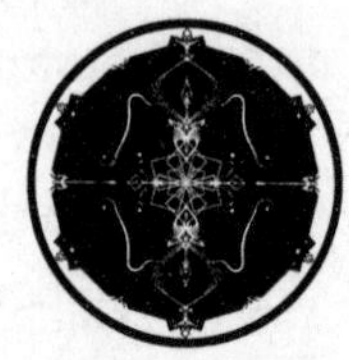

Grief Reflection Page

A Sacred Space to Feel, Remember, and Release

Beloved One,

As you arrive at this reflection page, know this: You are not broken because you grieve. You are not weak because you feel deeply. You are human. More than human. You are a soul.

Grief is not simply about what has been lost; it is about what has lived inside you, what shaped you, what mattered so deeply it left an imprint. Grief is the soul's sacred way of remembering love, processing change, and making room for your next becoming.

This page is not here to fix you or force closure. It is here to hold space for your honesty. Here, you are invited to lay down the masks, the strength, the silence, the stories you've carried. You are invited to speak from the ache. You are invited to honor what your heart knows.

Let your pen become your witness. Let your tears be your medicine.

Let this reflection be a spiritual bath that clears not just pain, but opens the heart and gives you permission to fully live again.

Take a breath. Place your hand on your heart. Say to yourself:

"I am safe to grieve. I am ready to feel. I am willing to heal."

And so, with love, begin.

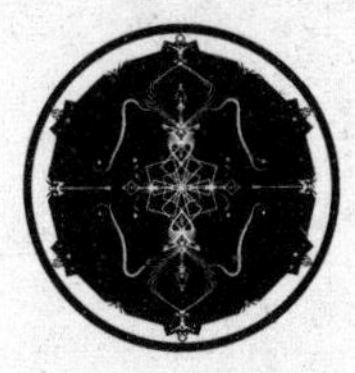

A Sacred Encounter with What Was Lost

Before you begin, create a soft, intentional space. Light a candle. Play soft music. Place a hand over your heart before addressing each inquiry. Breathe deeply.

1. **What are you grieving right now?**
   (Write honestly. It could be a person, a relationship, a lost opportunity, a former version of yourself, a dream deferred, or even something intangible—like safety or innocence.)

   ....

   ....

   ....

   ....

   ....

   ....

2. **Have you ever given yourself permission to fully feel this grief? Why or why not?**

   ....

   ....

   ....

3. **What did this person/experience mean to you? What part of you was or still is connected to it?**

4. **What emotions live beneath your grief?**
   (☐ Sadness ☐ Anger ☐ Guilt ☐ Relief ☐ Numbness ☐ Shame ☐ Gratitude ☐ Other)
   Describe them honestly:

5. **What are the stories you've told yourself about this loss? Are they true? Are they kind? Are they yours?**

6. What has your grief come to teach you?

7. What are you ready to release now, with love and reverence?

May this reflection be your altar. May your grief become your teacher. May your heart be restored to wholeness, piece by sacred piece.

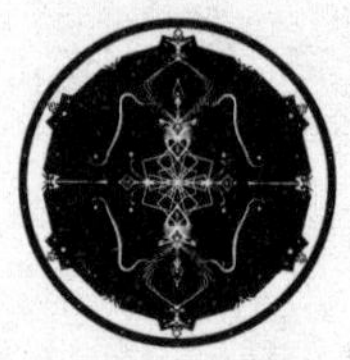

Ceremony of Mourning and Release

A Sacred Ritual to Cleanse the Heart and Honor the Loss

This ceremony may be done alone or in the company of others. It can be spoken aloud, written, danced, or silently held in presence.

PREPARATION

- Find a quiet space.
- Gather three sacred items: one that represents the grief, one that represents healing, and one that represents your spiritual strength.
- Have a bowl of salt water, a candle, and a piece of paper nearby.

Step 1: Name the Grief

Say aloud or write:

> "I name my grief today, not as a weakness but as a witness."
>
> "I am grieving the loss of ____________________."

"I am grieving the way it shaped me, held me, and left me."

Step 2: Honor the Emotion

Place your hand over your heart.

Whisper:

"I feel you."

"I do not resist you."

"I do not judge you."

"I welcome you as sacred."

Let yourself cry. Let your body speak. Let silence surround you. Stay present.

Step 3: Offer the Release

Write down what you are ready to release.

Speak:

"I release the pain that no longer serves."

"I keep the love."

"I honor the lesson."

"I surrender the rest."

Burn (*safely*) or bury the paper. You may also dissolve it in salt water.

Let the act be symbolic and complete.

Step 4: Anoint with Peace

Dip your fingers in the bowl of salt water.

Touch your heart, forehead, or shoulders, saying:

"I cleanse the sorrow."

"I reclaim my breath."

"I anoint myself in remembrance and in peace."

Light the candle.

Step 5: Sacred Declaration

Speak these words as your final rite:

"My grief is holy."

"My heart is whole, even when it aches."

"I carry the memory, not the weight."

"I am cleansed."

"I am clear."

"I am free to live and to love again."

Your Closing Whisper

Grief is not your enemy. It is your womb. It does not come to destroy you. It comes to deliver you to your truth, to your tenderness, to your throne. You are not broken because you grieve. You are becoming whole because you finally do.

So cry if you must. Wail if you need to. Sit in silence if that is all you have. Do it all as a sacred act. Do it now as a return to yourself.

This is your permission to grieve. This is your first breath of healing. This is your sacred release.

I acknowledge your courage.

I honor your strength.

I stand with you and for you in sacred remembering and healing.

Amen. Aṣẹ Aho.

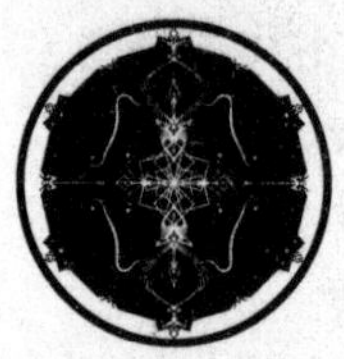

Closing the Gate of Level I

There comes a time on the healing path when silence no longer means safety. When hiding no longer feels like home. When the ache within can no longer be outrun by performance, denial, or survival. This is the sacred threshold of Spiritual Hygiene.

In this first gate, Level I: Healing, you have entered the terrain of your inner world, not to judge it, but to *clean it*. Whether the stories and offerings you have encountered stirred something within you or if you simply took them in as something to consider, the cleaning has begun. The energetic intention of this work is such that your presence is enough.

You have stood at the mirror of your mind, your heart, your habits, and your history. You have remembered what it feels like to truly see yourself. You have been awakened to the gift of **self-awareness**, the light that reveals what has been hidden. You have been exposed to the practice of **self-honesty**, the sacred art of telling yourself the truth, especially when it's hard, especially when it hurts. You have seen how to confront the patterns of **emotional dishonesty**, the masks, the suppression, the pretending not to feel. And then you did what many never find the courage to do: You accepted your **energetic responsibility** by turning the page and continuing to read.

You looked not just at what happened to you, but at how your energy responded. In doing so, you began the process of reclaiming your inner authority by not blaming others, by choosing how you will carry the stories, the sorrow, and the sacredness of your journey. Whether it happened consciously or unconsciously, the process has begun. You have the right to choose whether you will continue the process or not.

You met the Voices of Trauma, those inner protectors disguised as saboteurs. The Voice of Performance. The Voice of Shame. The Voice of Delay. The Voices of Avoidance, Inheritance, Blame, Anger, and Fear. You learned that they are not evil. They are echoes of a soul trying to stay alive in a world that asked it to be silent. They are the residue of what your strength and your courage have already walked you through.

You named the price of pretending. You examined the residue of unforgiveness toward others, and most tenderly, toward yourself. You acknowledged that what you did to survive came at a cost, and you chose to forgive yourself for the toll it took on your soul. And at last, perhaps for the first time in your life, you gave yourself **permission to grieve**. To cry. To remember. To break open without falling apart. To let go of the idea that being strong means being silent. To feel the sacred truth that grief is not the end. It is the *beginning* of healing.

You are not who you were when you began this path. You may not yet be who you are becoming. But you are **cleaner**. Clearer. Softer in the right places. Stronger in the right ways. You have returned to yourself, not as a performance, but as a presence.

This is your sacred return, to the throne of your mind, to the altar of your heart, to the center of your soul. I salute you. I honor you. I thank my beautiful baby girl, Nisa, for guiding me and us through this phase of the journey.

May you carry these teachings as blessings, not burdens.
Not as rules, but as revelations.
Not as pressure, but as presence.

You are worthy of your healing.
You are trustworthy with your truth.

You are whole, even in the becoming.
You are clean.

Level I is complete.
When you feel ready, let the sacred work continue.
And so, it is.
Amen. Aṣẹ Aho.

LEVEL II

SOUL CLEANSING AND DETOXIFICATION

A Sacred Descent into the Body

Welcome, Beloved, to Level II: Soul Cleansing and Detoxification.

At this level, our work is about creating a sanctuary for sacred release and inner purification. We now move into the space of ascending higher in our mind and heart by descending deeper into our feelings and body. The intention is to touch the places in yourself that are tender, forgotten, or buried beneath the dust of survival. This work is not about striving. It is the work of uncovering, of peeling back the layers that no longer serve your truth, of honoring the memories your body has been carrying quietly for years. This is your sacred permission to feel, to remember, to cleanse, and to return to the inner throne.

For this work, you are not expected to be strong. You are invited to be honest. We are not chasing healing. We are making room for it. Here, your body becomes your altar. Your emotions become your offerings, and the wisdom of your soul will become your guide. We are crossing into a space of radical tenderness, where the residue of trauma, memory, and emotional stagnation is no longer something to be afraid of or ashamed of; it will be acknowledged, honored, and released. This is a sacred unraveling, not because we are broken, but because something holy is breaking through.

In Level II, we will travel through five sacred territories:

1. **The Body As the Archive of the Soul**
2. **The Language of Pain**
3. **Permission to Feel**
4. **Rituals of Release**
5. **Returning to Rhythm**

You will encounter stories of people who may feel familiar, either as demonstrations of your own experience or that of someone you know and love, perhaps your Nisa.

To support our work, we will:

- **Learn the Language of Your Body** as a guide for healing: understanding how trauma is stored in the cells, muscles, and breath

- **Identify and Release Emotional Congestion** through sacred movement, water rituals, and gentle practices that invite the body to speak, tremble, weep, and remember

- **Cleanse Inherited Patterns and Ancestral Residue** by clearing energetic imprints that do not belong to your soul's true essence

- **Reframe Pain as Holy Information** by understanding your symptoms, shutdowns, and stories as messengers calling you back to wholeness

- **Restore Your Physical and Emotional Rhythm** by learning to live in alignment with your body's natural intelligence and cycles

As you encounter these teachings and recommendations for the work you can do, remember this is not about perfection, and you cannot do it wrong. This work is about presence, your presence for yourself, within yourself, authentically. This work is not about denying, avoiding, or bypassing pain. It is about learning how to bless and release it. This is where you cleanse not just what you experienced, what was done to you, but this work is also about acknowledging and clearing everything you were forced to carry because of it.

As you move through the pages of Level II, I encourage you to do what you can, what feels right, no matter how often the deceptive intelligence whispers, *"It's not going to work for you. It may work for everybody else, but not you!"* That is something Nisa often said to me. I share with you what I shared with her: *"A little bit of something is better than a whole lot of nothing."*

May your breath deepen.

May your tears baptize.

May your body remember.

May your soul cleanse itself through the grace of embodiment.

You are not alone.

It is not too late.

You are exactly where your healing can begin again.

As always, we begin with prayer.

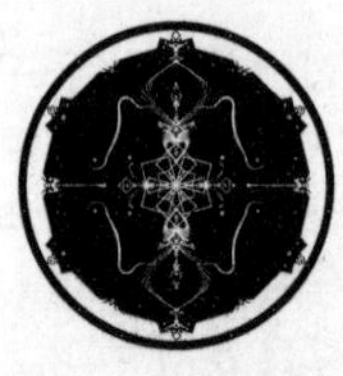

OPENING PRAYER

The Sacred Descent into My Holy Body

Beloved Presence of Divine Grace,
I come now to the altar within, not in search of answers,
but in devotion to truth.
I stand now not as performance, but in presence.
I choose now not to be strong, but to be seen, felt, and freed.

I invite the sacred light of remembrance to descend
gently into my body.
I allow it to illuminate the silent spaces, my clenched jaw,
my tender belly, the ache in my back, the breath I forgot to take.

I am here not to escape. I am here to enter.
I am ready to touch the grief I silenced,
I am willing to encounter the shame I inherited,
I now choose to bless the stories trapped in my flesh.

This is my sacred descent. The deeper I go, the higher I rise.
I call upon the wisdom of my ancestors, the prayers of the unwept,
and the courage of my inner child who is still waiting to be held.
I ask for and open myself to receive cleansing of the dust of survival.
Detoxification from the expectations that hardened me.
Freedom from the illusions that told me feeling was dangerous
and wrong.
Make room, oh Blessed Spirit, make room for healing to arrive
in waves, in weeping,
in trembles, and with truth.

Let my body become the sanctuary.
Let my breath become the balm.
Let my willingness be the testimony that something sacred
is being made new.

I do not need to know how.
I only need to be here.
Willing. Present. Honest. I Am.

May this work become a flowing river, a powerful movement,
a sacred rhythm that leads me back to my original wholeness.

And so I begin.
Washed in grace.
Held by Love.
Restored with elegant ease.

I Ask. I Allow. I Receive.
Amen. Aṣẹ Aho.
And so, it is.

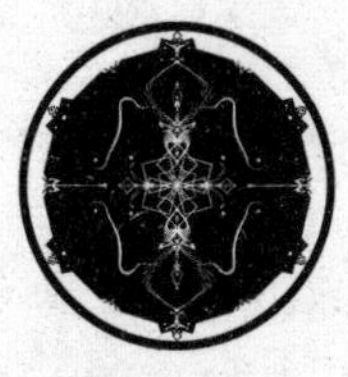

CHAPTER 6

The Holy Unbinding

Allowing the Body to Speak

"What the soul cannot express, the body will remember. What the body cannot release, the spirit will carry. Until it is witnessed, it will remain."

There comes a moment on every healing path when the soul no longer asks for more insight, analysis, or explanation. It seeks relief and release. This is the holy work of Spiritual Hygiene for the body. This is no longer a process of "*fixing*" what is broken. It is time to detoxify and cleanse what is buried, withheld, or heavy. This is the work of returning to the body's natural rhythm of feeling, flow, and freedom. For some, these states of being may feel unfamiliar, even unreachable, yet they are your birthright. In the sacred context of Spiritual Hygiene, these are not luxuries; they are sacred intentions.

At this stage of your journey, you are invited to step into the temple of your body and listen deeply to what still lingers there. The ache in your spine. The weight in your chest. The tightness in your jaw. These are not random discomforts. They are echoes of the voices that have something to say. These are prayers of unspoken grief, unexpressed anger, unmet needs, waiting to be heard, honored, and released. The body remembers everything that the mind could not process, and that the heart was afraid to feel.

The Soul's Cry for Cleansing

Have you ever felt like something inside you was broken or missing? A mental or emotional ache that refuses to go away, no matter how many workshops you attend, books you read, or "*self-help*" tools you try? Have you cycled through countless modalities, therapies, rituals, even mood-altering substances, only to end up in the same relentless search for relief? This may be the voice of your body calling out for healing. Trauma leaves behind energetic residue that settles into the body, mind, emotional field, and soul. Whether the trauma is personal, ancestral, or even culturally inherited, its residue can manifest in every aspect of life—relationships, health, work, finances, and especially how you relate to your own body. I do not speak this from theory. I speak it as a witness. The journey from Ronnie to Rhonda, and from Rhonda to Iyanla, was shaped by hidden pockets of trauma lodged deep in the crevices of my body, places I did not know existed. The unhealed residue of these traumas delayed my healing, distorted my self-perception, and depleted my strength for years.

In 2016, I traveled to Jamaica for a speaking engagement. While there, my colon ruptured. At first, we thought it was food poisoning. I had just gotten dressed and put my makeup on. I was ready to take the stage to address an eager audience when, suddenly, I began vomiting uncontrollably. I thought it was the result of the wonderfully spicy food I had eaten the night before. Twenty minutes in, I realized something else was going on, but I had no pain; I felt perfectly fine. My wonderful daughter-in-law was feeding me Pepto Bismol tablets, and my manager was right at the edge of panic. In my normal, *"Superwoman, I've got this"* posture, I decided I would take the stage anyhow. With a trash can in tow, I went out to the audience and announced to them that I was not feeling well, but I did not come all the way from the United States to disappoint them. I told them that if it became necessary for me to use the trash can, I would, and we could continue with the event. They applauded. Funny how people will unknowingly support you in maintaining trauma-driven, self-destructive behaviors. I spoke for about twenty minutes, my stomach flipping like a 747 amid a tornado. By then, I was also feeling weak and dizzy. I asked myself, *"What would you say if someone in the audience asked you what they should do if they had a commitment to do something but felt deathly ill?"* In that moment, I shared what I was feeling. I told them I had to go take care of myself. I promised them that if I were better, I would come back tomorrow. If I couldn't, I would make sure they received a refund for their tickets. To their credit, the audience stood up, applauded, and told me no refund was required.

A doctor who was in the audience attended to me. She prescribed an anti-nausea medication, believing, like we all did, that I had food poisoning. I made it through the night because my stomach had been emptied of all food. Dry heaving took the place of vomiting, which rendered me physically exhausted. We booked the first plane off the island, which put me in a middle seat for the two-and-a-half-hour flight with my son and a stranger sharing the row. As soon as we sat down, my son instructed the flight attendant to call for an ambulance when we landed.

Morphine and a drug cocktail stopped the heaving long enough for me to do blood work and have a CT scan.

It turned out there was a rupture in my colon, and they could see a mass. I was septic, and they detected some other bacterial virus, which meant I needed to be quarantined. Everyone coming near me needed to wear a gown, face mask, and gloves.

Wait! What? I am contagious? I've got cooties? Physical cooties? It was all too much for my Virgo sensibilities. Not only was I contagious, but I was also being scheduled for emergency surgery. I told the doctor that before any surgery could be performed, I needed to pray and ask God if it was necessary. In his most respectful tone of voice, he replied, *"Oh, I'm a Christian too, but you better pray fast because you are scheduled for eleven o'clock."* It was 10:20.

When I woke up from the surgery, the first face I saw was Nisa's. They told me that she refused to leave the room. She was masked, gowned, and gloved when she stood up and said, *"Hey, old girl, welcome back."* For the eleven days I spent in the hospital, she never left my side. Nisa had worked for the past seven years as a home health aide for an elderly woman. Everything she knew, everything she had learned, she used on me. She was wonderful, gentle, kind, and patient because, as someone who had never been ill, I was a horrible patient.

The mass they detected in my colon was actually my left ovary. Somehow—no one knew how because they had never seen anything like it—the ovary had plugged the hole in my colon. There was no hemorrhaging. No scar tissue. Somehow, the ovary made its way into the colon and plugged up the hole.

The Body Does Not Forget

Before the mind can form a memory, the body has already registered the experience. This is not metaphor. This is sacred physiology. Long before we could speak the language of emotions, our nervous system was fluent in safety and threat, touch and tension, breath and bracing. The body, unlike the mind, does not argue, negotiate, or analyze. It simply records. This is the foundation of somatic memory, the understanding that the body stores the emotional, spiritual, and energetic imprints of our lived experiences. Every sigh we stifled. Every scream we silenced. Every time we tightened our jaw, clenched our fists, or folded into ourselves instead of being allowed to fully express, we encoded a message into our muscles, our fascia, our bones. The body becomes the archive of the soul, a living, breathing, remembering entity that houses both what has been processed and what has not.

Nisa did not cry when her father left. She smiled. She helped. She performed. I am now aware that the sorrow lodged itself in her chest. Twenty years later, she described it as "*a tightness I feel when I breathe too deeply.*" This is why she gave up on meditation. The tears never reached her eyes, but her lungs never forgot. The body remembers the stories we tried to skip over. The silent heartbreaks. The things we tolerated. The betrayals we internalized. Our bodies carried them when our hearts could not.

These imprints may look like:

- Migraines that coincide with conscious or unconscious emotional triggers

- Autoimmune conditions tied to suppressed rage or grief
- Sexual numbness or pain where there was once violation
- Digestive disorders linked to anxiety, lack of safety, or betrayal

Avoid the ego's temptation to make this about blame. For Spiritual Hygiene, it is recognition. The body is not punishing you. It is signaling, faithfully, where love and release are still needed.

From Suppression to Stagnation

During a retreat I facilitated, I encouraged participants to give themselves permission to participate fully in whatever they felt. Whatever came forward. A woman stood up and asked how she would know if it was working for her if nothing happened. She said, *"I don't cry. I just can't."* I explained that crying, while helpful, wasn't necessary. I also asked her if she was willing to give her body permission to cry even if she didn't. Later in a ritual I conducted, where we did gentle pelvic rocking and breathwork, her entire body began to tremble. Immediately, she tensed up. I asked for permission to touch her. She nodded her head, saying it would be OK. I stroked her cheeks and forehead. I held and squeezed her hands. I waved a tissue drenched in rose oil under her nose. When her body finally relaxed, she sobbed for forty minutes. Afterward, she said, *"That wasn't even about today. That was my ten-year-old self. She finally felt safe enough to grieve."* That is the power of the body when it is given space to speak. The emotions were not gone. They were dormant. They were waiting.

The Vessel, Not the Vault

If you want to feel energized, grounded, and spiritually clear, your body must become a vessel, not a vault. The body is a sacred vessel, a living altar; just as you would never leave dust and debris on an altar in a church or temple, you must not allow emotional debris or energetic smog to linger in the sanctuary of your physical form. Through rest, movement, breath, and ritual care, you create a physical environment where the Divine can dwell fully within you. Spiritual Hygiene for the body is not limited to food and fitness. It includes the release of stored grief, unmetabolized fear, and inherited pain that is often embedded in cellular memory.

Because we are addressing the physical body, we must use physical means. Sight. Scent. Sound. Movement. Touch. These are the sacred languages of the body that can be honored through sacred tools of purification, such as sound baths, healing oils, dance, stretching, sweating, bathing, weeping, stillness, and ceremony. Meditation, prayer, and affirmation are sacred and powerful. However, some traumatic memories are not released through words or thoughts alone. Some require your hands, your breath, your hips, your feet. Some require sweat, salt, and sound. This is sacred work.

Your Body Is a Portal, Not A Prison

The greatest lie many buy into is the belief that their body is betraying them. That it is weak, broken, or burdensome. In truth, the body is the most loyal companion you have ever known. It has kept you alive through everything. It wants to be listened to, not managed, not silenced, not rushed. The body wants to be understood and reverently honored. Spiritual Hygiene for the body means you make space for holy unbinding, letting the body unwind from what has offended or abused it. It means you must become willing to learn to be attentive to your body's language.

The language of a body is not always linear or literal, but it is always true. The language of the body is universal in its form but intimately personal in its meaning.

- A racing heart may signal panic in one person, but excitement in another.
- Tears may mean sorrow, but they may also mean freedom.
- Stillness may feel like safety to one person and shutdown to another.

This is why Spiritual Hygiene teaches us to listen deeply and to discern compassionately. No two bodies speak exactly alike, but everyone's body tells the truth of its experience with *radical honesty*.

The ninety days I spent with a plastic bag hanging from the side of my body were the longest, most significant days of my life. It was Nisa who helped me put it on and take it off. I had a deep aversion to the sight and the smell. She handled it as if it were a common, everyday event. It was Nisa who rescued me from the restroom at my hairdresser's the day I put the bag on incorrectly and left little piles of poop in the corridor on my way to the salon. I had lost a great deal of weight—thank goodness, because with that bag protruding from the side of my body, formfitting clothes were a thing of the past. That was my everyday experience. On the spiritual level, I recognized with painful awareness that I had not been nice to my body. I didn't drink or do drugs, but neither did I eat regularly or rest properly.

Around week two, when I could get the bag on and off without support, I had an epiphany: For most of my life, I had been holding on to a lot of *s#*t.* My grandmother's meanness toward me, bordering on emotional abuse, which was often demonstrated as physical abuse; my brother's silent support of the way Grandma abused and neglected me. My father's silent accommodation of his mother's, my grandmother's, mistreatment of me and her inappropriate coddling of my brother. My aunt, making me her emotional sounding board and insisting that I continue calling my uncle *"Daddy"* after she knew he had raped me. The silent whispering about my *"mother,"* who was actually my stepmother, because she was "light-skinned" and had "good" hair, and all the other inappropriate conversations I was privy to and was expected to remain silent about. These sudden flashes of remembrance also gave me a deeper insight: Even as a child, I was usually the sanest one in the room, which no one appreciated.

Another thing I learned during those ninety days was how careless I had been about what I ingested, not just with my body, but also with my mind. When you're forced to see everything you put in your mouth, you gain deep clarity about what to eat, when to eat it, and what it will look like when it comes out. You get very clear about the importance of chewing well so that your food will digest completely. It's one thing when you are talking about food, which you can monitor and control, but when it comes to what you see, hear, and feel, you are upping the ante. I had heard and passed on gossip and malicious speaking. I had tolerated and engaged in name-calling and intentional misrepresentations of myself and others. I had rehearsed angry conversations in my mind that never made their way to my lips. I held on to them. I replayed them. I expanded them, and eventually, I owned them as my truth. *I was stupid. I was ugly. I always thought that I was better than everyone else. I was ungrateful and arrogant. I needed to stay in my place. My big ideas and I were headed for a great big fall.*

There were hundreds of them floating around in my mind. Things I had heard or been told that I ingested and digested without any consideration for their impact on my body. During those ninety days, that bag hanging off my body brought me face-to-face with every fear I had ever experienced. I finally understood why I hesitated when the time came to execute a plan. I also became aware that once my mind had figured out how to move through the voices of the trauma, I drove my body like a Mack truck, an eighteen-wheeler, determined to reach my destination in record time, at any cost.

What Is the Language of the Body?

The language of the body is not made of words. It is made of:

Sensation (tightness, tingling, heat, numbness)

Emotion (tears, joy, fear, rage)

Impulse (the urge to move, to cry, to rest, to scream)

Rhythm (breath patterns, heartbeat, energy levels)

Posture (how you hold or protect parts of yourself)

Symptom (pain, fatigue, illness, disease)

Pain, tension, hunger, and fatigue are not enemies. They are nuggets of information. When you ignore or deny the body's language, you will become "neck-down-dead."

"Neck-down-dead" is the condition of being energetically disconnected from the body while still functioning in the world; alive in thought, moving through tasks, but numb, silent, or shut down below the chin. It is the state of spiritual and emotional disembodiment, where the body becomes a vessel of function rather than a sanctuary of feeling, flow, and Divine presence. In Spiritual Hygiene, this phrase reflects a soul that is no longer listening to the wisdom of its own body, a self that has become so mentally dominant or trauma-protected that the sensations, signals, and sacred messages of the body have been muted or ignored.

When you are "neck-down-dead," the mind becomes the ruler, and the body becomes the servant. You might be able to speak truth, teach wisdom, or offer help to others, but you do so while being unavailable to yourself. This condition often arises in:

- Survivors of physical and sexual trauma who learned to detach from bodily pain or threat
- Highly spiritual people who prioritize transcendent theory over sacred embodiment
- Over-functioners and caretakers who tend to focus on others while neglecting their own needs

The cost of being "neck-down-dead" is that your inner altar goes unattended. You stop feeling fully. You know what to do to get things done, and it becomes the priority. You may lose desire, passion, pleasure, or vitality, or you may be overcommitted, constantly moving, too busy to feel, so you think about what to feel and perform that outwardly. In the process, the body begins to store grief, shame, fatigue, and inherited pain. Over time, this becomes spiritual smog and emotional clutter. It can also manifest as autoimmune issues, inflammation, hormonal imbalance, and physical stagnation. The path back from "neck-down-dead" is not mental. It is *movement*, *breath*, *sound*, *scent*, *sacred sensation* (i.e., *massage*), and *ritual*. To return to life, you must return to the body.

Spiritual Hygiene for the body requires reverence. It means treating your body as a sacred space. Listening to it. Speaking kindly to it. Nourishing it with food and rest. The body does not lie, nor does it hold grudges. As I learned in Jamaica, it does not wait for approval or the most convenient time to speak. This incredible vessel that we have been given to journey through life tells the truth about how your soul is doing, every single day. Learning the language your body speaks is about communion. It is how you return to yourself with reverence.

Learning Your Body's Language

Learning your body's language means becoming fluent in the subtle messages it sends: the flutter in your belly, the tightness in your throat, the ache in your chest. These are not random signals; they are sacred communications from your inner world. To learn your body's language is to build trust with your own temple, to honor what it feels, and to respond with presence instead of dismissal. This is the foundation of embodied Spiritual Hygiene.

Track Sensations Instead of Stories

Instead of saying "I feel anxious," say:

> *"There's tightness in my chest. Body, what do you want me to know?"*
>
> *"My jaw is clenched. Body, what are you feeling right now?"*
>
> *"My belly feels hot. Body, is there something you want me to know?"*

This helps you learn to decode the body's signals without layering interpretation too soon.

Honor the First Impulse

The first movement your body wants to make is often the most honest.

> Stretch?
>
> Lie down?

Walk fast?

Rock back and forth?

That is the body speaking. Listen to it. Let it do what it is requesting.

Journal the Messages

Keep a Body Language Journal. Ask each sensation:

"What are you trying to tell me?"

"What do you need?"

"What are you holding that I haven't acknowledged?"

Ritualize the Response

Once you receive the message, offer a response.

If the body says: *"I'm tired,"* rest becomes your Spiritual Hygiene.

If the body says: *"I'm holding grief,"* tears and movement become your ritual release.

A Word About Ritual: Returning to Sacred Rhythm

In the practice of Spiritual Hygiene for the body, ritual is not regarded as religion, restriction, or rules. For the purposes of healing and restoration, ritual is about rhythm, reverence, and reconnection. Ritual is the way we honor what matters. It is how we bring presence to our breath, intention to our movement, and soul into the everyday. Many fear the word "ritual" because it has been misunderstood, misused, or disconnected from love. Truthfully, ritual is simply the art of turning ordinary acts into sacred ones. Lighting a candle with intention is a ritual. Bathing with prayer, stretching with gratitude, breathing consciously, all of these are rituals when they are done with awareness and sacred purpose.

In Spiritual Hygiene, ritual becomes the bridge between what your body carries and what your soul is ready to release. It creates containers of safety for cleansing what is heavy, restoring what is sacred, and welcoming the Divine into your physical form. Ritual is not always something you perform with or for others. It is something you do with Divine intention, for yourself. This means that ritual is not something to fear. It is something used, engaged, and employed to remember and realign. It is your birthright to make meaning, to move with intention, to turn the mundane into the miraculous. Ritual is the way the body prays.

Sacred Movement as Spiritual Hygiene

Just as we brush our teeth and bathe to maintain physical cleanliness, the soul asks for Spiritual Hygiene through movement to stay clear and whole. Movement is not always exercise. It is not for performance only. It is also used to establish presence and connection. *Sacred movement* is movement with intention. It is the act of letting the body speak in ways that words cannot. It may look like:

- Gentle stretching with deep, slow breathing
- Shaking out the limbs to discharge held energy
- Rolling the hips to reclaim sensual flow
- Placing your hands on your heart and rocking slowly
- Letting your body dance, weep, crawl, or kneel without inhibition

When movement is intentional and sacred, it becomes medicine. Medicine is not meant to fix us. It is meant to bring us back to ourselves. Just to get in the flow of sacred movement, try this simple exercise, one you can use to start your day. Begin with stillness and curiosity. Say, *"Body, what do you need to say today?"* Place one hand on your heart, one on your belly. Wait. Listen. Don't rush.

Even if nothing comes, the question opens the channel.

Surrender the need to do it right. Be OK if it takes several attempts before the body responds, particularly if you are becoming fluent in your body's language. You are not performing. You are releasing. You are awakening. You are reconnecting. How does it feel?

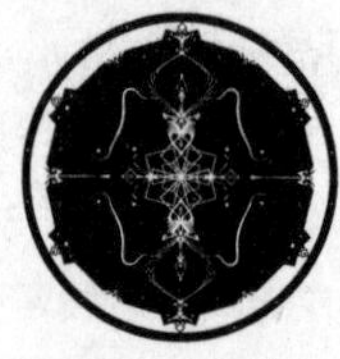

The Wisdom of the Body

It began with a tightness in her chest. She said it was not pain, exactly, but a persistent pressure that pulsed like a silent cry beneath the surface. Nisa had been "holding herself together" for so long that she had forgotten what it meant to feel. When her feet started to swell, she bought larger shoes. When she felt weak and dizzy, she practiced her smile. Her presence, dutiful and attentive, was beginning to show signs of disconnection and fatigue. One evening, as she collapsed into bed, her body began to tremble without cause. No tears came, but her hands shook, her breath shortened, and her heart pounded as though it were delivering a message in a code she had long forgotten. *"I'm sick,"* she finally whispered aloud. The room was still. In that stillness, the body finally spoke, for the first time in years, Nisa was ready to listen. The truth is, she had no other choice.

What Is Somatic Stewardship?

Somatic Stewardship is the sacred art of reclaiming a relationship with the body. It begins with not holding the body as a burden to manage, but rather considering it a sacred site of memory, meaning, and Divine intelligence. It is the daily practice of honoring the body as a living oracle: a revealer of truth, a transmitter of wisdom, and a sanctuary for soul embodiment. Your body is not a machine to be operated or an image to be perfected. It is a living altar that is breathing, sensing, and remembering.

To steward the body is to enter into a holy relationship with its sensations, to regard a tight chest not as an inconvenience, but as a sacred message. To recognize fatigue not as failure, but as a Divine call to rest. It is to slow down enough to listen to the rhythms beneath the noise, and to move with your body rather than against it. In the framework of Spiritual Hygiene, Somatic Stewardship means caring for the body as the altar, the antenna, and the archive:

- As altar, it is a sacred space worthy of reverence, cleansing, and devotion.
- As antenna, it is your energetic receiver, picking up subtle truths from your environment and your spirit.
- As archive, it is the storage site of unspoken stories, ancestral memory, and emotional residue seeking release

Modern culture teaches you to numb, override, or judge the body, to push past its signals, to distrust its needs, to mold it into something externally acceptable. Somatic Stewardship teaches the opposite. It asks you to slow down, soften inward, and reinhabit the home you've always lived in. This practice is not about control. It is about connection. It is not about domination. It is about dialogue. It is not about perfection. It is about presence. To become a Somatic Steward is to reclaim your wholeness through the body, and to allow your healing to be more than an idea. Your healing and wholeness must become a felt, lived, embodied experience, in the quiet of your cells and the language of your breath, so that your true authority begins to rise.

To be a Somatic Steward is to live in a conscious relationship with the sacred terrain of your body, and to see it as a Divine companion on the path of remembrance. This stewardship requires spiritual integrity. It requires the humility to listen when your body says "enough," and the courage to respond when it says "rest." It is not rooted in vanity, force, or appearance. It is rooted in reverence, where every breath becomes a communion, every sensation a message, and every ache an invitation to return to what has been exiled within. Somatic Stewardship is a sacred reclamation of the body as a spiritual teacher, a witness to the unseen, and a living map of your soul's journey. This is not theoretical work. This depth of work is intimate, cellular, and holy.

The Body as Truth-Telling Temple

Nisa had been in the hospital for three days before I knew she was there. It wasn't that we hadn't spoken. We had. One evening, she called and told me she was sick. Without a second thought, I made the forty-five-minute drive to her apartment. Once there, I knocked on the door feverishly. She didn't answer. I called her. No answer. I called her son. He had not spoken to her. I asked her neighbor if she had seen her. She had, three or four hours earlier. By this time, my mouth was dry, my hands were trembling, and I was about to call the police to break down the door. Nisa called. She had gone to the supermarket to get some juice. *"I told you I was coming. I could have picked it up for you."* She said she needed a few other things and didn't think I would be coming right away. *"How did you get to the store?"* She called an Uber. *"Where are you? I can pick you up."* She decided that since she was out, she would get her nails done. The salon was right next to the store. My body was screaming, *"She is not telling the truth."* Now, if I went to the closest supermarket and didn't find her, what would I do? If I didn't find her in the nail salon, what would that mean? *"Nisa, you said you didn't feel well, and I am here to support you. What do you want me to do?"* She felt better. She was alright. I could go home. She would call me later and maybe come over tomorrow. I knew something was off, but I had no idea how off. I discovered later that she had been admitted to the hospital that same day.

Your body is the first to know and the last to forget. Long before your conscious mind has made meaning of an experience, your body has registered it. The tightening of your jaw, the flutter in your belly, the tension behind your eyes—these are not random discomforts. They are messages from your inner sanctum, the subtle language of truth trying to rise to the surface. The body cannot lie. It may be silenced. It may be overridden. It may be numbed. Unlike your mouth, it cannot lie. While the mind can rationalize betrayal, the body will still tremble in its presence. While the voice may say, "I'm fine," the shoulders may slump, the breath may be shallow, the spine may curl. These are not betrayals of your will. They are confirmations of wisdom. They are an invitation to treat the body as a temple and to consider it to be sacred ground. Not only because your body houses your spirit, but also because it is your most faithful truth-teller. It reveals what is unresolved. It reflects what is unspoken. It remembers what was unsafe to express. The messages and signs the body sends are not meant to punish you for poor treatment or the absence of Spiritual Hygiene. They are your invitation to healing.

Listening to the Language of the Body

There is a language beneath language. A rhythm beneath words. A sacred communication system that predates logic and transcends intellect. It is the language of sensation. This is the first language your soul used to speak to you in this life. Before you formed sentences, you knew safety by the feeling of a heartbeat against your ear. You knew danger not by explanation, but by a rising wave of fear in your stomach. You learned belonging not from words, but from warmth. The body does not speak in words. It speaks in signals:

- A flutter of anxiety before a boundary is crossed
- A lump in the throat when truth goes unspoken
- A sudden headache when your mind is trying to override your intuition
- A heaviness in the chest when grief is unexpressed

To listen to the body is to learn to interpret these sacred signals with tenderness. Most people only listen to the body when it screams in the form of illness, exhaustion, or breakdown. Somatic Stewardship asks us to listen when it whispers. To pay attention to the faint tightening, the subtle shift in posture, the breath that doesn't fully land. When you attune yourself to the body's voice, you begin to hear the soul's echo. The body is not separate from your soul. It is your soul's sacred instrument.

Listening to your body can be uncomfortable at times. The body might say *"Slow down"* when your life demands acceleration. Sometimes, it says *"This is not safe"* when your ego is trying to impress or be accepted. You may have heard it say *"Leave"* before your mind has found the courage to act. Your body will not abandon you even when you have abandoned it. It waits patiently for you to return to your own sacred ground. This, then, is the first vow of Somatic Stewardship: *I will listen to my body as I would listen to God. With reverence. With patience. With trust.*

Detoxing Internalized Oppression Stored in the Body

I taught my children not to tell me things until it became overwhelming for them. This was because I was usually overwhelmed. Fighting off my husband. Maintaining the appearance of having it all together for my children, the neighbors, and anyone else who was looking. When I discovered that Nisa had been in the hospital, alone, for three days before her son called me, I did not ask why. I immediately said, *"Forgive me."*

What we call internalized oppression is not just an idea or a belief; it is a felt condition. It shapes the way the body folds inward, tenses in crowds, shrinks under scrutiny, and braces under pressure. It is not always conscious. In fact, it often becomes so deeply ingrained in the somatic fabric that we confuse it with our personality.

Spiritual Hygiene is the way we can detox from this oppression in a sacred sense. It is the way we move beyond blame. It eliminates the requirement of an acknowledgment or apology. It says to the body *"I am here now. We can release this memory"* to make room for truth in your tissues.

This detoxification goes beyond the third-dimensional physical realm. It is energetic, emotional, ancestral, and soul-deep. It may look like:

- Shaking out stored fear through dance or trembling practices

- Wailing from the belly to release grief held in the womb space
- Massaging the jaw to loosen generations of silenced truth
- Practicing movements that take up space as a reclamation of worth

It may look like naming aloud the lies you have believed about your body:

"I am too much."

"My pain is not important."

"I must earn my place."

"My pain is a burden to others."

"My body is not worthy of care unless it is productive or pleasing."

These are not truths. These are inherited constraints. Somatic Stewardship invites you to exhale them. To sweat them out, shake them free, and let your body tell the truth rather than the story it was taught. This is holy work. It is not always gentle, but it is always liberating. You are not just cleansing the body; you are decolonizing it. You are sanctifying it. You are releasing the residue of oppression so that your sovereignty may once again take up residence in your flesh.

Nervous System Overload from Hyper-Responsibility

There is a particular exhaustion that lives in those who carry what was never theirs to hold; the tiredness behind the eyes of the over-functioner, the shallow breath of the leader who never lets herself fall apart. This is not just physical fatigue; it is nervous system fatigue. A chronic state of inner alarm rooted in the belief that your safety, survival, or significance depends on how much you do for others. Hyper-responsibility is a trauma-informed adaptation. It is what the body learns when boundaries are never respected, when needs are unmet, and when love must be earned through over-giving. It is a deeply embodied orientation toward managing, fixing, pleasing, and performing. You may tell yourself that you are "dependable" while the body tells a different story. Behind the competence may be a rapid heartbeat. Behind the smile, shallow breathing. Behind the caregiving, clenched fists. Behind the endless capacity, an overwhelmed inner child whispers, "Will someone ever care for me the way I care for everyone else?" When you are living in chronic hyper-responsibility, your nervous system remains in a near-constant state of activation—fight, flight, freeze, or fawn. You are not relaxed. You are braced. You may not even notice it anymore, because this is the only rhythm you've known.

Somatic Stewardship means tending to this inner turbulence with sacred compassion. It means gently restoring your body to a state of rest and safety, with boundaries, through deep breathing, and saying no when your body urges you to do so. It means acknowledging that your worth is not in what you do, and your value is not in your usefulness to others. Spiritual Hygiene reminds you that your Divinity is not determined by how much you hold for others. Spiritual Hygiene for the body means clearing your energy of obligations that have suffocated your freedom. You are not here to be the savior. Nor are you here to be the strong one all the time. You are here to be whole. Wholeness includes stillness and receiving. It also requires the radical act of letting others grow by not rescuing them. This is the body remembering *"I am not a machine. I am sacred."* This is somatic sovereignty. This is the nervous system's path to peace. And the path is holy.

Diet and Spiritual Hygiene

Consumption of food, drink, and other substances is not just physical; it is also spiritual. Food is not just fuel; it is frequency. It carries memory, intention, vibration, and ancestral influence. This means you take in energy, frequency, and intention with every bite, breath, and belief. Every experience, every meal, every emotion becomes part of your energetic field. Just as your thoughts, relationships, and environments can either cloud your clarity or elevate your consciousness, what you feed your body can have a similar effect.

In the practice of Spiritual Hygiene, diet is not reduced to rules, restrictions, or shame. It is reframed as sacred nourishment. A daily opportunity to honor your temple with the things that support vitality, clarity, and alignment. The question is not simply, "Is this food healthy?" The deeper questions are:

- *"Does this food bring life into my cells?"*
- *"Does this food align with the frequency I desire to hold?"*
- *"Does this food feel grounding, clean, and honoring of my inner sanctuary?"*

The Energetics of Food

Each food carries a unique energetic signature:

> **Living, Whole Foods** (fresh fruits, vegetables, herbs, spring water) are high-frequency and support vibrancy, intuitive sensitivity, and cellular regeneration.
>
> **Highly Processed Foods** (like artificial additives, excessive sugars, and hormone-altered meats) tend to carry lower vibrations, often leading to stagnation, inflammation, or energetic heaviness.
>
> **Culturally Sacred Foods** (like ancestral grains, herbal teas, or soul food prepared with intention) can carry deep spiritual resonance when made with reverence and balance.

Your body is a living altar, and what you place upon that altar matters. Food becomes part of your blood, your bones, your breath. It impacts the clarity of your thoughts, the depth of your meditation, and the stability of your emotions. Eating perfectly may be a far reach for many. Eating consciously is quickly becoming a requirement for us all. Conscious eating is a form of spiritual integrity. It is a way of saying: "*I honor this vessel that carries my spirit. I treat it as sacred ground."* When you notice yourself reaching for food to numb out, to distract yourself, or because you think it is time to eat, pause. Place your hands over your belly and say: *"Body, what do you truly need right now? What are you asking for?"* You may find that what you are truly hungry for is comfort, rest, joy, or a self-honoring ritual. Good Spiritual Hygiene requires that we learn to let food be nourishment for the soul, not a substitute compensating for our pain or habits.

Sacred Pause

Eating as a Sacred Act

- Before your next meal, pause in silence.
- Place your hands over your heart or the plate.
- Bless the food aloud or silently.
- Ask that it nourish your body, your clarity, your courage, and your calling.
- Eat slowly, with attention.
- Taste, breathe, and give thanks for each mouthful of food.
- As you finish, place your hands on your belly and affirm:

  "I honor the sacred in me through what I receive to nourish me."

A Note About Drugs, Alcohol, and other Mind-Altering Substances

The question for anyone who consumes drugs, alcohol, or any other substance is, what is your intention? Many cultures believe that using plant medicines or other mind-altering drugs like ayahuasca can expand your experience and conscious awareness, which is a sacred aspiration. However, if you're drinking alcohol or smoking weed mindlessly, to numb yourself, you will only hinder the journey toward clarity.

It is also possible that when you are sitting around at noon watching *Judge Judy* and smoking a bong, or drinking, or doing anything that dulls your senses, you may have a wound that you are ignoring or denying. When you want to be clean in your heart and your mind, God is the only high.

Many years ago, on my show, *Iyanla, Fix My Life*, I asked the late hip-hop artist DMX if he wanted to get sober. He responded, "No weed, no drinking, nothing?" I can recall his pained expression when I responded, "Yes. Nothing." I explained that to be a clear, pure vessel for the voice of God, he might want to consider cleaning himself up, to which he said, "I think I'm exactly where I need to be with God." Sadly, about nine years later, he died at the age of fifty from a drug overdose.

I've heard that Justin Bieber quoted that interview on his social media, and I can only pray that he drew a different conclusion. If I were to learn that he, or anyone else, were abusing drugs and alcohol, I would ask, *"Tell me where it hurts. What's the part of you that you wish had never happened? What don't you want to look at? Does it hurt in your career? Does it hurt in your relationships? Does it hurt in your finances? Does it hurt when you're alone in the shower? That's where we need to begin."*

Exercise and Spiritual Hygiene

Physical movement is not a chore. It is a ceremony. When approached with presence, exercise becomes a sacred act of remembrance. Building muscles, flattening the tummy, and tightening the glutes is not the only intention. Exercise is also about partnership. It is a way of returning to the breath, to rhythm, to sensation. It is how the body unclogs what the mind cannot articulate. In today's world, exercise is framed through the distorted lens of control: *"Burn it off." "Get smaller." "Tighten up."* However, in the practice of Somatic Stewardship, movement is about revelation. It is how the spirit stretches itself back into shape and form.

When your body is stagnant, your energy becomes congested. When your energy is congested, your thoughts grow heavy. When your thoughts become heavy, your spiritual clarity dims. This is why physical movement is a vital aspect of Spiritual Hygiene. It is the process that clears the static that accumulates in the energetic field, flushes out emotional residue stored in the tissues, and restores the natural flow of chi, prana, or life force. Sacred somatic movement can take many forms:

- Walking as Prayer. Step by step, with intention and gratitude.
- Stretching as Offering. Creating space in the body to allow new insight to land.
- Dancing as Liberation. Shaking off stories, releasing shame, embodying joy.
- Doing Breath-Centered Yoga as an invitation to Intuitive Flow. Recalibrating the nervous system through conscious connection.

When exercise becomes part of your Spiritual Hygiene practice, you don't need a gym or equipment. You only need presence. What matters is not how much you do. What matters is how deeply you are in and connected to your body while doing it. Before your next workout, take a few moments to ask yourself:

- *"What am I clearing?"*
- *"What am I offering my body today?"*
- *"What does my body want to experience, not just achieve?"*

In this way, movement becomes a spiritual bath, a cleansing of the energetic pores. Your conscious movement also becomes a return, a reconnection, and a process of repair. When you move with consciousness and love, you send the message to your body: *"You are worth being taken care of."* This is a healing message. This is a holy message. As a commitment to Spiritual Hygiene for the body, each time you engage in physical exercise, let your sweat be a sacrament. Let your breath be a benediction. Let your movement be your medicine.

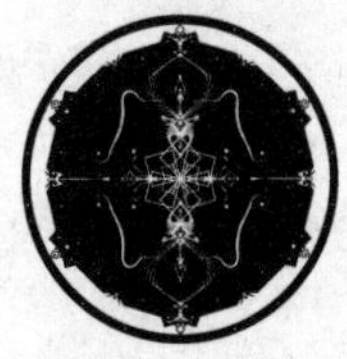

OPENING PRAYER

The Sacred Permission to Feel

Beloved Presence, Holy Source of All That Is,
I enter this moment with no answers, but with willingness.
I stand not with certainty, but with a trembling yes to what is real.
I lay down the armor of performance, the mask of composure,
and the burden of being strong.
I give myself permission to return to the sanctuary within
where all feelings are welcome, and nothing sacred is denied.
I give myself permission to feel.
I give myself permission to feel what aches,
without offering an apology.
I give myself permission to feel what has been buried,
without rushing it away.
I give myself permission to feel what is rising, coming alive within me,
without controlling its shape.
I give myself permission to allow the tears that never had a voice
to become my baptism.
I give myself permission to allow the rage that had no room
to become my holy fire.
I give myself permission to allow the numbness that silenced me
to be lifted by grace.
I give myself permission to allow every emotion I've ever exiled
to find its way home to love.
I no longer choose to shame what I feel.
I no longer choose to delay what is true.

I no longer choose to confuse silence with healing.
I allow this chapter to be my return to what is honest.
I allow my emotions to become sacred messengers.
I allow my soul to know the safety of full expression.
I allow the truth of my feeling nature to become a river
that carries me back to wholeness.
I surrender the need to be strong.
I reclaim my right to be real.
I celebrate my desire to be free.
Amen. Àṣẹ Aho.
It is done.
And so, it is.

CHAPTER 7

Cleansing the Inner Atmosphere

The Voice of Silencing is born from trauma.
The Voice of Truth is born from the Divine.

Malika's Healing

Malika was a mother and a strong presence in everyone's lives—friends, family, and even coworkers. Yet over the years, something started to close in on her. At church, she raised her hands in praise but felt nothing. During prayer, her mind wandered. She knew all the rituals, but they had become hollow. She didn't think she was angry, but she snapped at minor things the children did. She didn't feel sad, but she was alarmed when she realized that she hadn't cried in months, maybe years. Her chest felt tight at night, so she started baking the chicken she would have fried. What caught her attention was the awareness that she often could not find the words for what she was feeling. What Malika was experiencing was *emotional congestion* and *spiritual smog*.

Malika reluctantly brought the matter to the floor at her monthly sister circle meeting. She was guided into a *sacred grief ritual*, as a Spiritual Hygiene practice. A grief process is a series of actions designed to honor what has been lost. It could be a person, a version of yourself, a dream, or even time. The intention of the practice is to give your grief a sacred place to be expressed and released. It took several attempts before Malika was able to weep for the baby she had lost but never named. She screamed into a towel the words she had not said to her ex after he cheated and left. She wrote a letter to her younger self about being bullied, overweight, and responsible for her younger siblings. When it was complete, she burned the thirty pages. Then she took a spiritual bath, anointed herself with myrrh oil, and sat in silence for the first time in months. The next morning, she breathed differently because something in her chest had lifted. Nothing in her life had changed, but she had made space for life to move again. Her emotional waters had cleared. Her mental sky had opened. Divine communion returned, and Malika was present in her body for the first time in many years.

Emotional congestion is a sign that the energy of your emotional flow has been interrupted in its natural cycle. Emotions are *the energy that moves us.* Emotional energy is meant to move, not settle. Every experience you encounter and every story you tell has an emotion or a feeling attached to it. When emotional energy does not move, the emotional body becomes congested like a clogged pipe. You will drip irritability, seep fatigue, and sometimes burst wide open, exploding in unexpected ways.

When Silence Became the Symptom

Talia had always been the *peace glue* in her family. When arguments sparked, she changed the subject. When someone cried, she brought them a drink. When her uncle said something inappropriate at dinner, she laughed it off to break the tension. She had done it this way for years, until one day, during a simple conversation about groceries, she burst into tears. She was not crying about food. She cried, almost uncontrollably, because her emotional body was full. Talia had gagged her truth for so long that her body had become the battleground of unresolved pain. She realized that her digestion was off after repeated bouts of heartburn. She knew that her shoulders ached. She told herself it was the result of wearing cheap bras. Her dreams were restless, and her waking hours seemed to last forever. Talia was *spiritually constipated.* She was backed up with words unsaid, tears postponed, truths denied, and feelings left to fester. She had been gagged, not by force, but by fear, tradition, and trauma. The silence that had once kept her safe had now become her sickness. She was filled with toxic spiritual smog.

Living With Spiritual Smog

As we explored in previous chapters, spiritual smog is the dense energetic residue that accumulates in your spiritual field when emotional disconnection settles in as your daily rhythm. Spiritual smog accumulates when there is a prolonged absence of spiritual practice. In Talia's case, it was the result of spiritual avoidance, emotional misalignment, and unconscious energetic entanglements. Other common causes of spiritual smog can include:

- Long-term exposure to untruthful or low-vibration environments
- Holding on to unforgiveness or outdated spiritual contracts
- Absorbing collective trauma or ancestral debris
- Saying one thing, living another *(This is the definition of spiritual misalignment.)*
- Abandoning ritual, prayer, or emotional presence

The Body as a Bridge

The body holds the residue of what you feel (*emotions*), what you believe (*mind*), and what you carry energetically (*spirit*). When spiritual smog thickens and emotional congestion settles, the body becomes the place of overflow, the final stop for all that has gone unprocessed. Spiritual smog clouds your connection to Source, causing you to feel disoriented, uninspired, or spiritually numb.

Every practice can be consecrated to the work of cleansing, aligning, or restoring the very issue that calls for healing. In this way, your practice becomes a living medicine, tailored by Spirit to meet the need before you.

Key Distinctions Between Emotional Congestion and Spiritual Smog

Emotional Congestion	Spiritual Smog
Rooted in the heart and nervous system	Rooted in the aura and energetic field
Comes from unexpressed or denied emotion	Comes from spiritual misalignment or energetic pollution
Feels like being emotionally blocked, heavy, or reactive	Feels like being spiritually disconnected, foggy, or stuck
Requires emotional expression and inner permission	Requires energetic cleansing and spiritual re-attunement
Involves body, breath, and feeling	Involves ritual, intention, and re-sanctification
Example: Holding grief and not allowing yourself to cry	Example: Praying while still holding resentment, or trying to manifest while out of alignment

Just as the lungs and the blood must be purified for the body to thrive, the heart and the aura must both be cleansed for the soul to radiate clearly. One without the other will create a misfire, emotional weight in a spiritually disconnected vessel, or spiritual potential that cannot move through an emotionally congested heart. With Spiritual Hygiene, we cleanse the emotional waters, and we clear the spiritual air, so that Divine life can flow without obstruction.

The Weight of the Unwept Tears

Emotional congestion does not always begin with a crisis. More often, the congestion settles in with a quiet compromise. It is not always in the moment of heartbreak that we choke back tears. Quite commonly, the congestion forms the moment we tell ourselves, *"Now's not the time." "It's not that serious." "I don't want to make things worse."*

In those sacred moments when truth wants to express—whether it comes up as sobbing, silence, or sacred rage—but we force it back down, something gets lodged in the body. The emotion becomes a phantom. It is felt but not freed. The body always remembers what the mind tells the mouth it cannot, should not say. The nervous system then braces itself for the next moment of suppression. The heart builds an invisible wall of protection. Over time, that wall becomes filled with graffiti, a home for grief, shame, and unmet needs.

Permission to Feel: A Sacred Return to What Is Real

Carlos never told his best friend how hurt he was when he wasn't invited to the wedding. He said, *"I totally understand!"* but a bitterness grew inside him like moss. He began not to return texts to his friend as quickly as he once did. When they went out drinking, he spoke less freely. The worst part of all was when he started questioning his own worth as a friend and within himself. Yes, it is true. Many men have a far more difficult time processing and expressing their feelings than women do. A man is far more likely to let his feelings *roll off his back* than his mother, sister, or the lady in his life. This not only creates major issues with intimacy and communication, but it also causes spiritual smog and emotional congestion that can lead to extremely *bad behavior.* In many cases, it is not the wound that hurts him, those around him, or those he loves. It is the silence that calcifies around it that causes the most significant problems. Unspoken pain nests. It festers. It rewrites the way we trust, love, and show up. What we do not speak becomes the quiet architect of our disconnection. Carlos didn't need revenge or retribution. He needed a voice. He needed to name the pain as the way to release it.

Emotional congestion is the residue of truths buried under politeness and fear.

The mind thrives on information, something to think about, something to dwell upon. Processing information keeps the mind active. When you are on the healing path, the heart does not need or want more information. The heart wants to feel. The heart does not need to analyze, justify, or perform emotion. When stimulated by energy or experience, the heart needs to feel it and process it. This is the tender, often terrifying edge where Spiritual Hygiene begins its deeper work, not in the mind, but in the sacred temple of the body and the heart. You may ask: *If a feeling is attached to a story, what are we truly feeling?* You are feeling the emotion itself: the grief, rage, shame, tenderness, and the residue of the meaning you gave to the story. You are feeling abandoned, not just because someone left, but because you told yourself it meant you were unworthy. You are feeling heartbroken, not just because the relationship ended, but because some aspect of you believes it confirms you are "unlovable." To give yourself permission to feel is not simply releasing an emotion; it is also reclaiming authorship of your inner truth. Permission to feel is akin to saying, *"I will no longer deny myself the medicine of my own inner authority."*

The mind believes that when we suppress our feelings, we can avoid the pain. That assumption is inaccurate.

Permission is:

- A spiritual agreement you make with yourself to be present with what is real
- An energetic yes to feeling, releasing, remembering, grieving, or resting—even when it is inconvenient, messy, or unfamiliar
- A cleansing key that unlocks the gates of suppression and allows your soul to exhale

When you think about what to feel, you are feeling without permission. Your everyday tasks become habitual, and your spiritual tasks become performative. You may pray, journal, or meditate and still carry tension in you body, grief in your center, and fear behind your smile.

You may recite sacred words and still feel disconnected. You may seek clarity, but confusion will permeate the thinking mind because the truth is trapped behind a locked inner door. That door is called *permission to feel.* Permission to feel is not about falling apart. It is an agreement with yourself to allow what no longer belongs to fall away. When you grant yourself this permission, the false self begins to crumble. The performance dissolves. The pretending dies. And what remains is the pulsing, naked truth. *You do not need to be strong.* You owe it to yourself and everyone you care about to be real.

In the sacred space of your permission to yourself, your soul returns to its center cleansed, baptized, reborn in the waters of truth. Your emotional congestion is your responsibility to clear. Not through force, not with logic, not because the intellect understands. You clear emotional congestion and spiritual smog by *allowing.* Let the tears come when they come. Let the truth be told, even if only in prayer. Let the body express what the ego was too afraid to name. This is how we unclog the heart. This is how the soul breathes again.

Spiritual Hygiene Practice: Meeting the Voice of Silencing

Name the Voice

When you hear the voice that says, *"Just let it go,"*

place your hand over your heart or your belly.

Respond with:

"Body, I hear your fear. This truth needs breath."

Let the body speak.

Let tears come.

Let your body shake.

Let your voice crack.

These are not signs of weakness. They are signs that trauma is exiting the body.

Rewire the belief. Create a spiritual affirmation that reclaims your right to express:

"My voice is safe. My tears are holy. My truth is allowed."

The Voice of Trauma that speaks louder than your sacred voice will always ask you to postpone. Your soul will always invite you to unfold. Remind yourself that only you can grant the permission to feel. You are safe to speak. You are safe to heal.

Spiritual Hygiene Practice: Removing the Gag

If this teaching speaks to your experience, I invite you to begin here:

Write the words you weren't allowed to say.

When you feel complete, burn the paper, bury it, or read it aloud to Spirit.

Speak Aloud to the Voice of Trauma

Tell the voice:

> *"I know you tried to keep me safe when . . ."* (Speak about what or who you needed to be saved from. Speak about as many things as you can remember.)
>
> *"Thank you."*
>
> *"I no longer need to be silent to survive."*

Create a Truth Altar

Place your journal, a candle, and something that reminds you of your younger self in a safe place.

Sit in stillness in this place.

Breathe deeply and call forth the words you have swallowed.

Give yourself permission to speak freely in this sacred space.

When it feels like you have nothing more to say, breathe and move.

Let your voice come back to life in whispers, sighs, prayers, songs, and movement.

Play your favorite song and dance.
Use a broom or mop as your partner.
This is the sacred antidote to the gag.

Spiritual Hygiene Practice: Releasing the Voice of Fear

For those who carry this silence, especially men, here is a beginning:

Name the Fear Out Loud:

"I am afraid to feel because I was never taught it was safe."

"I am afraid to speak because I fear I will lose control."

Ritual of Safe Release:

Light a candle. Place your hand on your chest.

Speak or cry the words you've been holding.

No performance. Just presence.

Reclaim the Inner Voice:

Create a new affirmation to counter the trauma voice:

"My truth is safe with me."

"I am not weak when I feel—I am wise."

Breathe Through the Breaking:

Emotional congestion will start to lift when breath and sound are introduced.

Let yourself groan, sigh, and exhale.
Let the voice come back to life.

Emotional congestion need not be the end of your peace, joy, or aliveness. It is simply the soul knocking from the inside, asking to be set free.

Final Blessing

Beloved, may you never again gag your truth to keep the peace.
May your voice return like rain.
May your heart unclog like a spring.
May your tears become sacred waters of cleansing.
May the silence that once suffocated you now become the space where healing sings.

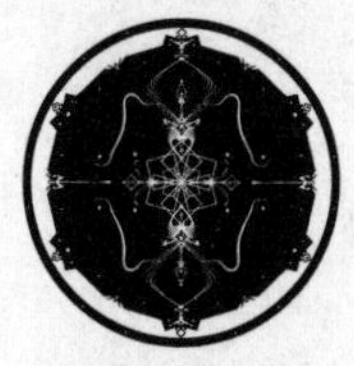

OPENING PRAYER

Precious Lord of the Universe,
Have mercy, Lord
Forgive *me*, Lord
Restore *me*, Lord
Your grace is *my* sufficiency.

Have mercy, Lord
Forgive *them*, Lord
Restore *them*, Lord
Your grace is *their* sufficiency.

Have mercy, Lord
Forgive *us*, Lord
Restore *us*, Lord
Your grace is *our* sufficiency.

I rest in Thee.
Amen. Aṣẹ Aho.
And so, it is.

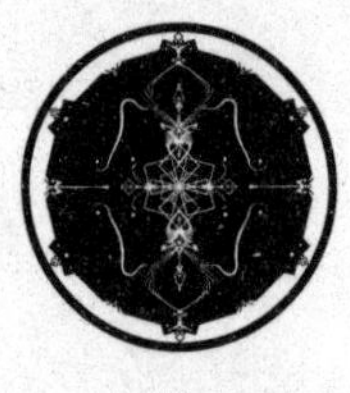

CHAPTER 8

Unbinding the Bloodline

Cleansing Trauma Patterns and Ancestral Residue

A Sacred Invitation: How to Engage This Chapter

Beloved, as you enter the truths within this chapter, let this be more than reading. Let it be a return. A return to yourself. A return to your truth. A return to your body, your breath, your spirit.

Take your time. Let each sacred truth settle into your awareness like holy water on dry soil.

This chapter is not meant to be consumed in one sitting. It is meant to be *sat with.* To be prayed through. To be honored. If something arises within you, an emotion, a memory, or a question, let it rise. The ego would have you stuff it down. The intellectual may motivate you to label what you feel as weakness. The heart is whispering gently, *"Do not skip past it this time. We can do this. We need to do this now."* Listen to your heart. It is speaking on behalf of your body and your soul.

You may find yourself needing to move, rock, stretch, or place a hand on your heart or belly.

You may need to speak aloud: ***"I am safe now." "That happened, but I am not there anymore." "I can face this with God, Source, Creator, the Divine. I can move through this with grace, with guidance."*** Call in your spiritual support, your ancestors, your angels, your Divine team.

Read a page, say a prayer. Read another, take a bath. Light a candle and read some more.

Let the sacred hold you. You deserve it. You are finally taking a stand for your value, worth, and freedom.

Most importantly, know this: *Nothing offered in this chapter replaces professional care.* If you have a counselor, therapist, or spiritual advisor, bring what arises here into your sessions. Use this work as a bridge, not as a bypass. Healing is layered. Restoration is gradual. Reclamation is a holy unfolding.

The work you will encounter here is not about bypassing your pain with spiritual practices. **This is the sacred work of gathering back the pieces of yourself you were forced to abandon. It is a holy unraveling of what burdened you, and a gentle return to the self that learned to hide to stay safe. Here, we lay down the weight that was never ours to bear, and call home the sacred parts of us that had to disappear to survive.** In this chapter, you will be offered several sacred tools. The ego may try to convince you that the work is too hard, or too easy, or that it will not work for you. *Do not be fooled by the ego or the power of simplicity*. The tools are:

> **Spiritual Hygiene Insight** is a sacred revelation that helps illuminate how unprocessed experiences, emotional residue, or energetic imprints are affecting your spiritual well-being. It brings clarity to what your body, mind, heart, or soul has been holding—and offers guidance on how to cleanse, release, and realign with Divine truth. It is not just information; it is *illumination,* a truth that invites healing.
>
> **Somatic Residue** represents the lingering imprint of unprocessed experiences, emotions, or traumas stored in the tissues, muscles, and nervous system of the body. It is the physical echo of what the mind, heart, or soul could not fully express or release in the moment of impact.
>
> **Clearing Movement** is a sacred, intentional practice that uses breath, posture, gesture, and motion to release stored trauma, tension, and emotional residue from the body. In

the context of Spiritual Hygiene, it helps restore flow, safety, and presence by reconnecting the soul to the body as a temple of truth and healing. It is movement for the purpose of purification.

Spiritual Hygiene Practice is a consistent, intentional act, such as breathwork, prayer, movement, anointing, or journaling, used to cleanse the body, mind, heart, and soul of energetic residue, emotional congestion, or inherited patterns. These practices are sacred tools that restore spiritual alignment, inner clarity, and embodied wholeness. They are rituals for detoxification, restoration, and liberation.

Hygienic Reframe is a conscious shift in thought, language, or belief that clears toxic narratives and restores sacred perspective. It replaces internalized shame, fear, or distortion with truth, dignity, and spiritual alignment. In the practice of Spiritual Hygiene, it is how we cleanse the mind and reclaim the voice of the soul. A reframe is not just a new thought; it is a sacred reclamation of how you see yourself.

This portion of the journey invites you to surrender what dimmed your light and welcome home the truths you silenced to protect your soul. It is the process of letting go of inherited pain and retrieving the innocence, truth, and beauty you tucked away to make it through. This is where you release the residue of survival and retrieve the sacred essence of who you truly are. This is not just healing; it is the holy act of shedding what suffocated your spirit and recovering the parts of you that still remember how to shine. So, breathe. Feel. Pause when you need to. Cry if it comes. Return when you're ready. You are not alone. God, Source, Creator, the Divine, the Sovereign Presence in all things, put this work in your hands for a reason. This is the work of returning to your true "*homes*," your heart and your body. Let us begin.

Everyday Trauma and the Call to Cleanse

There are things we do every day with no awareness of the impact they have on our body, our mind, our heart, or our soul. There are things we have endured, accommodated, and tolerated for so long that we no longer question them. They have become woven into our routines, our relationships, and our responses. Some of these experiences never had a name. They were never acknowledged, never questioned. They were inherited, accepted, or passed off as "*normal*," but "normal" is not the same as healthy. "*Common*" is not the same as harmless. While society may not recognize them, while our families may have normalized them, the soul does not forget. They are betrayals we minimized. They are silences that bruised us more deeply than violence. They are glances, gestures, rejections, assumptions, and expectations that did not register on the emotional Richter scale, but shook the foundation of our safety, value, worthiness, and trust. **These are everyday traumas, the small, consistent ruptures in the soul.** Left unattended, they accumulate like dust on the altar of the body. They disguise themselves as the personality traits anxiety, irritability, perfectionism, and people-pleasing. They appear as chronic tension, emotional numbness, or a quiet disconnection from the center of our being.

Spiritual Hygiene for the body is the sacred practice that reveals what has been buried and restores what has been broken. It is not merely a New Age woo-woo healing modality. It is how we cleanse the residue of our chaotic human experiences. It is how we reclaim the parts of ourselves taken by force or left behind in places of silence, confusion, and survival. In this chapter, we will name what was once unnamed. We will acknowledge what once had no space to be acknowledged. We will begin the process of gentle, holy release through spiritual practices that cleanse not only the body but also the imprints left on the mind, the wounds of the heart, the residue in the body, and the echoes in the soul. **This is the sacred truth:** *You do not have to justify your pain to heal it.* You do not need to call it "*trauma*" for it to be cleansed. What your soul remembers, your healing must honor.

Sacred Scars the Body Carries

Your wounds are a testimony to the strength and courage of your spirit. They are badges of power.

Spanking As Trauma

Trauma is not only the unspeakable, but is also often the *unsaid*, the normalized, the minimized, the passed down. There are stories written into the body that never made it into family conversations. And yet they live in the curvature of your spine, in the way your shoulders tighten when someone raises their voice, in how your breath shortens when you're told to "just get over it."

So many of us were told, *"I did it because I love you,"* while being hit. The inner child received another message entirely: "*Love hurts. My body is not mine. Pain is how I learn. Obedience keeps me safe.*" Spanking teaches the body to flinch. To brace. To prepare for violation under the guise of correction, in the name of love. Spanking, though normalized, imprints fear into the nervous system and pollutes the energy field with confusion between love and control. For some, it becomes the foundation of *shame-based discipline,* where the nervous system never fully relaxes and trust is equated with submission. Spiritual Hygiene reminds us that ***pain is not a prerequisite for discipline***, pain is not purification, and love never violates the body.

Spiritual Hygiene Insight:

Spiritual Hygiene teaches that love does not violate the body. Spanking leaves an energetic imprint of fear and confusion. Spiritual Hygiene restores boundaries and safety with self-touch and breath.

Somatic Residue:

The lingering imprint of unprocessed experiences, emotions, or traumas stored in the tissues, muscles, and nervous system of the body. It is the physical echo of what the mind, heart, or soul could not fully express or release in the moment of impact. Spanking contributes to:

- Tight glutes and pelvic clenching
- Constant muscle tension or lower back pain
- Hypervigilance or startle response to sudden sounds
- Deep, unconscious distrust of authority figures

Clearing Movements:

- Grounding movement on the floor: lying belly-down and feeling supported by the earth
- Rocking motions with breath to restore safety and self-soothing
- Gentle touch and affirming statements: *"I am safe in my body. No one can harm me here."*
- Repatterning through self-holding: hugging the inner child and tapping the sternum softly

Spiritual Hygiene Practice:

Cleansing this imprint requires clearing the shame and guilt embedded in the body's cellular memory. Through sacred movement and affirming touch, we restore energetic boundaries and reestablish safety as a birthright, not a reward for compliance.

Hygienic Reframe (Affirmation):

> *"I cleanse the belief that love must hurt. I purify my energy field of punishment disguised as protection. I restore safety in my body."*

Poverty As Trauma

Poverty is more than a lack of money. It is the chronic exposure to instability. Poverty is not only economic; it is also the psychic and emotional residue of unworthiness, lack, and inherited survivalism. It is watching your caregivers stretch, panic, sacrifice, and sometimes shatter under financial pressure. It teaches the body to live in *survival mode*, to brace for not enough, to equate worth with struggle. Poverty also creates an energetic fog, cluttering the energy field with fear, overwork, and injustice. Spiritual Hygiene calls for clearing that fog with stillness, beauty, and trust. It addresses the energetic fog of poverty by reinforcing the truth of Divine provision. Because poverty embeds fear into the nervous system, the residue of the traumatic experience can linger, even after circumstances change.

Spiritual Hygiene Insight:

Poverty is not only economic; it is also the psychic and emotional residue of unworthiness, lack, and inherited survivalism. It is watching your caregivers stretch, panic, sacrifice, and sometimes shatter under financial pressure. It teaches the body to live in survival mode, to brace for not enough, to equate worth with struggle. Poverty also creates an energetic fog, cluttering the energy field with fear, overwork, and injustice. Spiritual Hygiene calls for clearing that fog with stillness, beauty, and trust. It addresses the energetic fog of poverty by reinforcing the truth of Divine provision. Because poverty embeds fear into the nervous system, the residue of the traumatic experience can linger, even after circumstances change.

Somatic Residue:

- Clenched jaw, tension in shoulders and hands (from constantly holding things together)
- Constant hypervigilance and inability to rest
- Overworking or self-sabotaging prosperity
- Nervous tics or insomnia rooted in "*not enoughness*"

Clearing Movements:

- Restorative movement focused on slowing down: restorative yoga, breathwork with long exhales
- Stretching the hands open wide and affirming: "*I release survival. I welcome support.*"

- Gentle walking in nature to reestablish a felt sense of abundance and provision
- Belly laughter as a form of energetic wealth and emotional breath release
- Daily affirmation spoken aloud: *"There is more than enough. I am more than enough. I am safe to receive. I am not in danger anymore."*
- Open palm stretching, reclining breathwork, slow walking in nature
- Affirmation: *"I release struggle. I welcome Divine ease."*

Spiritual Hygiene Practice:

Stillness, softness, and restorative movement act as a counterforce to hustle. By tending to the overworked body and reclaiming pleasure, we detoxify the nervous system from the addiction to lack and the identity of struggle.

Hygienic Reframe (Affirmation):

> *"I cleanse the addiction to struggle. I honor my energy as sacred wealth. I live from Divine abundance."*

Hunger As Trauma

To feel hunger and not know when, or if, you will be fed is a *primal rupture* in the nervous system. Food is survival. For many, childhood hunger was normalized, and the body remembers that emptiness. Hunger affects more than the stomach. It distorts the notion of safety, care, and provision. Spiritual Hygiene for the body invites us to honor nourishment as a spiritual principle. Hunger trauma clogs the field with scarcity patterns, imprinting the belief that survival must be earned or that satisfaction is dangerous. This trauma can lead to hoarding food, bingeing, or dissociating from hunger cues altogether.

Spiritual Hygiene Insight:

- Scarcity imprints survival panic into the body. Hunger trauma teaches the body to distrust satisfaction. Spiritual Hygiene invites nourishment as a ritual act of restoration.

Somatic Residue:

- Tight belly or shallow breathing in the solar plexus
- Eating quickly, nervously, or not at all
- Blood sugar instability, adrenal fatigue
- Overproduction of cortisol (stress hormone) from childhood food scarcity

Clearing Movements:

- Rhythmic rubbing of the belly with loving words: *"You are nourished now."*
- Slow, mindful movement before eating (e.g., swaying or placing feet on the ground to create safety)
- Walking meditations that restore connection to rhythm, abundance, and the environment
- Belly blessing with warm hands, hand-to-heart pause before eating, and grounding the feet
- Movement with affirmations like: *"I am fed." "I am sustained." "I am provided for now."*

Spiritual Hygiene Practice:

Movement before eating becomes a cleansing act that resets the nervous system to receive with trust. Through breath, blessing, and belly-touch, the field is cleared of the energy of scarcity, even ancestral scarcity, and restored to flow.

Hygienic Reframe (Affirmations):

> *"I cleanse the fear of not enough. I sanctify nourishment. I receive fully what I once feared to ask for."*
>
> *"I am fed. I am nourished. I receive now."*
>
> *"I sanctify nourishment. I receive fully what I once feared."*

Neglect As Trauma

Neglect is the trauma of *absence*. It is the ache of what never came. The touch that didn't soothe, the words that were never spoken, the protection that never arrived. Neglect teaches a child that their needs are too much or that they are not worth meeting. Unlike loud, visible traumas, neglect often hides in the shadows. It becomes the trauma of invisibility. Neglect is not always an act of cruelty. Often, it comes from caregivers who are overwhelmed, therefore emotionally unavailable, or spiritually disconnected. The body of the neglected child does not recognize or understand the nuances of the experience. In the child's experience, it registers as a lack of safety, a lack of attunement, and a lack of nurturing.

Neglect Teaches:

- *"Don't ask for help."*
- *"No one is coming."*
- *"You or your feelings are too much."*
- *"Being alone is safer than being disappointed again."*

Spiritual Hygiene Insight:

Neglect is the absence of care, which leaves emotional debris in the heart space. Spiritual Hygiene to address neglect includes the restoration of presence, tenderness, and self-recognition.

Somatic Residue:

- Numbness in the body, especially in the chest and extremities
- A "frozen" nervous system; rather than fight or flight, the person will collapse or withdraw
- Shallow breath, sunken posture, or sensation of "disappearing"
- Difficulty trusting intimacy or receiving care without guilt
- Fatigue that feels soul-deep, but has no medical explanation

Behavioral Imprints:

- Over-functioning and self-parenting from a young age
- Anxious attachment or deep fear of abandonment
- Hyper-independence masked as strength: *"I'll just do it myself."*
- Emotional detachment or dissociation during vulnerability

Clearing Movements May Include:

- **Heart-Touching Practices:** Place both hands on the chest and whisper affirmations.

  "You matter." "I see you." "I am here with you."

- **Slow Spiraling Movements:** Gentle circular motions with arms, torso, or hips to invite fluidity and connection
- **Blanket Wrap Ritual:** Wrapping oneself in warmth, rocking side to side, and affirming:

  "I give myself the nurture I once needed. I am worth this care."

- **Mirror Gazing with Movement:** Looking into one's own eyes while swaying or stretching, offering a consistent, loving presence

- **Silent Stillness Practice:** Sitting with the body, hands over heart or womb, and simply witnessing what arises with no agenda to fix
- **Daily affirmation spoken aloud:** *"You are worth being seen. You are enough."*

Spiritual Hygiene Practice:

Learning to hold, comfort, and honor yourself becomes sacred hygiene for the heart. These practices regulate the emotional field, remove the residue of abandonment, and reestablish self as a worthy caretaker of the soul.

Hygienic Reframe (Affirmation):

> *"I cleanse the pain of invisibility. I sanctify my presence. I am worthy of love, care, and emotional tenderness."*

Movement for Self-Reclaiming Worth After Neglect:

Healing neglect begins by restoring presence where there was once absence. The goal is to reparent the body by slowly rebuilding trust that the body is safe to live in, feel in, and be witnessed in.

Daily Remembrance:

To be written or spoken aloud:

> *"What was missing was never my fault."*
>
> *"What I needed is allowed now."*
>
> *"I am no longer invisible—I am holy, and I am here."*

Abandonment As Trauma

Many of us were left not always by doors slamming or people vanishing, but by emotional absence, broken promises, and love that was inconsistent, unavailable, or withdrawn as punishment. The inner child received a message: "I am not worth staying for. My needs are too much. Love always leaves. I do not need anything to be safe." Abandonment is not always physical. It is the moment someone chose their silence over your safety, their discomfort over your care. It is the wound that teaches the heart to close preemptively, to leave before being left, to shrink before anyone asks you to go. The body begins to recognize the departure and carry the absence. Abandonment creates the smog that precedes intimacy, that fears the beauty of connection, that distrusts even the presence of love.

Spiritual Hygiene Insight:

Abandonment leaves a hole or hollowness in the soul's energy field. It is a vacancy that echoes. Spiritual Hygiene teaches us that abandonment is not simply an emotional experience; it is a spiritual fracture, where the self learns to disconnect from itself and everyone else to survive. We spiritually abandon ourselves when we suppress needs, silence feelings, or seek love from sources that cannot sustain us. Healing abandonment requires a return, a daily, sacred act of showing up for the inner child who still waits by the door.

Somatic Residue:

- Tightness or aching in the heart center or solar plexus
- Shallow breathing or holding the breath unconsciously
- Numbness in the chest or arms, especially when receiving affection
- Clenching of the jaw or chest during moments of intimacy
- Sudden withdrawals or dissociation during moments of vulnerability
- Restlessness when alone, or an anxious urgency to secure connection

Clearing Movements:

- Heart-opening postures such as seated chest lifts, gentle backbends, or arms extended outward with breath
- Swaying from side to side while hugging the self, offering rhythmic reassurance
- Kneeling or seated postures while rocking forward and back to soothe the nervous system
- Mirror movement with eye contact and spoken affirmations of presence and worth
- Breath-infused tapping over the sternum and heart with the mantra, "I am here."

Spiritual Hygiene Practice:

To cleanse the imprint of abandonment is to restore the soul's sense of sacred belonging. We begin not with others, but with the Divine covenant to never leave ourselves again.

Through breath, ritual, movement, and spiritual affirmations, we tend to the space where love once disappeared, and we fill it with presence.

Hygienic Reframe (Affirmation):

> *"I cleanse the lie that I am unworthy of lasting love. I return to myself with devotion. I am never alone in the presence of my own soul."*

Bullying As Trauma

So many of us were told to *"Toughen up," "Just ignore it,"* or *"Don't let them see you cry."* But the inner child received another message entirely: ***"You are not safe. Your voice is not enough. You must change to belong. You are alone."*** Bullying is the slow erosion of self-worth through repeated emotional, verbal, physical, or psychological harm, often while those in authority remain silent or complicit. Whether in childhood, adolescence, or adulthood, bullying imprints a somatic message of ***"Shrink to survive"*** and ***"Stay silent to stay safe."*** The body internalizes bullying as a form of social exile and emotional terror. It begins to anticipate rejection, critique, and abandonment—even in safe environments.

Spiritual Hygiene Insight:

Bullying does not just bruise the ego; it distorts the heart's radiance. It covers your light in layers of self-doubt, over-adaptation, and quiet shame. In Spiritual Hygiene, bullying is a spiritual pollutant: a force that clouds your Divine image and clutters your energetic field with fear of visibility and rejection. To cleanse this trauma is to remove the residue of unworthiness left by others' projections:

- You are not what they said.
- You are not what they laughed at.
- You are not their fear dressed up as cruelty.
- You are radiant.

Somatic Residue:

- Rounded posture, sunken chest (from learned invisibility)
- Tight jaw, tension in neck and shoulders (from silenced expression)
- Nervous laughter, people-pleasing, or apologizing for existing
- Heightened social anxiety, hyperawareness of others' reactions
- Inability to receive praise or feel safe in visibility

Clearing Movements:

- **Postural Reclaiming:** Standing tall, lifting chest, opening arms wide while breathing deeply

- **Vocal Release:** Sounding out (yells, sighs, chants) to restore expression
- **Mirror Affirmation Movement:** Eye contact in the mirror while moving with strength or grace
- **Stomping or Power Poses:** Reclaiming space in the body and environment with phrases like: *"I belong here." "I am not invisible." "I take up space."*

Clearing Movement Practice:

- Begin with open-arm movement, chest lifted, breath deep
- Place hands on the solar plexus and affirm:

  "I am strong. I am safe. I am not what they said."

- Mirror work with eye contact and posture expansion
- End with grounding—feet planted, voice spoken:

  "I take up space. I stand in my worth. I belong."

Spiritual Hygiene Practice:

Cleansing the imprint of bullying involves clearing the energetic field of humiliation and restoring the sacred identity of self. Through embodied declarations, posture reclamation, and spiritual affirmations, we reestablish the field as one of dignity, presence, and rightful belonging. **This is the holy work of reclaiming your space, body, breath, and voice. It is the courageous return to your soul's full stature, unapologetic and whole. Here, we reclaim sacred ground: in your body, in your field, in your voice. This is where you rise into the full measure of your soul, without shrinking, without shame. This is about embodying your truth without apology—inhabiting your voice, your energy, your presence without leaving pieces of yourself behind. The path of healing is a return to wholeness. It is where you rise in the full presence of your spirit and no longer ask permission to be.**

Hygienic Reframe (Affirmation):

> *"I cleanse the residue of shame and rejection. I reclaim my right to be seen, to be heard, and to be honored as I am."*

Sexual Abuse in Women As Trauma

The sacred space of the body is not just physical; it is also spiritual. When that space is violated, especially in childhood, the soul often *disassociates to survive.* Many survivors learn to leave the body long before they can leave the circumstance. Sexual trauma fragments the sense of safety, worth, sensuality, and even self-identity. It can create both hyperawareness and numbness. It often replaces pleasure with shame. Sexual violation of the sacred body leaves an energetic residue and ignites the trauma voices of guilt and shame. Movement, breath, and sound are important to cleanse shame from the body's temple.

Spiritual Hygiene Insight:

Spiritual Hygiene teaches that the womb and body are *holy temples*, and when those temples are desecrated, the soul fragments. Sexual trauma is not only physical, but also a spiritual defilement that can congest the energetic field with shame, secrecy, and soul silence.

Somatic Residue:

- Numbness in the pelvic region or inability to feel sexual sensation
- Cycles of pain or inflammation in the womb, hips, or lower abdomen
- Difficulty with eye contact or vulnerability in intimacy
- Panic or shutdown responses to touch

Clearing Movements:

- Womb breathing and hip-circling to reconnect safely with the root and sacral chakras
- Guided self-massage of the thighs, hips, and belly to restore autonomy
- Sound and breath movement to reclaim voice: sighing, humming, groaning with intention
- Movement done in a mirror, clothed or unclothed, to slowly reintegrate the gaze with self-love
- Affirmation to speak aloud:

  "My body is mine. My pleasure is mine. My safety is holy and untouchable now."

Spiritual Hygiene Practice:

Sacred movement becomes a ritual of reclamation. Cleansing the inner sanctuary includes affirming the right to pleasure, safety, and sacred embodiment. Sound, breath, and movement help detoxify energetic imprints from the root and sacral chakras.

Hygienic Reframe (Affirmation):

> *"I cleanse my womb space with love. I release the residue of violation. My body is sacred, and I now live in it fully."*

Sexual Abuse in Men As Trauma

The sacred body of a man is often left out of conversations around sexual trauma. Conditioned to be strong, silent, and untouched by vulnerability, many men carry wounds in silence, buried under shame, confusion, and suppression. When the sacred boundary of the male body is violated, especially in childhood, the soul often splits, dissociating to survive. The body becomes a battleground of mistrust, and the spirit may retreat from physical sensation altogether. What remains is a quiet war between numbness and rage, shame and silence.

Sexual trauma in men fractures the inner altar of power, identity, and presence. It can distort the sense of self, sever connection to pleasure, and silence the voice. Many men internalize the violation as weakness, believing they should "*move on*" while their soul is still frozen in time. Others hide the violation, taking on the burden that sex between males is "*sinful*" and wrong. Men, more often than women, fall into the trap of believing *"Something I did made this happen,"* **which invites the trauma voices of guilt and shame to become the *Killer Critic* and the *Hanging Judge*. At its worst, the experience can morph into the belief, *"If I were a real man, this wouldn't have happened or I would have stopped it, so I deserved it,"* which can result in lifelong self-identity issues.**

Spiritual Hygiene Insight:

This healing is not about explaining the trauma. It is about cleansing what that trauma left behind: shame, silence, dissociation, and false identities. When a man's (or a boy's) body is defiled, his spirit may leave the room. His voice may shrink. His presence may become performative rather than embodied. Spiritual Hygiene for the masculine is about restoring sovereignty, bringing the soul back into the temple of the body, and the body back into communion with Divine truth.

Somatic Residue in the Male Body:

- Chronic tightness in the jaw, fists, or lower back
- Erectile dysfunction, genital numbness, or hypersensitivity
- Startle response, muscle clenching, or flinching from touch
- Avoidance of emotional vulnerability or physical intimacy
- Internalized rage or mistrust of one's own body or desires

Clearing Movements:

- **Grounded Kneeling with Breath:** Sit or kneel on the ground, breathe into the belly, feel the spine. This posture honors humility and connection to self.
- **Shoulder Rolling and Arm Circling:** Reclaiming the chest and heart space, softening the armor of protection
- **Pelvic Rocking or Seated Hip Circles:** Gentle, clothed movement to restore sensation and sacred connection to the root chakra
- **Sound Practice:** Releasing breath through low, grounding tones (e.g., "hummmm," "ohhhh," "ahhh") to restore voice and vibrational trust
- **Mirror Presence:** Stand or sit in front of a mirror, clothed or unclothed. Make sustained eye contact. Speak your name. Reclaim your image with compassion.
- **Spoken Affirmation:**

  "My body is sacred. My truth is safe with me. I reclaim my power from the shadows of silence."

Spiritual Hygiene Practice:

- Begin with prayer: Invite your spirit back to the body. Acknowledge the violation without reentering the story.
- Anoint your body: With oil or water, touch your chest, belly, and thighs while affirming, *"This is mine. This is sacred."*
- Create safety rituals: Wrap yourself in a blanket, listen to grounding tones (417 Hz, 528 Hz, 396 Hz), or surround yourself with symbolic masculine protectors (e.g., stones, symbols, ancestral tokens).
- Daily mirror breathwork: Eye contact + breath = Truth Restored

Hygienic Reframe (Affirmation):

> *"I am not what happened to me. I am the sacred witness who survived. I now choose to live, feel, and reclaim my body in full truth."*

Ancestral Trauma

Ancestral trauma is not just your personal story; it is the unprocessed grief, fear, silence, and survival encoded into your DNA. It is the cry of your great-grandmother's womb. It is the echo of your grandfather's shackled choices. It is what your ancestors could not speak of, yet you feel it every time you try to rise beyond their pain. Modern science calls it "epigenetics": the study of how trauma is passed down biologically through gene expression. However, long before science, the *Spirit knew*. Your bones knew. The soul recognized that what is unhealed in one generation is carried by the next.

Energetically and spiritually, ancestral trauma can linger for *seven generations* and beyond. In many traditions, African, Indigenous, and Eastern spiritual systems, it is taught that seven generations always live within you:

- You are the **dream of those who survived.**
- You are the **burden-bearer of what was never released.**

If your ancestors endured slavery, genocide, famine, addiction, abandonment, sexual violation, or systemic erasure without the space or power to process that pain, that energy did not disappear. It descended. You inherited it. This means that you, the healing one, the aware one, are often the first in the line to say: *"This is not normal,"* and to start asking, *"Where did this pattern come from?"* and *"What is this pain trying to teach me?"*

Spiritual Hygiene Insight:

You carry more than your own story. Ancestral trauma is encoded in your energy field. Spiritual Hygiene includes ritualized movement, spoken release, and reverent return of what was never yours to hold. Spiritual Hygiene acknowledges that the body is not just a personal vessel; it is a lineage altar. Ancestral trauma is the energetic inheritance of unprocessed sorrow, fear, shame, and silence that lives in your field until it is named and released.

Ancestral Trauma	Voice of Inheritance
Energetic, emotional, and spiritual residue from unhealed trauma passed down through bloodlines	Internalized beliefs, coping mechanisms, or emotional patterns learned from caregivers or culture
Present in the body without a conscious awareness of the cause (e.g., "*I've always felt this grief.*")	Repetitive thoughts like: *"This is just who we are." "In this family, we don't . . ."*
Often rooted in events you never experienced personally but were shaped by (e.g., *migration, enslavement, forced silence)*	Rooted in family rules, traditions, roles, and emotional modeling
Healed through somatic ritual, energetic clearing, and lineage reclamation	Healed through awareness, reframing, and conscious disruption of patterns
Feels like weight without origin or stories without words	Feels like voices in your head or beliefs that support your behavior

Somatic Residue:

- Heaviness in the legs, hips, or lower back
- Chronic fatigue without clear medical cause
- Tightness in the chest or throat when speaking truth
- Sensations of carrying weight in the shoulders or spine

- Sudden tears or emotional waves when hearing family stories
- Persistent anxiety or guilt when surpassing family limitations
- Tension that deepens in moments of success or joy, as though joy itself must be earned or explained

Spiritual Hygiene Practice:

Ancestral Release Flow serves as a hygiene ritual for the soul's lineage. Movement becomes intercessory prayer. Sound becomes invocation. Shaking becomes clearing. What was once carried in silence is returned to the earth in ceremony.

Cleansing Movement Practice (Ancestral Release Flow):

- Stomp, spiral the spine, shake the limbs, seal with prayer

Begin seated or lying down.
Wrap arms around self and rock gently.
Place hand over heart and belly.
Breathe slowly.
Say aloud:

"I will not leave you."

"I am here. I see you. I love you."

Repeat while touching your own face or arms with reverence.
End by placing one hand on your altar or womb and say:

"This is my home. I belong to me."

Hygienic Reframe (Affirmations):

"I cleanse my bloodline with breath and movement."

"I release the burdens of those who came before me."

"I carry forward only what is sacred, whole, and aligned."

CHAPTER 9

Restoring Physical and Emotional Rhythm

In the journey, there comes a sacred pause, where noise dissolves because you no longer feed it. What remains is a gentle rhythm, ancient, trustworthy, calling you back to the sound beneath your survival. What remains is a quiet pulse, steady and soft, waiting for you to listen. This is the rhythm of your body.

This rhythm, this sacred rhythm, is not forced by alarms, deadlines, and calendar alerts. It is not the rhythm dictated by the cultural obsession with productivity or the pressure to stay "on" at all costs. This is the rhythm underneath all of that. It is the sacred metronome of your being. It breathes when you're not looking. It heals without your permission. It knows the seasons before your mind does. To live by it, you must choose to remember it. This final chapter of Level II is that remembering.

The Language of the Body

Your body is the first truth-teller. It is the *first responder* to trauma. It is the most accurate prophet of your needs. Yet many of us have spent years, sometimes lifetimes, betraying its messages. We eat when we are numb, not hungry. We sleep when exhausted, not when our cycle asks for rest. We override pain, suppress tears, and call it strength. In doing so, we fall out of rhythm, physically, emotionally, and spiritually. The cost? Exhaustion that no nap can fix. Mood swings without a cause or name. Chronic inflammation, brain fog, and spiritual disorientation. All while we tell ourselves, and anyone who will listen, that we are doing just fine. Rhythm is not just how you move; it is how you *feel* about what you're moving through. When your emotional rhythm is off, your physical rhythm follows. The breath shortens. The heartbeat hardens. The body tightens, and the body becomes a container for spiritual smog.

A Story of Misalignment

Nia, a forty-seven-year-old mother of three, had been diagnosed with adrenal fatigue and thyroid imbalance. No matter what supplements or diets she tried, her exhaustion never lifted. She was waking up tired, going to bed wired, and living in a near-constant state of emotional numbness. During our work together, I asked her one simple question: *"When was the last time you followed your body instead of your schedule?"* She said, *"I don't understand."* I replied, *"Well, your body knows. Have you checked in with it?"* She paused. Tears welled up.

"I don't know," she whispered. *"I've been on everyone else's clock for so long. I forgot I had one of my own."* I shared with Nia the process of beginning a rhythm restoration practice.

She started waking up without an alarm on weekends, letting her body decide when to rise. She paused for ten minutes mid-morning to breathe—not check off a to-do list, just breathe. She tracked her emotions like a weather pattern: noticing when joy felt like sunlight, when grief moved like rain. She canceled meetings when her womb asked for rest. She danced barefoot when words wouldn't come. Three months in, she sent me a message: *"I feel like I'm back in my own skin. Not fighting time. Moving with it."* Her body hadn't been broken. Her lights were on, but she wasn't home.

The Wisdom of Rhythm

Rhythm is a sacred order. It is the universe's way of organizing energy. It is why the tide knows when to rise, how flowers know when to bloom, how babies know when to sleep, and you are no different. You and your body have a rhythm.

Living in alignment with your body's rhythm means:

- Sleeping when your soul is weary, not just when your schedule is clear.
- Moving not to punish, but to circulate life.
- Eating to nourish, not numb.
- Crying without apology.
- Pausing without guilt.

Restoring the Rhythm: Sacred Practices

1. Morning Rhythm Ritual:

Before checking your phone or clock, place your hand on your chest. Ask: *"What does my body need right now?"* Move from that answer.

2. Emotional Weather Tracking:

At the end of each day, write one word to describe the emotional rhythm of your day. Was it stormy, still, fast, tender? Learn your emotional patterns like moon cycles.

3. Sacred "No Clock Day":

Once a month, live without a clock for twenty-four hours. Eat when hungry. Rest when tired. Move when moved. Let your body lead.

4. Rhythm of the Womb (for women):
Track your menstrual cycle. Notice your energy, appetite, emotions, and desires at each phase. Align creative work with ovulation, rest with menstruation. This is embodied Divinity.

5. Somatic Dialogue:
When you feel a symptom or sensation, ask: *"What are you trying to tell me?"*

Then wait. Let the body speak. Do not rush the answer. To restore rhythm is not to add more to your life. It is to *remove* everything that dishonors your unique pace. It is to refuse urgency as a lifestyle. It is to stop dancing to a rhythm that was never yours. The world around you may rush, but your soul is not a track star. We are here to breathe in cadence with the Sacred. We are here to rise and rest in alignment with love. We are here to remember that the body is never late, which means your healing is not running behind. Your rhythm, unlike anyone else's, will guide you back to your sacred home. Your return.

Emotional Rhythm: Letting Feelings Flow Instead of Freeze

The body speaks the truth of what the soul has lived. Your emotions are the sacred messengers that tell your story. They speak in the rhythm of that truth. Grief moves slowly, like a river carving its way through stone. Anger arrives hot and fast, often igniting without warning. Joy rises wide and full, spilling light into everything it touches. Each emotion has a tempo. A current. A cycle. When the cycle of your emotions is interrupted, the rhythm of your body is thrown off. You feel it in the way you breathe. It may be a tightness or churning in your gut. Since they always have a story to tell, your emotions will find a way to let you know it is time for them to speak. When your emotional rhythm freezes, and the body starts to carry what the heart could not say, the body will let you know—"you've got a problem."

Jalen: The Pace of Performance

Jalen was a thirty-eight-year-old project manager. Driven. Focused. Reliable. He prided himself on always being available. He read and sent emails at 1 a.m. During the day, he was in meetings back-to-back. He went to the gym at 5 a.m. even when his body was begging for sleep. He ate what he could, when he could, and called it healthy if it wasn't fried or two days old. When he felt tension creeping up the back of his neck, he brushed it off. When his digestion slowed and his mood began to dip, he doubled down on supplements and caffeine. He had no consistent spiritual practice. No time for breathwork. No space for silence, and stillness made him anxious. When asked how he was doing, his answer was always the same: *"I'm good. Just a little tired."*

Tired became his baseline. He began waking up exhausted. His memory became increasingly foggy. His patience was thin. He was constantly craving sugar and stimulation. Eventually, his body issued a louder warning: chronic inflammation, rising blood pressure, and a deep, persistent sadness he couldn't explain. Jalen was not sick in the way that labs could measure. He was rhythmically misaligned. His body had been trying to slow him down for years. But he was living by pressure, not presence. He had become a man of reaction, not rhythm, a man who was trying to outrun his own truth.

Devin: The Practice of Presence

Devin, age forty-one, was a father, a business owner, and a man with many responsibilities. His mornings began with conscious breath, not email. He rose with the sun and paused in stillness before the day pulled at him. Devin consciously tracked his energy in cycles. He noticed that after high-output weeks, his body called for restoration. He listened. He had a simple rhythm of checking in with himself before saying yes to anything. He meditated when overwhelmed.

He wept when he felt grief stirring. He moved slowly when his body felt tight. When he didn't know what he was feeling, he got still enough to ask. There was no perfection in his rhythm.

There were hard days. Stressful moments. But he knew how to return to center. He knew how to reset. His spiritual practice was his pulse. A way of coming back to himself, repeatedly. Devin's body responded in kind. He slept deeply. He laughed often. He made decisions from the inside out. He didn't wait to break down to justify rest. He lived in his rhythm, not by reactivity.

Living against your rhythm is a symptom of spiritual disconnection. When the world sets your pace, your body begins to forget its truth. You lose touch with what feels good. You become numb to the early signs of exhaustion. You live on adrenaline instead of alignment. Over time, that disconnection will morph into dysfunction:

- Insomnia
- Brain fog
- Chronic fatigue
- Irritability
- Hormonal imbalances
- Silent inflammation

They are sacred signals. Whispers from your body asking: *"Will you return to me? Will you honor me?"* You were not put on earth, in a body, to race against time. We are all here to move with our own Divine timing. To walk, breathe, and choose in a way that honors our cycles, not just our goals. A spiritual practice creates a rhythm of return. It teaches the body that it is safe to rest. Safe to feel. Safe to slow down without losing value. This is the gift of rhythm: When you live in harmony with your body's truth, you stop needing crisis to justify your care. This is the place where many stand: at the edge of return or resistance, and the doorway of deeper listening. Each of us is given the same invitation, though it may come in different forms:

- A breakdown
- A diagnosis

- A relationship ending
- A deep, unexplainable emptiness

Whatever the form, the message is clear: Come home. Come back into sync with yourself.

Come back to the Divine tempo within. We all have the choice to honor the body's sacred rhythm or not.

Reclaiming the Feminine Flow

A woman's womb is not just an organ; it is a temple. A timekeeper. A transmitter of Divine rhythm. For too long, women have been taught to override the sacred cycles that live within them, to see their "*flowing*" time, their monthly cycle, as an inconvenience. To push through fatigue. To ignore the subtle and powerful shifts in mood, energy, and creativity that naturally occur. Modern life is not designed for the feminine rhythm, but a woman's soul is.

To reclaim the feminine flow is to remember the intelligence that lives inside the womb, the wisdom that doesn't move in straight lines, but in spirals. It is to understand that your energy, emotions, and embodiment are not meant to be the same every day. They move through a sacred order. And when you live in alignment with this inner order, you stop fighting yourself. You begin to honor what your body has known all along. Your womb cycles through four distinct energetic seasons each month. Whether you are actively flowing, in perimenopause, or postmenopausal, this energetic blueprint still lives in your field.

Inner Winter (*Menstrual*):

A time for rest, reflection, and releasing.

The veil is thin. You are deeply intuitive.

The body asks for stillness and silence.

Inner Spring (*Follicular*):

Energy rises.

Ideas blossom.

Motivation returns.

A time for visioning and gentle action.

Inner Summer (*Ovulation*):

Magnetism, clarity, expression.

You are most radiant here—emotionally, physically, and spiritually.

This is a time for creation, communication, and connection.

Inner Autumn (*Luteal*):

Energy begins to wane. Focus turns inward.

A time to complete, organize, and prepare to release again.

Sensitivity rises, not as weakness, but as truth-teller.

Each phase offers a gift, a sacred shift. Women have been taught to live in a constant state of output, productivity, and performance, mimicking the masculine rhythm, just to feel accepted, safe, or seen. To live with the womb is to listen, to refuse to apologize for needing rest at certain times. To survive and flourish in the many earth changes that are unfolding, women must learn how to stop pushing through the wisdom of fatigue or the clarity of mood shifts, and to see the feminine energy cycle as a portal rather than a problem.

Mariah's Return to Herself

Mariah, age thirty-six, was a high-performing therapist and mother of two. She hadn't taken more than two consecutive days off in several years. Her cycle had become irregular. She dreaded her flow time. In her hurried life, she experienced it as a nuisance. Like so many women, Mariah had been conditioned to believe that needing rest made her lazy, emotional shifts made her unstable, and asking for space made her selfish. When she began the work of Spiritual Hygiene and reclaiming her rhythm, everything shifted. She started tracking her cycle, not just the days she was flowing, but her energy, emotions, and cravings throughout the month. She noticed she was most creative and outspoken during ovulation, but deeply introspective just before her cycle began. Rather than resisting the sensitivity of her *luteal phase*, she began protecting it by scheduling fewer meetings, creating space for journaling, and finding much-needed solitude. She allowed herself to flow in stillness, sometimes even anointing her womb with oil, whispering blessings of release and renewal. For the first time in her life, she didn't feel *broken*. She felt whole. Within three months, her body responded. Her cycle stabilized. Her sleep improved. Her anxiety decreased. Self-awareness taught her how she had abandoned herself and how she had dishonored her feminine rhythm. The state of her mind, heart, and life improved once Mariah learned to live *with* her womb, not despite it.

The feminine body does not thrive in constant output. She blooms in rhythm and cycles. She renews through rest, not resistance. Reclaiming the feminine rhythm is not about the monthly flow. It is about a *relationship*. A conscious relationship to your inner timing. An honoring relationship to your emotional tides. Relationship to the part of you that is constantly and Divinely moving between birth, bloom, death, and rebirth. The shame around rest, slowness, and sensitivity is inherited. It does not belong to you. It is not holy. It is not yours to carry forward. Surrender the belief that you are not too much. Remember, you are not inconsistent. You are rhythmic.

Spiritual Hygiene Practice: Womb Rhythm Restoration

Track Your Cycle Energetically:

- Each day, journal your emotional tone, energy level, and bodily sensations.
- Begin noticing your inner seasons.

Rest on Purpose:

- During your flow phase, create a ritual of stillness, e.g., light a candle, take a bath, say no without explanation.

Speak the Rhythm:

- Speak aloud: *"I am allowed to be slow. I am allowed to change. I am allowed to follow my flow."*

Offer Gratitude to the Womb:

- Place your hands on your womb and say:

> *"Thank you for holding, for releasing, for guiding, for creating. I live with you now. Not against you."*

How Women Without a Physical Womb Align with the Teaching

1. The Energetic Womb Remains

- The womb space, located between the sacral and solar plexus chakras, remains active, even without a uterus.
- It holds memory, creativity, intuition, and the energetic blueprint of cycles.
- This space is still a center for gestation, release, and regeneration.

2. Rhythmic Living Is Still Sacred

- The four-phase rhythm *(menstrual, follicular, ovulatory, luteal)* reflects energetic archetypes: Rest, Initiation, Expression, Reflection.
- These phases can be mapped onto moon cycles, seasonal energy, or inner emotional patterns rather than physical bleeding.

3. The Moon As a Mirror

Women without a flow cycle can align with the moon:

- New Moon (***Menstrual***): Rest, renewal, deep listening
- Waxing Moon (***Follicular***): Clarity, inspiration, gentle action
- Full Moon (***Ovulatory***): Expression, magnetism, creativity
- Waning Moon (***Luteal***): Completion, discernment, release

4. The Body Still Speaks in Rhythm

- Even without monthly flowing, the body still cycles through energy fluctuations, emotional patterns, intuitive waves.
- Tracking these rhythms can reveal a unique, personal sacred flow.

5. The Feminine Flow Is a Birthright, not a Condition

- Whether you have a womb or not, **the feminine flow lives in your field.**

- It is your right to rest, to rise, to speak, to feel. It is your right to honor your rhythm without apology.

Spiritual Hygiene Practice for Women Without a Physical Womb:

The Inner Moon Journal

Each day, reflect:

"What phase do I feel I am in today—new, waxing, full, or waning?"

"What does my body need?"

"What emotion is most present?"

"What is rising to be created or released?"

Womb Touch Ritual

Place your hands below your navel.

Whisper:

"Though I do not flow monthly, I still hold life."

"Though I no longer carry the womb, I still carry her wisdom."

"I am rhythmic. I am whole."

"I honor the spiral that lives within me."

"I release the shame of needing rest."

"I remember the rhythm of my womb."

"I reclaim the sacred flow of my life."

Reclaiming Rhythm Is a Return to Sacred Listening

The journey of rhythm reclamation is a call to *listen* and *hear more,* not to do more. To shift from the 3D physical world of doing to the 5D experience of *being,* it is important to remember that stillness and rest are your birthrights. Spiritual Hygiene practices teach that you must honor what has always been speaking through your breath, your fatigue, your longings, and your aches. Neither your mind nor your body was designed to be governed by urgency or hardened by suppression. You were not created to live in a state of performance, constant output, or apology for needing a pause. You were not born to race toward *the end.* You were born to *respond* to the pulse of breath, the ebb and flow of emotion, the quiet wisdom of the body's sacred cycles. You were designed to move in rhythm with life itself. Family and society have conditioned you to be in competition with it.

This reclamation is not about managing your time better. It is about *reentering your timing,* your unique rhythm. It is about remembering that Divine rhythm is *within you.* Waiting. Whispering. Returning. When you listen to your body, you do not fall behind. You do not miss out. You come back into alignment with a deeper intelligence. You stop measuring your value by productivity. You stop silencing your soul for the sake of survival. You begin to walk out of the rhythm of stress and walk with the rhythm of Spirit.

Throughout this chapter, we have explored the many ways the sacred rhythm of the body and emotions becomes disrupted, and how it can be restored. You are being invited to see that:

- **The body keeps time** not by clocks, but by connection, through sensations, breath, and emotional flow.
- **Emotional rhythm** requires movement, not management. Emotions are not fixed points, but energetic waves with a beginning, middle, and end.
- **Living out of rhythm** leads to spiritual and physical depletion. One who ignores the body's truth will eventually be brought to their knees by it.
- **Women carry sacred rhythm in their wombs,** whether physical or energetic. Living in alignment with these cycles is an act of spiritual sovereignty.

- **Rest is not passive.** It is active restoration. A return to trust. A healing balm for the overused nervous system, the overloaded heart, the overlooked soul.

This is the practice now: ***releasing the lie that your worth is measured by motion***. When you pause, you do not lose ground or waste time. You *return to it*, firm, rooted, and whole.

Rest As Reclamation

Rest is not a luxury. Rest is not something you earn after proving your value. Rest is a spiritual stance that you can embrace as a lifestyle. Honoring your body's need to rest says:

> *"I trust the rhythm of my body more than the rhythm of the world."*
>
> *"I am not here to be consumed. I am here to be consecrated."*
>
> *"I do not hustle for healing. I create space for it to arrive."*

The body heals when it is not being hurried. The nervous system unwinds when it feels safe.

The soul reveals itself when silence is honored. Sacred rhythm begins with sacred stillness. Stillness is an invitation. In stillness, your next breath becomes holy. Your next step becomes intentional. In stillness, you remember that exactly where you are, as you are; you are becoming whole and holy.

Let this be your declaration:

> *"I reclaim my rhythm."*
> *"I honor my body's truth."*
> *"I restore what I once ignored."*
> *"I no longer rush my healing."*
> *"I no longer apologize for my pace."*

"I walk in the rhythm of Spirit."
"I rest because I am wise enough to know what is sacred."

This concludes Level II*: Soul Cleansing and Detoxification*.
You have listened.
You have felt.
You have released.
Now, rest.
You are not taking a break from your life.
You are preparing for a sacred return to it.

THE BRIDGE

Key Teachings on Level I and Level II

A Descent into Sacred Alignment

There comes a moment on every path of inner evolution when deeper clarity calls for a fuller turning inward. The soul no longer seeks explanation. It seeks release. It seeks renewal. It seeks to live without the heaviness it has silently carried for far too long. This is the work of Spiritual Hygiene that you have begun. This work is not an intellectual exercise; it is a spiritual imperative for the time and energy in which we live. This is the journey of uncovering, unburdening, and restoring the radiant alignment between your inner world and your sacred truth. It is a reclamation of your spiritual integrity, which is mental, emotional, physical, and energetic.

Level I: Becoming Conscious of What Lives Within

The first opening arrives gently: a whisper to pay attention. To notice what you've normalized. To notice the exhaustion behind the smile, the tension behind the spiritual talk, the unshed tears tucked into your everyday strength. ***Self-awareness*** is not a skill. It is a sacred doorway. It is a soul vow: *"I will not abandon what I see in myself."*

Yet awareness alone is incomplete without the courage to be real, to not just see it but name it. This is the heart of ***self-honesty***, and it, too, is sacred. It is the turning point where pretending ends and presence begins. You no longer aim to be perfect. You choose to be aligned.

But truth often collides with the performances we've rehearsed for years. Emotional dishonesty, masked as politeness, responsibility, or spiritual maturity, becomes exposed. It is not just what we say; it is what we deny ourselves permission to feel, to need, to question.

From this honesty blooms the awakening of ***inner authority*** and ***energetic responsibility***, the spiritual maturity that says: *"My inner state is not their burden to carry or their fault to fix."* No more blaming. No more bypassing. This is the moment the soul stops outsourcing its power and chooses to steward its energy with intention. Still, as we begin to listen more deeply, we discover that not all the voices within us belong to the truth. Some belong to pain.

Here is where the ***Voices of Trauma*** reveal themselves, those familiar echoes that shaped our survival strategies: shame, blame, delay, avoidance, performance. They are not flaws. They are fragments. We learned that they were our wounded parts, doing the best they could without a map for healing. And so, the soul begins to grieve. Not the kind of grief wrapped in silence, but the holy grief that tells the truth of what was lost. What mattered. What was missed. This was the invitation to *grieve as a form of spiritual clarity*, to allow feeling to become a current of cleansing rather than a weight of sorrow. This is where the teaching becomes personal.

I shared the story of my youngest daughter, Nisa, Beloved soul of my soul. She lived in this place for years, in the silent grip of unreleased grief. Her body bore what her mouth could not say. She smiled through the weight of unmet needs. She laughed through the ache of disappointment. And her body, faithful and wise, began to speak louder than her words. Diabetes was never just a diagnosis. It was the physical expression of stories she had no space to name.

Nisa never gave herself *permission to grieve*; she didn't know how, and I could not teach her. The voices were too loud, the pain too entrenched. She continued pretending she was OK. She insisted on holding up the world, her broken and distorted world. She did not trust the messiness of her tears. She was afraid to breathe, to feel, to know. Her healing did not begin with answers. It began with pain.

With sadness. With anger. Finally, her soul said, *No more!* That is when her healing began—with a transition. Her evolution. A change in form that she did not trust she could do in her body. It was her choice, and as sad as it makes me, I respect her choice. This is what grief does when it is allowed to flow: It softens the soul and begins the sacred repair.

Forgiveness, then, becomes the next invitation. Not a demand. Not a deadline. But a sacred threshold. Because we learn that what we will not forgive, we continue to re-create, and not as a conscious process of creation. We create and re-create in the patterns we repeat, in the walls we build, in the fatigue we cannot explain. This is not punishment. It is feedback. It is the soul saying: *"There is still something here that wants to be felt, to be faced, and to be freed."*

Level II: The Descent into the Body Temple

If Level I is the awakening of the inner temple, Level II *is the consecration of the body as sacred ground.* This is where healing becomes embodied, where language gives way to sensation. Where the story gives way to stillness. Your body is not a shell. It is an altar, and it remembers. This is where we learned to descend into the wisdom stored in the cells. In the belly, the spine, and the hips. In the places where breath gets shallow and motion becomes guarded. This is where we met *somatic memory,* the body's holy language of truth. We noticed the physical expressions of what the soul had been managing silently: jaw tightness from withheld anger, womb pain from inherited shame, shallow breath from years of suppression. These are not dysfunctions. They are sacred signals.

We invite *cleansing through movement* as prayer. Grounding. Swaying. Shaking. Rocking. The natural rituals of restoration that we forgot we were allowed to do. Each gesture becomes a way back into the self. Each breath becomes a declaration of return. We learned to honor *ritual not as religion, but as regulation.* It is a sacred rhythm that brings the body back into presence, a living ceremony that says: *"I will no longer abandon my nervous system in the name of productivity."* In this descent, we grieve again. This level of grief is older, deeper. Ancestral. The grief of lineage. The grief of women who were silenced. The grief of men who were never permitted to weep. The grief of children who adapted before they could speak. In this holy descent, the trauma once lodged in the body becomes visible. Not just in the memories, but in the chronic pain. The fatigue. The inflammation. The autoimmune flare-ups. These are not merely health conditions. They are also spiritual messages. This is where we reclaimed *permission to feel* not as indulgence, but as responsibility. Emotional presence becomes our protest. Our praise. Our medicine.

As we have done the work, we begin to feel and flow differently. We let go of the myth of constancy. We align with inner seasons. We listen to the wisdom of rest. We recognize that some days are for doing, but others are for being, shedding, softening. And that both are holy. This is the rhythm of the feminine. The rhythm of the soul. In that rhythm, we have given ourselves permission to remember that *nothing real was ever lost.* It was only waiting to be welcomed home.

Reflection: A Sacred Integration

Take a breath, Beloved. Let these words become more than concepts. Let them become companions. Remember, you have lost nothing. You are becoming whole again. You were never broken. You *were* and *are* in the process of a sacred transition. One which you prayed for, even when you did not know what it would look like, or how it would feel. You are not too much. You are filled to the brim with what needs to be honored, released, or reshaped. So now, reflect gently:

- What unspoken truth is ready to be voiced, not to be fixed, but to be freed?
- Where does your body still carry the weight of what your heart never had permission to name?
- What if the fatigue isn't failure, but a signal of sacred over-functioning?
- What new rhythm are you being called to honor?

This journey is not about becoming someone new. It is about *unlayering* what you are not. Releasing the false, the forced, and the forgotten, until only what is true remains. As we move forward into Level III, allow these to be your soul's affirmations:

> *"I am no longer holding what isn't mine."*
>
> *"I am no longer silencing what wants to speak."*
>
> *"I am no longer racing to be enough."*
>
> *"I am the sacred returning to itself."*
>
> *"I am in rhythm. I am in alignment."*
>
> *"I am a vessel of truth, a temple of light, and a well of rest."*

You are ready.
You are remembered.
Your healing has begun.
Amen. Aṣẹ Aho.
And so, it is.

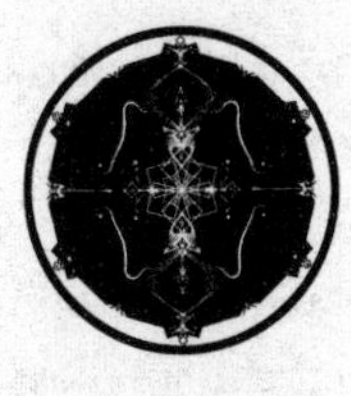

LEVEL III

RECLAIMING: THE SACRED SELF

The Tails of Two Monkeys

This is a timeless tale of two monkey clans as told by spiritual mystics, teachers, and sages throughout the ages.

In the dense southern regions of the world, a clan of monkeys existed that had sixteen tails. Their tails were not merely appendages; they were tools, weapons, and status symbols. The bigger and stronger their tail, the greater the monkey's source of power and pride. In their natural habitat, the monkeys were surrounded by fruit trees of all kinds. They played and swung from the highest trees, gathering fruits and nuts as they went along. They enjoyed competing against one another while swimming in the numerous ponds and rivers scattered throughout the region. In each generation, the males strengthened their tails by wrapping them around the branches of one tree or several trees and then dangling from those tree anchors for hours. It was a painful process, but the males who vied for rulership in the clan would engage in this stretching and strengthening process for days, sometimes weeks, at a time. The monkeys who watched the process knew to stay away from these monkeys, as they were the ones who used their tails to attack the males with weaker tails, usually to steal their female partners. When males fought, the victor was always the one with the longest and strongest tails.

The female monkeys used their tails to gather fruits, hold on to the nuts they gathered, and to carry their babies. A female monkey could carry up to twelve babies with her tails. It was not unusual for the hungriest baby to use one of its tails to snatch food from the mouth of one of its siblings. This meant that the smallest or weakest baby might wait for days to eat because the stronger ones had no qualms about using their power to take what they needed or wanted, which often went unnoticed by the mother. The spirit of competition was implanted among the monkey siblings before they took their first steps on the ground. For them and their mother, survival became a dance of get more, carry more, do more, produce more, all while hanging on by their tails.

The female monkeys also knew that the strongest adult male monkeys, the ones who could protect them from predators, were attracted to females who could carry the most babies at one time. For a fruitful mating to occur, all sixteen of her tails needed to be occupied so that when a male approached her, his advances *would* not, *could* not be resisted. While the two mated, the babies hung from their mother's tails, attached only by their tails, which left the little ones prone to falling. It also meant that a predatory adult male who did not get to mate with the female of their desire could snatch, and maybe even kill, the unattended baby. It was essential for this species of monkey to mate often because they typically died young, usually at the age of five to six years. If the species were to survive, constant repopulation was necessary. Unfortunately, the increasing population led to food shortages and increased *survival aggression* within the clans.

On the opposite end of the world, in a very high and extremely cold territory, there lived a clan of monkeys that had no tails. The species did not begin that way. It happened as nature adapted to the demands and needs of their environment. When the species first emerged, they had very long, wiry tails. Since there were very few trees in the region, the tails were not particularly useful. In the winter months when the temperatures dropped below freezing, the monkey's tails, covered with snow and ice, fell from the monkey's body, leaving just a tiny nub of gristle and bone protruding from the monkey's hind parts. When that happened, the hole in the monkey's body exposed them to freezing. In response, once a monkey lost its tail, it retreated into one of the dens or caves naturally carved out on the sides of the mountain until the worst of the weather was over.

It was not uncommon for hundreds of monkeys to be in a cave, braving the winter together, their bodies pressed against one another for warmth. Elders were given first place in these sacred hollows. It was also during these times that the tailless monkeys would mate, emerging from the caves with bulging bellies or newborns in the somewhat warmer weather. Over time, without intervention from external forces, the monkey babies were born with no tails. They were not necessary, and they exposed the monkeys to peril. In the presence of the community, mating was gentle. The tailless monkeys survived not by aggression, but through adaptation. Through the community. Through stillness. Through reverence for the gifts and rhythm of nature. These monkeys lived longer, with a lifespan of fifteen to sixteen years. Their lives were marked not by dominance, but by dignity. When a monkey died in the cave, its body was returned to the earth, becoming nourishment for the sky and soil. Nothing was wasted. Everything was sacred.

This tale is not simply about monkeys and their tails. It is a mirror for us. A *soul-teaching* in disguise. Spiritual Hygiene begins with the same question: *"What are you growing that you no longer need?" "Where are you strengthening survival strategies that exhaust your spirit?" "How have you mistaken suffering for strength and endurance for identity?" "What part of your inherited environment, physical, emotional, cultural, or spiritual, asks you to freeze, contort, compete, or conform to belong?"*

The first half of our sacred journey, **Healing and Releasing**, asked us to *become aware of and tell the truth about* the ways we have stretched ourselves for approval, validation, or survival. Now we are being asked to notice the ways we are still bracing, clinging, or performing for belonging. With this awareness, we will begin the sacred act of *choosing*. We begin the path of soul reclamation, by letting go of the tales we have told and the "*tails*" we have used to control ourselves and the environments in which we find ourselves. This awareness is not the end of the journey. To reclaim is to *remember*. To remember is to *return*. This return requires *responsibility*. This is where we cross the threshold into **Level III of Spiritual Hygiene: The Return to the Sacred Self**. This will not be a simple return to joy and peace, or a better way of doing what you have done in the past. This return requires all the skills we have examined: *awareness, honesty, permission, inner authority,* and *spiritual integrity*. This will be a return to your soul's *rightful seat of power.* Maintaining this seat is your *Sacred Responsibility*.

The tailless monkeys learned from their experiences. They did not question or resist change. They did not mourn the loss of their tails, nor did they carry them into the caves once they fell frozen to the ground. They learned to surrender and honor what no longer served their evolution. They protected their young by accepting the changes in their being. They honored their elders by creating and restructuring their space. They aligned with the wisdom of their environment, thereby protecting the lineage of their ancestry. This is what Spiritual Hygiene prepares us to do: to *clear* so we can *claim*. To *release* what was inherited and what no longer serves, so we can *return* to what is eternal and holy. To release what was traumatic so that we can reclaim our Divine identity. As we enter this next phase, you are invited to sit with the sacred question that leads us forward: "*What are you now ready to release so you may return to yourself?*" We begin by examining why this release and reclamation is your responsibility and identifying the ways of living you are being called to embrace.

As established, we begin with prayer.

OPENING PRAYER

Holy Presence, Ancient and Near,
I bow at the altar of remembrance, seeking to become, ready to *return.*

I choose to return to the center where You dwell within me.
I choose to return to the truth that was covered, not lost.
I choose to return to the throne of my being,
where my soul remembers its name.

Today, I lay down what is no longer needed.
The false strength.
The inherited stories.
The broken agreements I made from fear.

I return not empty but *emptied.*
I Am emptied of the clutter that clouded my knowing.
I Am emptied of the roles that ruled my worth.
I Am emptied of the noise that drowned out Your whisper.

I ask and open myself to receive cleansing in the crevices
and corners of my consciousness.
I ask and open myself so that the residue of my resistance
will be washed away.
I ask and open myself for the restoration of what
has always been mine:
Sacred Responsibility. Soul authority. Divine inheritance.
I acknowledge this return as holy.
I honor the reclamation as sacred.
I walk forward in the name of all who have forgotten

and are now awakening.
I remember who I Am.
I remember what I carry.
I remember what is mine to raise and restore.
I Ask. I Allow. I Receive.
Amen. Ạṣẹ Aho.
And so, it is.

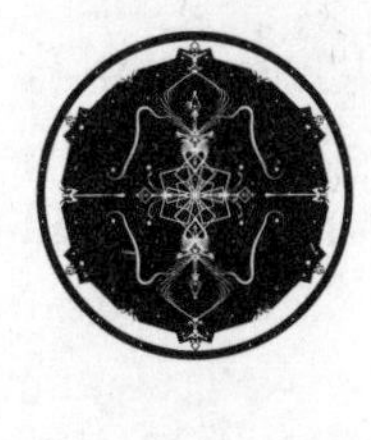

CHAPTER 10

SPIRITUAL RESPONSIBILITY

The Call to Reclaim the Sacred Self

Your Creator can only do for you what can be done through you.

The Survival *Tails* We Have Outgrown

Some patterns that were once required survival strategies are now burdens. Like the southern monkeys in the teaching tale, many of us have stretched ourselves in painful ways to feel strong, worthy, or loved. Strength born of suffering cannot sustain true joy, and it denies the authentic identity that lies beneath the pain of the survival skill. I can recall many times when, in an effort to "keep the peace" with her sons, Nisa would deny or silence her intuition. She would stretch herself in ten different directions to please them. She would try desperately to manage their emotions by hiding her truth until her energy frayed. I remember looking at her one evening, her eyes filled with tears that she wouldn't allow to fall, and saying: *"My love, if their peace costs you your peace, it is not peace. You can stop stretching yourself into their structure and share your heart with them. You can't just be their mother. You also must be yourself."*

Like the monkeys who stretched their tails for battle, we sometimes train for wars we no longer need to fight. We mentally rehearse arguments that never take place. We defend ourselves against old ghosts. We armor up daily, forgetting we are no longer in danger. Exhaustion becomes our normal state. People-pleasing becomes our daily intention. In

Nisa's 3D consciousness, with her sons and with me, she believed she had to over-give and over-function to prove her worth. In my 5D consciousness, I have learned the importance of shedding thoughts, beliefs, and behaviors that no longer serve me and those in my environment. Spiritual Hygiene helped me prune the overgrowth in my ways of being, allowing me to grow in alignment with Divine truth.

On the journey of growth, we all encounter fear and resistance to change. Yet even within the roles we hold—whether as a mother, partner, or guide—our personal healing remains our Sacred Responsibility. Each of us must choose the time, process, manner, and method by which we grow. Others may not agree with our path or accept our methods, but the responsibility for transformation rests within our own hands.

The Practice of Spiritual Responsibility As Sacred Responsibility

Spiritual Responsibility is the conscious and consistent commitment to care for the unseen parts of yourself. This includes your *thoughts*, your *energy*, your *emotions*, your *breath*, your *body*, your *heart*, your *presence*, and your *purpose*. A helpful way to think of responsibility in this context is that you are "*response-able.*" You can respond, rather than react, to what shows up in the moment because you are grounded in your spiritual core, your *spiritual center*. To be spiritually responsible means that you no longer treat your pain as someone else's fault, your healing as someone else's job, or your energy as someone else's dumping ground. You accept this responsibility not as a duty you perform under pressure or to receive external rewards, but as a devotion to yourself and for yourself that you hold with reverence. It is the Divine act of reclaiming *stewardship* of your energy field and inner world, so that you may become a clearer vessel for God, for good, for grace.

Sacred Responsibility

Sacred Responsibility is the holy charge entrusted to every soul to honor, protect, and embody the Divine within and around us. It is more than duty; it is a covenant with Spirit to live in alignment with truth, love, and integrity. Unlike ordinary responsibility, which can feel like an obligation, Sacred Responsibility is born of reverence. It calls us to recognize that our choices, actions, and presence carry spiritual weight and ripple into the lives of others and the unfolding of creation.

Sacred Responsibility Asks Us to:

- Revere Life: To treat all beings, including ourselves, as expressions of the sacred
- Guard Our Gifts: To care for our talents, relationships, and resources as blessings given for a Divine purpose
- Walk in Integrity: To live so that our inner truth and outer actions are in harmony
- Serve the Whole: To remember that our healing, growth, and awakening are not just for ourselves but for the upliftment of the collective
- Remain Accountable to Spirit: To continually return to prayer, reflection, and alignment, seeking Divine guidance in all things

At its heart, Sacred Responsibility is not a burden; it is a blessing and a service. It is the recognition that we are participants in the holy work of creation and keepers of Divine order. It is the awareness that spiritual responsibility for self is a Sacred Responsibility to the world.

Spiritual Responsibility

Spiritual Responsibility is **personal**. It is the call to tend to your own inner life—your thoughts, emotions, choices, and energetic presence. It is about being accountable for your growth, your healing, and your alignment with the Divine.

- **Focus: Self-awareness and self-mastery**
- **Emphasis:** Cleansing the mind, heart, body, and soul
- **Nature:** An **inner covenant** that says, "***I am responsible for my spiritual state.***"
- **Example:** Choosing to release harmful thoughts, practicing forgiveness, or committing to daily prayer/meditation

Sacred Responsibility

Sacred Responsibility is **relational and collective**. It recognizes that your life is part of a larger whole and that you hold a holy duty to live in ways that honor the Divine in yourself, others, and creation.

- **Focus: Service and stewardship**
- **Emphasis:** Protecting life, honoring gifts, walking in integrity, serving the greater good
- **Nature:** A sacred covenant that says, "I am responsible to Spirit and creation."
- **Example:** Using your voice to speak truth, caring for community, protecting the earth, or living as a healing presence

Spiritual Responsibility is the foundation, how you care for your own soul. Sacred Responsibility is the extension, how you embody that care in a relationship with the world.

In practice, Sacred Responsibility means taking the time to clear your energetic field before sharing your presence with others. When you speak to teach or share, you don't just speak from memory or charisma. You do what is required to cleanse the remnants of yesterday's fears, projections, conversations, and distractions so that what pours through your speaking is holy, not hurried.

Sacred Responsibility means you learn to speak truth even when silence would be safer. You choose alignment over approval. Integrity over image. You tell the truth, not to be loud, but to be free. And you honor the cost of truth as part of your calling. It means you develop the discernment to know what is yours to have, hold, or carry, and what must be released so that you move in the world with clarity and cleanliness. You stop dragging people, pain, and problems into new experiences and relationships because you have done your work. You return other people's projections to them as a function of Somatic Stewardship. You unhook your soul from the false sense of responsibility for everyone and their healing. Sacred Responsibility means brushing your teeth *and* brushing off the thoughts, beliefs, and behaviors that shame or diminish you. It is eating well and digesting the emotions you've swallowed whole. It is going to sleep at a reasonable hour and tending to the dreams and messages that visit you at night. It is saying no, not just to people, but to anything that dishonors your wholeness, your rhythm, your breath, and the truth you know in your soul. Yes, all of these things are personal, yet, doing them serves the world.

Sacred Responsibility shows up in the little things too. It means you *ritualize your daily choices.* They are not rigid. They are relevant. You cleanse your altar and your calendar. You choose foods that nourish not just your body, but your vibration. You place boundaries where your peace has been bleeding. You speak to yourself with the same kindness you give others in prayer. Sacred Responsibility is a choice you make in every moment to remain clean, clear, and connected. It is not something you do because you are afraid of falling apart. It is what you become because you are finally ready to live whole.

The tailless monkeys learned to listen to their environment. They stopped growing what no longer served them. They shared space. They honored rhythm. They created harmony. This is Spiritual Hygiene in motion. In my own home, I had to learn to create an environment where spirit, rather than chaos, was the center. It meant waking up early for moments of silence, choosing stillness over noise, creating altars instead of arguments. My soul began to bloom not because my life got easier, but because my atmosphere became sacred. Your sacred return does not begin with *addition,* adding more things to do in an already packed day and life. It begins with subtraction. You do not need more affirmations, more rituals, more approval. You need to release. Your return to yourself and your center begins with asking: *"What must die so I may live? What tail must I stop growing?"* In the 3D world of physical reality, we continue to accumulate, gathering things and people to make ourselves feel good or safe. In the 5D consciousness where energy is safe and sacred, we embrace simplicity, stillness, and silence. Spiritual Hygiene clears the noise so you can hear the whispers of your soul and the Divine.

Coming back to yourself, your true self, your authentic self, is a sacred act. When lived fully, Spiritual Responsibility becomes Sacred Responsibility. It is the recognition that your body is not just biology functioning to keep you alive. Your body is a living altar. In fact, it would serve us to spend some time in recognition of those who may be challenged by the concept of "*an altar*":

Just because it was taught doesn't mean it is true.

Just because it was modeled doesn't mean it is aligned.

If the Altar Scares You

An altar is more than an arrangement of sacred objects. It is a mirror of your soul, your truth, and your Divine relationship. To build one is to say: *"I believe in something greater. I believe I'm worthy to be in conversation with it."* Fear related to altars often reveals itself in *four deep energetic layers*:

1. Fear of Exposure

Altars bring the invisible into the visible. They are declarations of belief, intention, and devotion. For some, this triggers a fear of being vulnerable. There is an unconscious fear that building an altar will:

- Expose spiritual beliefs others may not understand
- Invite judgment or misunderstanding (*especially from religious upbringing*)
- Require a deeper level of accountability you may not feel ready to fulfill

Altars are not a site of religious or spiritual performance. They are portals of intimacy.

2. Unworthiness Wounds

For many, creating an altar stirs up the unhealed lie: *I'm not pure enough, holy enough, spiritual enough.* This is rooted in religious trauma, shame, and separation consciousness.

There's a fear that:

- They are not "*ready*" or "*worthy*" to commune with Spirit
- They must earn the right to create sacred space
- God or their ancestors will judge them
- An altar does not require your perfection. It invites your presence.

3. Fear of Power

Altars *amplify intention*. They open channels of communication with your higher self, your ancestors, and your guides. Some part of us knows that once we step into this sacred space, our lives may start to realign. This may trigger a fear of:

- Receiving instructions from Spirit they will be afraid or unable to follow
- Inviting truths they are not ready to face
- Activating a deeper level of spiritual responsibility

Altars do not demand transformation. They gently call it forth.

4. Cultural or Religious Conditioning

There is a deeply ingrained fear, often rooted in colonized theology, a system of religious belief and practice that has been shaped, distorted, or controlled by colonial power structures or ancestral disconnection, that people use to associate altars with:

- Idolatry or witchcraft (due to religious fearmongering)
- Family beliefs that condemn personal spiritual practice
- Superstition around "*what could come through*"

Altars exist in every sacred tradition. They are places of prayer, honor, remembrance, and peace.

In the framework of Spiritual Hygiene an altar is:

- A place to engage in conversation between your soul and the Divine
- A spiritual home for your intentions, prayers, and remembrances
- A reflection of your sacred worthiness

You are not required to build an altar with objects. However, if you feel drawn to one and fear arises, you must know that fear is not truth. That fear is the old guard: a voice of limitation, shame, or programming that seeks to block the door to your new becoming. It could be the part of you that asks: *"Who am I to create something sacred?"* The truth is, you already are something sacred. *The altar has always been you.* Unfortunately, you may have been "worshipping" things that were no longer necessary.

Awakening to your sacred self, to your body as an altar, your mind as a temple, your heart as a chalice, Spiritual Responsibility invites the consideration of an altar as a sacred space where Spirit dwells, *where intention is placed, where presence is honored, where offerings are made, where truth is revealed*. When you are reminded that *"Your body is a living altar,"* it means:

- Your breath is an offering
- Your skin is a sanctuary
- Your womb is a portal
- Your tears are libation

- Your boundaries are sacred fences
- Your stillness is a ceremony

The body becomes the space where Divinity is not just worshipped, it is embodied. It also means that if your body is the altar, it is nothing to fear. Instead, your daily choices, energy, and emotional care are what either nourish or neglect it. Just as a physical altar must be dusted, tended, and revisited, the body requires:

- Rest
- Anointing
- Emotional honesty
- Movement
- Surrender
- Secure boundaries
- Breath

When you cleanse your body, you make space for Spirit to dwell there more fully. When you listen to your body, you hear the voice of God more clearly. If this teaching triggers discomfort or concern, *pause and breathe*. Your response is not a rejection of your body or spiritual awareness. It is revelation.

A trigger is often:

- A stored memory rising for acknowledgment
- A limiting belief resisting a new possibility
- A part of you that was taught to disconnect from your body for safety

It is not a sign that something is wrong. It is a sign that something wants to be cleared. The trigger is the teacher. Allow it to lead you into healing without judgment.

Tending to the Altar of the Body

Place your hands over your heart and whisper: *"This is holy."*

- Anoint your body with oil, blessing each part with gratitude.
- Cleanse your emotional field by writing down what you have been holding about altars or your own sacredness. You can burn it as a love offering.
- Listen to where tension lives, and ask: *"What am I holding that is not mine?" "What am I growing that is no longer required?"*
- Offer a prayer for purification.

You do not need permission from anything or anyone outside of yourself to be, see, or hold yourself as sacred. You do not need tools to make yourself holy. Your body is not the obstacle. It is the altar. The more gently you tend to it, the more clearly you will hear the Divine whisper back: *"Thank you. Welcome home."*

Your Mind Is a Temple

The distinctions between third-dimensional consciousness and fifth-dimensional consciousness are important at this level of our journey. In 3D, we often overlook the inner world of thought in our pursuit of the outer world of intellect and sensory stimulation. In 5D, we are more concerned with listening, aligning, and adapting with reverence. Spiritual Hygiene fosters the conditions for our mental life to flourish, as it recognizes the mind as more than a file cabinet of memories. *It is a temple of consciousness.* This means your mind is a site of sacred architecture where thoughts are prayers, beliefs are altars, and imagination is prophecy.

Your mind is not just a thinking device; it is a spiritual chamber that shapes your reality through energy, vibration, and perception. What you allow to dwell in this temple becomes the atmosphere of your life. To tend the mind with respect, love, and presence is to keep the temple clean for Divine wisdom to flow freely. When you cleanse what's within, you change what flows without.

Again, let us consider the monkeys. One clan stretched and strained for dominance. The other adapted and evolved for harmony. One clung to inherited survival strategies. The other listened to the land and let go of what was no longer needed. This is a tale of two states of *consciousness*, two ways of being. It is the turning point in your own sacred return.

Sacred Responsibility in Daily Life

A Sacred Responsibility is not burdensome or overwhelming. It is not about pleasing or fixing other people. Your Sacred Responsibility for yourself is *the commitment to stay* ***in right relationship*** *with your own energy, your own truth, your own choices.* It may look like:

- Whispering into the water you are drinking: *"This body is holy."*
- Saying "No" and meaning it without fear or guilt
- Saying "Yes" and honoring the commitment by showing up fully
- Choosing personal and spiritual integrity when avoidance is easier
- Pausing to pray to get into or stay in alignment
- Journaling instead of gossiping
- Giving yourself permission to feel rather than numbing out
- Resting without a need or reason and without guilt

The Spiritual Responsibility of returning home to your heart and soul is a blessing. It is the radical choice to become the clean vessel. You are not seeking praise or approval. You are devoted to your own internal experience of peace. Turning to and embracing Spiritual Hygiene not only neutralizes or eliminates the voices of trauma, the pain of history, and the dysfunction of what has been inherited, but it also demonstrates your willingness to cut off the tails of duty, overwhelm, and numbness. You are replacing the tails of denial, avoidance, fear, and resistance with the warmth of truth, clarity, and light in every aspect of your life. It begins right here, right now, by opening your heart and turning your attention to each of the following inquiries being offered to reacquaint you with your spiritual core, your center, because you were always meant to *live from the center of your soul.*

FINAL REFLECTION

With a notebook and pen or recording device, give yourself permission to unearth and bring forward your authentic response to each of the following inquiries:

How many *"tails"* or *"tales"* do you have?
What are they holding on to or holding in place?

....

....

....

....

....

What are you growing, nursing, nurturing that you no longer need?

....

....

....

....

....

How have you mistaken suffering for identity?

What inherited behaviors have you mistaken for truth?

Where are you strengthening something or someone that exhausts you?

What in your environment must be attuned to in order for you to thrive?

Where have you "outsourced your power" and over-performed to feel worthy or receive love?

....

....

....

....

....

Remember and embody this:

> *The trigger is the teacher.*
> Let it lead you into healing, without judging it as bad or wrong.

OPENING PRAYER

Beloved Divine Presence, Source of All That Is,
Anchor me now in the truth of who I Am.
Still the noise of the outer world so that I may hear the whisper within.
Clear the static of fear, comparison, and inherited belief.
Make way for the sacred knowing that cannot be taught,
only remembered.

Let the breath be my guide.
Let the heart be my altar.
Let the core of my being rise in recognition of its own radiance.

Where I have drifted, call me home.
Where I have betrayed myself, bring forgiveness.
Where I have forgotten, awaken the seed of truth that
has never left me.

I come now because I Am reclaiming all that I Am.
I Am here because I Am willing.
I welcome the clarity, the courage, and the stillness to live from the
place within me that has always known that you love me.

Amen. Aṣẹ Aho.
And so, it is.

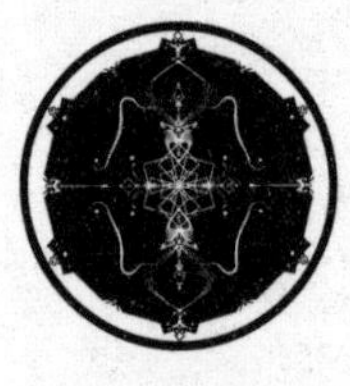

CHAPTER 11

Finding Your Center

Returning to Your Spiritual Core

There is a place within you that has always known everything about you, and everything you need to know. This place existed before your name, before the world told you who to be, before you were derailed by betrayal, confusion, or applause.

Although it is referred to often, perhaps as your "*center*" or "*the real you,*" your spiritual core is not something you can be taught. It is a truth you remember. It is the compass of the soul, a Divine code that is etched into your being. That etching is like a song being sung to you and for you as you move through every experience of life. No matter how complex or painful the situation may seem, this song is playing on repeat. The words of the song are, "*. . . if only you knew how much I do, I do love you.*" That love, which has never, can never, and *will* never leave you, is your spiritual core.

How do you recognize your Spiritual Core?

I recall a woman who shared with me that when she was five years old, her parents were fighting in the living room. Plates were being thrown. Doors were being slammed. Her father's voice boomed like thunder, and her mother's cry filled the house like broken glass. I listened to her intently because her story was also my story. Her learning was my learning. Her healing was my healing because we are all connected at the core. She said that she was small, too small to stop, change, or fix what was unfolding before her, so she crawled into a dark linen closet, wrapped herself in a towel, and whispered: *"God, if you're real, hold me now."* She didn't know why she said it. Her parents had not taught her how to pray, but somehow, she knew. Something in her knew. Years later, she would understand that moment as her first encounter with her *spiritual core*, the unshakable part of her that believed in something greater, even in the dark.

I remember the first time I encountered my core. I was about five, and my brother was having a severe asthma attack, which necessitated yet another mad dash to the emergency room. When the taxi screeched to a halt in front of the hospital, my father and stepmother threw the doors open, scooped up my brother, and ran into the emergency room, leaving me sitting in the back of the taxi. I don't remember the driver saying anything because he was as shocked as I was, but something within me spoke to me. It said, *"You are OK. You've been here before. You know where to go and what to do."* And I did, so I did. The driver helped me out of the car. I walked into the emergency room and sat in my usual seat by the vending machine. When my stepmother came looking for me, she sat down next to me and said, *"He's going to be alright."* She didn't apologize for leaving me in the car, but she did give me a nickel to buy some candy from the vending machine.

Your spiritual core is not something you earn. It is not reserved for the holy, the healed, or the well-behaved. It is the inner seat of truth and trust that has always been present. Some people discover it in silence. Others in times of crisis. Often, we discover our spiritual core through the very experience that we believe has come to separate us from ourselves. It is at that exact time, in that most troubling experience, that your spiritual core whispers:

"Even now, you are not alone."

"Even here, there is a way through."

"Even this, I can use for your remembering."

Imagine you are on a yacht cruising on a vast ocean, and the skies grow dark. The waves rise, slamming furiously onto the side of the yacht. You lose sight of the shore, and you lose your footing. You are being tossed around the deck like a rag doll. In that moment, your intellect and all your degrees cannot save you. Your ego panics. Your conditioning fails. Then, there it is, like a compass on your chest, but it is within you. It does not scream. It does not demand. If and when you hear it, it doesn't even frighten you. It simply turns you toward what is true. It tells you what to do and what not to do. That is your spiritual core. It does not promise you comfort or ease. It gives you direction. It does not ask for your approval or agreement. It offers you alignment. Think back to a moment in your life when everything was unclear, perhaps chaotic or frightening, yet something inside you *knew.* Maybe you left the job. Or maybe you said yes to the move, the calling, the risk. Maybe you finally told the truth. That knowing. That pull. That song. That whisper, which felt more like a *remembrance*, was your spiritual core. In a world that teaches you to outsource truth, to obey demands, and to numb the ache of disconnection, your core remains intact, available, and accessible. It is the sacred place where your soul and the Divine are still in conversation. All it asks is that you pause long enough to listen.

You *can* begin Spiritual Hygiene without being fully grounded in your core, but your practice will be limited to the surface level. It will be like dusting the altar without ever entering the sanctuary. Like lighting candles for a God you do not speak to. Like scrubbing the mirror but never looking into your own eyes.

When you are not anchored in your spiritual core:

- Spiritual Hygiene becomes a ritual of control rather than communion.
- You may perform the spiritual cleansing but not listen to what the residue is trying to teach you.
- You may pray, smudge, bathe, or affirm, but still feel foggy, fragmented, or "off."

Without your core being activated, you are clearing energy without direction. You are tending to the field, without asking: *"What am I protecting? What am I remembering? What sacred truth am I making space for?"* Spiritual Hygiene without connection to your core is like washing your hands when you are afraid of water. You are spiritually misaligned.

Misalignment happens when you perform rituals (i.e., *praying, meditating, even attending church*) while denying the emotions that need to be released. It happens when you strive for connection to the Divine while ignoring the fracture within. You can pray while misaligned. You can teach, serve, lead, and love while misaligned. Unfortunately, your actions will feel hollow; they will echo, as if the spirit of your intention has not caught up to the performance you deliver. You can tell that you are not living from or choosing from your core when:

Your decisions lack clarity.

- You say "yes" when you mean "no."
- You say "I'm fine" when you're unraveling.
- You ask others for answers your soul already knows.

Your energy leaks.

- You become emotionally drained without understanding why.
- You tend to attract confusion, chaos, or chronic friction in your relationships.
- You are constantly managing how you think you are being seen because you no longer know who you are.

You struggle to feel joy or peace.

- Even in success, something feels hollow.
- Even in rest, you are restless.
- Even in prayer, you feel disconnected because you are speaking from the mind, not the core.

You repeat the same painful cycles.

- Misalignment creates loops.
- You date the same lesson in different bodies.
- You find yourself in spaces that shrink you, jobs that drain you, or dynamics that dishonor you.

When you live misaligned with your core, *you cannot access the full wisdom of your soul*. Instead, you are fending for yourself with intellect, ego, and at its worst, trauma.

Your spiritual core is the *why* behind every Spiritual Hygiene practice. It is the truth you are returning to when you mentally or physically detox, when you journal, when you cry, when you fast, when you forgive. The core gives you *direction*. It gives you the courage to say, *"This energy or person or situation must go because it is not aligned with who I truly am." "This pattern ends here because I am no longer a match for it." "This boundary is sacred, not because I am angry, but because I am holy."* Spiritual Hygiene is meant to address the most common forms of spiritual misalignment that happen when:

- You **silence the voice of your heart** to avoid rejection or maintain belonging.
- You have **inherited beliefs or roles** that no longer match your lived truth.
- You have **abandoned yourself**, bit by bit, to stay safe, be accepted, or to maintain the illusion of control.

Sometimes the misalignment happens slowly. Sometimes it happens all at once after betrayal, burnout, trauma, or awakening. In all cases, it leaves you far from home, far away from your heart. The good news is that no matter how far you drift, your spiritual core never leaves you. It waits to welcome you back to your center. It waits until *you choose* to come home.

The Compass Within: Heart vs. Intellect

Your spiritual core is connected to your heart—not your physical heart, not the heart that beats only blood, but the heart as the seat of the soul. This is why we often default to the mind and the intellect; many of us have broken hearts. The way our survival strategy functions, we think about what we should feel, and bypass what we know in our core. Your heart will always tell you the truth. It is the center of knowing, the sanctuary of Divine communion. On the other hand, the intellect will lie to you, not because it is bad or wrong. It distorts the truth because it is limited. The intellect is attached to third-dimensional reality. It depends on what it sees, what it hears, what it can measure or understand. It asks: *"Where is God when children are dying?"* and *"Why do good people suffer?"* The heart doesn't need these answers. It knows love. The heart recognizes truth even when the facts don't make sense. It trusts what the mind cannot grasp.

The mind is not the temple of revelation. It is the chamber of analysis. The soul does not speak in bullet points. It speaks in resonance. Your spiritual core is accessed not through facts; it is accessed through awareness, truth, and energy. To live from this place, we must *renew the mind of the soul*, which is the *heart*, not the brain. In this very moment, your mind is probably thinking, *"But wait a minute! You said earlier that the mind is an altar and that I must remove the illegitimate leaders so that my mind would be sacred. Now you are saying the mind is a liar! Unreliable! Please explain!"* This is a legitimate concern, so let us examine it step by step.

Imagine that you are a castle:

- *Your brain* is the control room. It helps you move your arms, speak words, solve puzzles, and remember what time dinner will be served.
- *Your mind* is like the room where all your thoughts live. This is the part of you that asks questions, makes decisions, and tries to figure out the world.

- *Your consciousness* is the light inside the castle that never goes out. It is not a room. It is the presence that sees it all, feels it all, and remembers who you are in your spiritual core.

That is the most basic, the simplest explanation. Let us go another step further.

The Brain: A Helpful Tool

The brain is a physical instrument. Spiritual Hygiene acknowledges the brain as part of the body's sacred design. It is like your body's computer. It helps you function. It's smart, and it's fast. However, despite its outstanding functionality, the brain does not know, recognize, or understand the truth of your soul. It can store information, but it cannot access what is sacred. The brain says, *"Let's figure this out. Let's organize the information. Let's protect you from potential harm."* The brain then digs through its stored files and retrieves what it believes is required to keep you safe from harm. That is its priority.

The Mind: The Thinking Chamber

The mind is an energetic and emotional chamber that holds memories, judgments, comparisons, beliefs, and attachments. The mind is where thoughts swirl like clouds. This is useful when you need to analyze, compare, or make plans; however, because it follows the lead of its cousin, the brain, the mind also gets frightened. It will ask: *"Am I safe?" "Will they love me?" "What if I'm wrong?"* The mind needs proof. It wants to be right. The mind will sort through all the information in the swirling thoughts and conclude, "*I need to understand this now.*" Unfortunately, it can only understand what it already knows, which keeps the mind stuck in the past. When you follow your mind, you also become stuck in the past, revisiting what you have already seen, heard, and experienced, even if it has no relevance to what is happening now. When you clear out fear, shame, and old programs, your mind becomes a temple again. Spiritual Hygiene practices clear the mind, allowing it to serve the truth.

Consciousness: The Eternal Light

Consciousness is your eternal essence. It does not need to be purified. It simply needs space. Consciousness is not thought or thinking. It is knowing. When someone calls your name, you don't think about responding because you know your name. This is how your consciousness functions. Spiritual Hygiene clears the fog that clouds consciousness, allowing Divine awareness to shine through your choices, thoughts, and actions. It is the part of you that watches the mind. It feels like stillness. Like breath. It is there, but you don't have to work on it or with it. It is the whisper that says, "*You are more than this moment.*"

So if your mind is asking, "*Wait . . . didn't you say the mind is an altar? Now you are saying I can't trust it?!,*" you can say, "*Yes. The mind is a beautiful altar, but only when I clean it, quiet it, and place my soul at the center.*" It is not *either/or*. It is *both/and*. The mind becomes sacred when it stops pretending to be God and starts listening for the voice of the heart, which speaks for God. When we practice Spiritual Hygiene, we are doing more than just smudging or praying. We are **clearing distortions, calming the mind, softening the body**, and making room for the **truth that never left**, our *spiritual core.*

Aspect	Role	What Spiritual Hygiene Does
Brain	Physical processor	Clears overactivation, grounds the nervous system
Mind	Emotional/ energetic filter	Cleanses beliefs, thoughts, distortions, and ego loops
Consciousness (Soul)	Divine awareness	Creates space for soul authority to rise

Aspect	**Role**	**What Spiritual Hygiene Does**
Spiritual Core	Living truth center	Realigns all levels to sacred wholeness

A Sacred Pause

Take a breath.
Get still.
Ask yourself gently:

"When was the last time I trusted my heart over my head?"

"What truth have I silenced because I feared I wouldn't be loved?"

"What would happen if I let the heart lead?"

Pay attention to your responses because they will give you insight about how close you are, or are not, to your spiritual core.

Come Back. Come Clean. Come Home.

I can almost hear inquiring minds asking, *"How can I connect to something I didn't even know I had?"* The sacred truth is, **you've never been *disconnected* from your *core in the literal sense*.** What has been disrupted is your ***awareness*** or ***recognition*** of it. Your spiritual core is the center of truth within you. It is the stable axis around which your values, beliefs, discernment, and sense of Divine identity revolve. Your spiritual core has always been present, quiet, constant, waiting. It does not need to be created. It needs to be *recognized.* Spiritual disconnection does not mean the absence of Divinity within you. It means you have *forgotten where it lives in you and how it speaks to you. As you read the list below of* behaviors that erode your spiritual core, *if you recognize something you do, or have done, stop reading. Take a deep breath. Resist the temptation to shame yourself. Accept the awareness with compassion by stating aloud:*

> *"I am grateful for this awareness."*
>
> *"This is no longer who I am."*
>
> *"I ask for and open myself to receive Divine correction."*
>
> *"It is done."*
>
> *"And so, it is."*

Chronic Self-Doubt

"Who am I to . . . ?"

Repeatedly questioning your intuition, worth, or ability weakens your spiritual authority. Any time you second-guess the quiet wisdom within, you hand your power to the outer world and silence the soul's knowing.

Self-doubt is not humility. It is an inherited hesitation that prevents you from trusting the Divine voice already seated within you.

Erosion Effect:

- Breaks trust in your inner guidance
- Makes you dependent on external validation
- Interrupts your ability to follow Divine guidance, even when it is clearly received

Overexplaining or Over-Apologizing

Constantly defending your boundaries, truth, or feelings causes your energy field to shrink. When you overexplain your thoughts, feelings, needs, or requests, you silently agree that your truth must be justified to be valid. Each time you apologize for how you feel, you abandon your inner authority in favor of someone else's comfort. Eventually, the soul stops speaking clearly because it no longer feels safe to be heard.

Erosion Effect:

- Depletes personal sovereignty
- Normalizes self-abandonment
- Trains you to distrust your own clarity

Compulsive Busyness

Being constantly in motion can be a trauma-adapted way to avoid presence. When we fill every space with doing, we leave no room for being. No space for the soul to speak. Busyness becomes a protective disguise, masking the ache of disconnection with calendars and commitments. Underneath the hustle is often a sacred silence waiting to be felt, honored, and healed.

Erosion Effect:

- Disconnects you from spiritual rhythm
- Exhausts your nervous system
- Leaves no room for spiritual recalibration

Judgment (*of Self or Others*)

Judgment is the ego's attempt to control what it does not understand. When we judge, we momentarily relieve ourselves of discomfort by placing distance between "*us*" and "*them*," even when that "*them*" is a part of ourselves. Judgment clouds the heart, clogs compassion, and locks the spirit in a cycle of separation. What begins as protection often ends in distortion, where the noise of opinion muffles the voice of Divine love.

Erosion Effect:

- Closes the heart center
- Blocks compassion and higher insight
- Fuels and feeds separation consciousness

Perfectionism

Perfectionism is the illusion that you must "*get it right*" before being loved, chosen, or spiritually approved.

Perfectionism is not a pursuit of excellence. It is a survival strategy rooted in fear. It is a trick used by the ego that causes you to believe that flawlessness earns worth, when in truth, it only deepens the ache of disconnection. When you chase perfection, you abandon your humanity. The soul cannot thrive where authenticity is denied.

Erosion Effect:

- Prevents authentic action
- Replaces Divine flow with control
- Traps you in cycles of never-enoughness

People-Pleasing

In its simplest form, this is saying "yes" to what you don't want, in reaction to fear of rejection, resentment, or discomfort. People-pleasing may appear as kindness, but it is often rooted in the belief that your truth must be softened or sacrificed for you to be loved. People-pleasing fractures your alignment and slowly teaches your nervous system that safety lies in silence. Each time you abandon your truth for someone else's comfort, the soul grows quieter, and the core grows dimmer.

Erosion Effect:

- Silences soul-truth
- Weakens energetic boundaries
- Creates spiritual fog and resentment

Avoidance of Emotion

When you prioritize function over feeling, you sever the bridge to healing. Avoiding emotion does not erase pain or the problem. It buries itself in the body, where it manifests as weight, illness, or confusion. This avoidance teaches your energy field that the truth is unsafe and that being present is dangerous. Every feeling you refuse to feel becomes a block between you and the guidance trying to reach you.

Erosion Effect:

- Stagnates energy in the body
- Blocks intuitive clarity
- Builds emotional scar tissue

Neglecting Sacred Ritual

Letting your altar gather dust, skipping stillness, or forgetting your daily practice is a sign of poor Spiritual Hygiene. Ritual is not just a routine; it is the soul's way of remembering itself. When sacred practices are neglected, the connection to Source slowly frays from the absence. This is not a punishment. It is a consequence. Without ritual, the spiritual core becomes undernourished. It is alive, but dim, like a flame needing breath to rise again.

Erosion Effect:

- Starves your spiritual core of nourishment
- Normalizes disconnection from Source
- Weakens your field of spiritual remembrance

Overconsumption

Constant scrolling, comparing, bingeing, or incessant information intake is a form of energetic contamination that clutters the mind, weakens the heart, and disrupts the soul's clarity. Overconsumption of social media floods the energy field with noise, leaving no room for the soul's wisdom to come through. The frequency and energetic vibration of social media also impacts spiritual sensitivity by distracting you from the inner world and tethering your attention to things that cannot nourish you. What you take in constantly, energetically, or emotionally, shapes what you are available to know or receive. Too much noise drowns the voice of knowing.

Erosion Effect:

- Drowns the voice of intuition
- Clutters the mental field
- Disrupts energetic sensitivity

Staying in Misaligned Environments

When you remain where you are, shrinking, diminished, or dismissed out of habit or in reaction to fear, it slowly teaches your spirit that survival is more important than truth. You begin to adapt, contort, and shrink to fit what no longer reflects who you are becoming. Over time, your spiritual light dims. It has faded, but the space no longer welcomes its brilliance.

Erosion Effect:

- Normalizes the compromise of your soul's truth
- Erodes confidence in your ability to choose differently
- Mutes your radiance

Certain comfortable or familiar patterns of behavior may seem ordinary, even polite, productive, or protective; however, each one can quietly disrupt the integrity of your inner field. Over time, these behaviors accumulate as residue, spiritual fog that extinguishes your inner glow, compromises your inner knowing, and distances you from Divine intimacy. Spiritual Hygiene is not only about clearing what's heavy; it's also about protecting what is holy.

For the purposes of Spiritual Hygiene, it is essential not only to recognize the behaviors but also to understand the stages involved in the process of disconnection from your spiritual core.

Stages of Disconnection from the Core

STAGE 1 Distortion – *Truth Becomes Unclear or Is Adopted From Others.*

This is the quiet beginning of disconnection, when what once felt true starts to blur beneath the weight of expectation, fear, or cultural conditioning. You may begin to doubt your own knowing or trade your inner compass for someone else's approval, hoping to feel safe, seen, or spiritually "correct."

STAGE 2 Distraction – *You Fill the Void with Noise, Activity, or Performance.*

Once the truth has been distorted, the soul begins to drift. Not in rebellion, but in quiet resignation. You fill the silence with noise; the emptiness with motion; the ache with approval, activity, or achievement. Distraction is deceptive because it feels productive. It gives you something to do while you slowly forget who you are.

STAGE 3 Dissonance – *Inner Conflict Emerges Between Belief and Behavior.*

The spiritual fracture becomes harder to ignore. What you say, what you do, and what you allow are no longer in harmony with what you believe deep down. You may speak of peace while feeling resentful, perform love while withholding truth, or stay silent when your soul wants to scream.

STAGE 4 Division – *The false self emerges.*

By this stage, the gap between your outer life and inner truth has widened into a canyon. You wear the mask well, perhaps even beautifully. Yet, on the inside, something sacred feels as though it is missing. You may still lead, give, serve, or succeed, but it is the performer who shows up, not the soul.

STAGE 5 Disillusionment – *Collapse or Crisis looms: The Holy* **Beginning.**

This is the breaking point, when the weight of the false self becomes too heavy to carry, and something collapses. What was once manageable now feels unbearable. You may experience spiritual exhaustion, loss of faith, profound grief, or a sense of hollowness where your fire once burned.

Disconnection from the spiritual core will not feel like a sudden fall. It unfolds as a gradual *forgetting* of the internal in pursuit of the external. The five stages are signals. Sacred invitations. Each one reveals where your soul is asking to be reclaimed. Even in the deepest disillusionment, you are not lost—you are being stripped of what no longer holds your truth. The return begins with one breath, one truth, one act of remembrance. Your spiritual core has not abandoned you. It has simply been waiting for you to come home.

Sacred Pause

Knowing Where You Are Matters

Because disconnection from your spiritual core doesn't always come with a crash, it is essential to recognize where you are in relation to your core, for spiritually hygienic purposes. The following personal ritual is a sacred and gentle way to discover where you are on that path, and what your spirit is asking of you now.

You Will Need

- 10–15 quiet minutes
- A journal or page on which to write your reflections
- A candle (optional, to symbolize the light of your core)

Set the Space

- Take three deep, reverent breaths.
- Place your hand on your heart or womb.
- Come to stillness.
- Speak aloud or whisper:

  "Show me gently where I am."

  "I release the need to perform or pretend."

  "I am willing to know the truth."

  "I am willing to return to it."

Read each of the inquiries below slowly.
Notice what your body, heart, or breath reveals in response.

Ask Yourself . . .	**If You Say "Yes" . . .**
Have I been believing in things I never chose?	**Distortion**
Have I been keeping busy to avoid myself?	**Distraction**
Do I feel misaligned with what I'm saying, doing, or allowing?	**Dissonance**
Am I showing up as someone I no longer fully recognize?	**Division**
Have I lost connection to meaning, guidance, or passion?	**Disillusionment**

Allow your *body* to show you the truth. You may experience tightness, tears, stillness, or warmth. What you feel is what your soul remembers. Do not give it a meaning. Simply receive the information and write it down.

Journal Prompt

Write the name of the stage you resonated with most:

....

....

....

Complete this sentence with the first thoughts or feelings that come forward:

"The truth I'm ready to face is . . ."

....

"What I most need to remember right now is . . ."

....

Let the answer come without force. Even one word is enough.

Closing Breath and Blessing

Take one final breath with your hand on your heart.

Whisper to yourself once or as many times as it feels appropriate:

"Even now, I am worthy."

"Even now, I can return."

"I honor where I am."

"I bless where I am going."

No matter how far you've wandered, how long you've been quiet, or how deeply you've disguised yourself just to survive, your spiritual core has never left you. It is not something you have to earn back or search for in the world outside you. Your core is the flame that flickers beneath every moment of stillness, every aching truth, and every whisper that says, *"This isn't who I am."* Your disconnection is not a failure. Again, *you haven't done anything wrong.* Your awareness of the depth of a disconnection from your spiritual core is an invitation. This is not a journey of doing or becoming. It is a journey of remembering. When you are willing, your heart will say, *"You are welcome."*

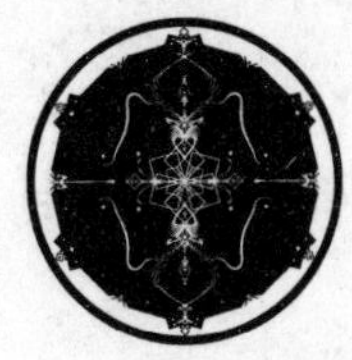

OPENING PRAYER

Beloved Divine Presence,
Seat of all Rhythm, Keeper of all Truth,
If I have given my time to what dims me,
If I have spent my energy without intention,
If I have tied my soul to unspoken pain,
or broken sacred trust with my own spirit—
I now ask to be forgiven.
I ask You, to return me to presence.
I ask You, to return me to truth.
I ask You, to return me to my center where my soul speaks clearly.
Let every place within me that has been scattered, neglected,
or disguised be called home by You.
May I not fear the mirror of self-awareness.
May I not run from the weight of what I have carried.
I ask that this be a time of release,
where the fog lifts, where the hooks are unfastened,
and the altar of my heart is restored to truth.
I declare this now:
I Am not my habits.
I Am not the disconnection.
I Am not the past distortions.
I Am the living light of the Divine,
cleansing and clearing the temple of my soul.
I Am ready to begin again.

Amen. Aṣẹ Aho.
And so, it is.

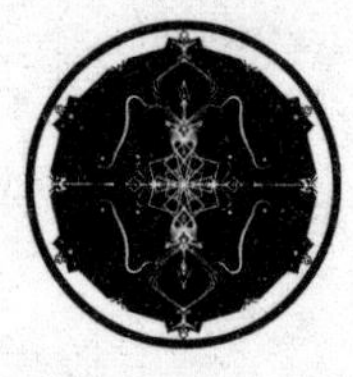

CHAPTER 12

When the Core Cracks

Unforgiveness, Misalignment, and the Cost of Spiritual Neglect

The Story of Amara

Amara was a beautiful soul—radiant, intelligent, giving. As a young girl, she aspired to be a nun, but her mother yearned for grandchildren. As an only child, she felt obligated to follow the traditional track of womanhood and motherhood. At age thirty-seven, she had not found the right match for her "*deeply spiritual lifestyle*." Amara knew how, and she loved to hold space for others in their times of need. She was frequently called upon to share wisdom in spiritual circles, where she performed rituals with great skill and grace. But quietly, beneath the glow of her candles, incense, and affirmations, something had begun to decay.

The wounds were so quiet, she forgot they were there, until someone spoke their name, until a scent or silence or shadow brought it all back. Amara didn't think she was holding a grudge. She had learned to rise above it. To move on. To rebuild. The betrayal had happened years ago. A trusted friend, and dare she say *lover*, had used her, lied to her, and humiliated her behind her back. At first, the rage was visible. But time buried it beneath layers of "*I'm fine*." She prayed. She taught. She smiled, but something wasn't flowing.

Since then, she repeatedly found herself overly protective in relationships. She assumed the worst before she hoped for the best. Her heart felt guarded, even when she allowed herself to experience fleeting moments of joy. Love didn't seem to land. Her affirmations felt hollow. Her connection to the Divine felt muffled. It was unforgiveness, disguised as strength and service.

Amara had not realized that the pain had built a throne in her soul. Her heart was no longer a place of truth. It had become a shrine to the wound. Unforgiveness had become an altar where she unconsciously worshipped with denied thoughts and avoided feelings. Daily, she offered her energy to the memory of the harm, rather than to the healing of her heart. She had forgiven with her lips and on her journal pages. Her heart, however, refused to participate or align. The betrayal of her former friend lingered like a cloud of smoke in her soul. She smiled when they were mentioned. *"It's fine,"* she would say. *"I'm over it."* But in the quiet moments, her chest would tighten. Her thoughts would spiral. She rehearsed her pain like a prayer, feeding the spirit of her wound instead of the altar of her truth. In the quiet moments when she gave herself permission to *feel* her truth, she felt ashamed. She took that shame into a mental cave of denial and ordered it to stay there because she did not have the time, would not give herself the time to unpack it.

Amara was exhausted. She was giving more than she had. She avoided confrontation like the plague. She kept saying yes when she meant no, then wondered why she felt so invisible. To keep the peace, she swallowed her truths. Her spirit, once vibrant, now felt faint. She also found herself gossiping more, disguising it as *"just processing aloud"* or sharing her feelings and observations honestly. She overcommitted and underdelivered, breaking quiet promises to herself and then compensating with public performance. She prayed often, but her prayers felt empty. One day, she realized that she could no longer hear the voice of God, which meant her intuition had dimmed. Her body ached for rest, but she kept going. Her soul ached for truth, but it felt overwhelming. Outwardly, she was seen as being deeply spiritual, while inwardly, she felt disconnected.

What Amara did not realize was that she was not experiencing a personal failure. It was an *erosion*, a slow, steady disconnection from her spiritual core, because she was afraid. Afraid to feel, afraid to grieve, afraid to rest in truth.

What We Must Remember

Your spiritual core is the inner sanctuary where alignment begins. It is the sacred intersection where your soul leads, your mind surrenders, and your energy flows freely in communion with the Divine. When your core is intact, you are clear, grounded, and in rhythm with your truth. However, when poor Spiritual Hygiene becomes your norm, the erosion begins. Each behavior or survival pattern may seem small on its own, but collectively, they create a spiritual smog. The conscious choice, failure, or resistance to clear the smog is the textbook definition of poor Spiritual Hygiene.

Unforgiveness: The Binding Cord

Unforgiveness is not simply withholding pardon; it is anchoring your spirit to a moment that no longer exists. Each revisit to the grievance feeds an altar of pain instead of presence. Unforgiveness rarely announces itself loudly. It shows up in tension behind the smile. In the sudden ache when a name is spoken. Unforgiveness is a spiritual tether. It not only binds you to the person, but it also binds you to the emotional frequency of the harm. Unforgiveness binds your breath to fear, your joy to suspicion, and your choices to the ghosts of what was never resolved. What you do not forgive, you begin to fear. What you fear, you begin to control. What you control, you cannot surrender. Without surrender, the soul cannot breathe.

As a **spiritual tether**, unforgiveness becomes an invisible cord that keeps your soul linked to the frequency, memory, and emotion of a painful experience. It may not be apparent in your day-to-day actions, but it resonates in your energy field. It informs your boundaries. It influences your expectations. You may think you've moved on, but your soul remains caught in a loop, revisiting what was done, reactivating what was felt, rehearsing what was lost. Whether consciously or unconsciously, every time you revisit the wound, replay the story, or suppress the emotion without transmuting it, the tether of unforgiveness strengthens. It becomes harder to live in the present moment because part of your spirit is still worshipping at an altar built in the past. Unforgiveness says, *"I'm not ready to be free."* This is not because you lack the capacity. It is because the tether has become familiar. It may feel like protection, but it is spiritual entrapment. You are trapped in the energy of unforgiveness.

Cracks in the Core

When what you say, feel, do, and believe are out of harmony, the soul becomes divided. Misaligned behaviors are not just habits. They are symptoms of erosion, a quiet separation from your center. They are also the result of poor Spiritual Hygiene that interrupts the flow of Divine presence in your daily life. These seemingly ordinary behaviors carry extraordinary spiritual consequences, and your commitment to healing begins by bringing them back into truth.

Telling Lies (Even "Small" Ones)

Lying fractures the inner voice. Even if no one else hears the falsehood, your spirit does. It becomes harder to hear the voice of God when you are consistently overriding the voice of truth within.

Spiritual Impact:

- Energetic static in your field
- Loss of inner trust
- Diminished ability to channel or discern Divine guidance

Gossip and Breaking Confidences

Gossip may be culturally normalized, but spiritually, it is a subtle poison. It leaks sacred energy. Breaking confidences fractures the energetic web of trust, and each fracture weakens the field of your own integrity.

Spiritual Impact:

- Misalignment between sacred speech and sacred presence
- Distorted energetic signature
- Exhaustion from masking and managing inauthenticity

Broken Commitments and Inner Betrayals

When you say yes and don't follow through; when you make promises you don't intend to keep—whether to others or yourself—your energy splinters. Others may feel disappointed, but your own field suffers most. Trust, once cracked, becomes difficult to restore.

Spiritual Impact:

- The voice of intuition weakens.
- Inner authority collapses.
- Relationships and spiritual clarity become clouded.

Mismanagement of Spiritual Resources

There is a sacred architecture woven into the life of the soul. Where your soul leads, your mind surrenders, and your energy flows in alignment with the Divine. This is the place of holy rhythm, sacred order, and inner clarity. When time is overspent, money is misused, or energy is scattered, this spiritual alignment begins to unravel. What once felt rooted becomes restless. What once moved with grace now grinds with resistance. The spiritual core, the center of your being, begins to dissolve beneath the surface of your daily doing.

Mismanagement of spiritual resources is the *unconscious misuse, avoidance, or distortion of time, money, and energy* in ways that disrupt your sacred rhythm, violate your inner agreements, and accumulate as spiritual interference or smog.

As resources, time, energy, and money are not just practical elements for living; they are also **spiritual currencies**. They are the Divine

Triad of Stewardship. Time is how you mark what matters. Money is how you engage with Divine circulation.

Energy is how you carry the vibration of your soul. These four things are the carriers of your values, your priorities, and your agreements with the Divine. When these currencies are mishandled through overcommitment, financial dishonesty, or energetic leakage, the channels of your soul become congested. To misuse, hoard, manipulate, or promise these without fulfillment is to mishandle a Divine trust. Whether it's your own income, borrowed support, a service you've agreed to pay for, or a tithe dishonored, these misalignments create spiritual weight.

The Misuse of Time: *When the Sacred Becomes Secondary*

Time is not just something you spend; it is something you sanctify. What you consistently give your time to, you anoint, whether it reflects your truth or not. When you overcommit, procrastinate, or fill your schedule with what does not serve your soul, you are not just disorganized; you are displacing the Divine. Time misused becomes time misaligned. Misaligned time becomes spiritual smog.

Signs of Misused Time:

- Constant busyness with little fulfillment
- Avoidance of sacred stillness
- Resistance to rest, reflection, or saying "no"
- Feeling behind, overwhelmed, or reactive

Sacred Pause

Take a breath.
Get still.
Place your hand over your heart.

Ask yourself gently:

"Where am I giving my time to things that do not reflect what I say I value?"

Overcommitment

When you say yes in fear or guilt instead of discernment, you violate your sacred rhythm. Overcommitment is not generosity. It is the soul's quiet cry for boundaries.

Spiritual Impact:

- Erosion of self-trust
- Emotional depletion masked as "productivity"
- Emotional congestion
- You lose the ability to be still in your own soul
- Sacred guidance becomes difficult to access
- Divine timing is drowned in urgency and distraction

Time As Avoidance

Sometimes we fill our time with noise to avoid what the silence would reveal. Busyness becomes a drug that numbs our spiritual core. Time as avoidance is a subtle form of soul abandonment. You fill your day to escape your depth. You check tasks instead of checking in with yourself. You surround yourself with motion to avoid the mirror of stillness, and by doing so, you leak energy in quiet, barely noticeable ways.

Resulting Erosion:

- Emotional truths are ignored or denied.
- The soul's wisdom is drowned out by tasks.
- Presence is lost in performance.

Sacred Amnesia

This is the forgetting of your origin, your authority, and your Divine rhythm.

It is what happens when your life becomes shaped by survival, repetition, or outside demands, until the memory of who you truly are begins to dim beneath who you've been told to be. When your energy is consistently spent on the wrong things, people, stories, worries, and performances, you slowly forget your essence.

Resulting Erosion:

- You become spiritually disoriented.
- The connection to your Divine assignment weakens.
- You begin to live reactively instead of intentionally.

The Misuse of Energy: *When You Leak Instead of Lead*

Energy is your essence in motion. It is the vibration of your soul made visible in your choices, boundaries, and presence. When you give your energy to resentment, performance, gossip, or emotional suppression, you are not just exhausted, you are leaking life force. Where there is leakage, there is erosion. When your field is not protected by clarity, your energy is spent managing distortion instead of magnifying your light.

Signs of Misused Energy:

- Feeling drained after certain conversations or environments
- Over-giving or caretaking to avoid rejection
- Holding emotional tension or unspoken truths
- Constant "on" mode without restoration

Sacred Pause

Take a breath.
Get still.
Place your hand over your heart.
Ask yourself gently:
"Where is my energy being drained, and what boundary or truth needs to be honored in its place?"

Dissonance Between Intention and Action

When *what you value* and *how you spend your time* are not in harmony, an energetic dissonance develops. The spiritual core, which requires congruence, begins to dim under the weight of contradiction.

Resulting Erosion:

- Inner confusion replaces clarity.
- Guilt or resentment silently accumulates.
- You feel spiritually off-center but can't name why.

Disregard for Rest

To ignore your body's need for restoration is to reject the Divine rhythm. Hustle culture, spiritual striving, and burnout are often normalized forms of sacred disconnection.

Resulting Erosion:

- Disconnection from the feminine principle of receptivity
- Reduced ability to hear Divine guidance
- Burnout interpreted as spiritual failure

Dulling of Intuition

The spiritual core speaks in the language of stillness, rhythm, and resonance.

When your energy is constantly being spent without replenishment, your intuitive senses become muffled.

Resulting Erosion:

- You second-guess your inner voice.
- Divine downloads are missed.
- You lean on logic rather than trust.

The Misuse of Money: *When Exchange Is Out of Integrity*

Money is a sacred currency. It carries the vibration of trust, value, and Divine circulation. When money is misused through avoidance, dishonored commitments, hoarding from fear, or spending without alignment, it creates a karmic disruption. The flow of abundance becomes entangled in guilt, shame, or fear of lack. To promise and not pay, to tithe in word but not in action, to manipulate or withhold in exchange—these are not just practical lapses. They are energetic debts.

Signs of Money Misuse:

- Financial avoidance or chaos
- Guilt around receiving or charging for your gifts
- Broken financial agreements
- Constant fear of not having or not being supported

Sacred Pause

Take a breath.
Get still.
Place your hand over your heart.
Ask yourself gently:
"Where am I mishandling the energy of provision, and what truth must be honored to restore trust?"

Financial Dishonesty

This is not just about unpaid bills or broken agreements; it is a fracture in the spiritual covenant of reciprocity. When you make a financial promise (to yourself or someone else) and do not honor it, it creates a distortion in your energetic field. That distortion clouds your relationship with provision, trust, and Divine flow.

Spiritual Impact:

- Blocks the flow of abundance by signaling unreliability
- Seeds doubt in the soil of your integrity
- Erodes trust between you and others, and between you and God
- Contributes to shame and avoidance in your relationship with money

Stealing (Material or Energetic)

Whether it is time, credit, attention, or creative expression, stealing begins with a belief in *not having enough,* which reflects *scarcity thinking* and *lack consciousness.* Both demonstrate spiritual forgetfulness of sufficiency. It tells the Universe, *"I must take what I do not believe will be given."*

Spiritual Impact:

- Repetitive experiences of scarcity
- Diminished flow of provision and creativity
- Loss of gratitude and sacred reciprocity

Sacred Pause

"My time is not mine alone. It is my offering to my life."

"My energy is not infinite, but it is sacred. I am the steward of its flow."

"When I spend my time on things that dim me, I agree to disconnection."

"When I honor my energy, I honor the Divine spark within me."

How Amara Mended the Erosion and Reclaimed Her Core

Amara's healing did not arrive in a single moment. It came in fragments, soft, subtle awakenings that arrived as invitations rather than instructions. She began with silence. Not the kind born from suppression, but the kind that listens. One morning, while journaling in frustration, she heard her inner voice whisper, not from her mind, but from the soul beneath the pain:

> *"You are not angry because you were betrayed. You are angry because you abandoned your own truth."*

That truth broke something open. Amara stopped trying to be strong. She stopped performing forgiveness. She sat with her grief like a guest she had long ignored. She wrote letters she did not send. The letters were for her release. She let her breath move through the spaces that had been tight for years. She cried. Not the shallow tears of surface pain, but the ancient ones, the kind that unclog memory from her bone marrow. She began to tell the truth. First to herself: *"I wasn't OK. I didn't say what I needed. I've been wearing a mask in God's name."*

She forgave herself and everyone else. Not all at once, but one hurt, pain, or memory at a time. Each time she named a hurt, she surrendered blame. Each time she honored her boundaries, she celebrated herself. Each time she said no, she offered no explanation. Each time she kept a promise to herself, a piece of her core returned. Her rituals changed. They were no longer acts of spiritual performance. They became holy appointments with her own truth. She created a daily space to feel. She no longer rushed to be OK. She allowed *a sacred pause* between each lesson and learning. Each day, with reverence, she asked, "*What needs cleansing in me today?*" When she became aware of the need and the answer, she addressed it. Amara learned to live in Spiritual Hygiene as a state of presence. Her truth became her altar, and that is how the erosion reversed.

Healing does not begin with power. It begins with presence. When you stop hiding your pain behind a facade of performance, your soul can find you again. The Divine never left you. *You left the place where the Divine could meet you.*

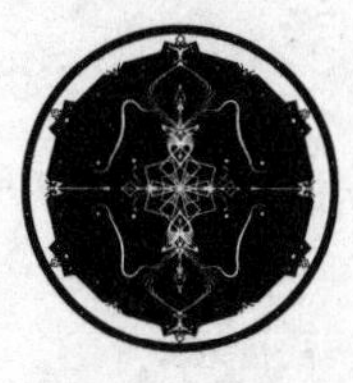

CHAPTER 13

Whole, Holy, and Home

Living from Your Core

You Have Known It All Along (Even Without Words)

There are truths you've carried since before you could name them. They lived in your bones, in your breath, in the way you looked at the stars or wept at beauty long before you understood why. You've known it all along, not with language, but with resonance. It was why you pulled away when something felt wrong. You felt it in the peace you experienced near water. You felt it around certain people, or in moments of silence, when something holy passed through you like wind. You may not have had the words, but your soul recognized the frequency. The truth was there, waiting for your awareness to catch up. That is the nature of the spiritual core. It remembers what the mind forgets. It holds the truth until you're ready to live it. You do learn it. You remember it when you see it, hear it, or even smell it. You know it's your core when:

- Before you could name it, you lived it.
- You've held this belief through multiple seasons of life.
- It speaks without effort and lives without permission.
- Even in silence, it feels louder than your fears.

- You feel it in your body, not just your mind.
- It anchors you, especially during chaos.

You Feel at Peace When You Act in Alignment with It

There's a kind of peace that does not and cannot come from getting everything right. This peace comes from what feels true.

Remember that story I told you earlier about leaving my law office for good one day? Well, it was much more complicated than it may seem in a quick anecdote. I left a career I had fought hard for—I became a professional when the odds were against me. And I had three kids I had to support on my own! But Spirit had much bigger plans for me. When my friend called me to create a program for women who were going from welfare to work, I developed a program. I would write these worksheets to teach them things like how to do breathwork, prayer, and meditation, along with practical things like how to fill out a job application, or create a résumé. After about a year and a half, I had a ton of material put together.

I shared it with another friend, and they told me, "That's a book. There's a lot of people that ain't on welfare that need it. I need it."

So I put everything together and took it to Kinko's. While I was there printing it out, a woman noticed it and told me I could self-publish it. So I did! *Tapping the Power Within*, my first book, was the workbook I made for women going from welfare to work. I went to Black bookstores and sold it on consignment, and eventually an agent called me and asked if I wanted to publish it formally with Harlem River Press. Once it was published formally, I got invited to do conferences and present my book to different audiences.

Eventually, a reader picked it up and shared it with Oprah Winfrey.

None of this was easy. There were times—and there *still* are times—when I didn't know where—or when—I'd get my next paycheck.

But if I hadn't listened to Spirit, I wouldn't have had the opportunity to touch millions of lives. Spirit has dictated everything I do since then. It's directly supplied the words for every book I've written from that point forward.

When your actions align with your core, there is no residue. No regret. No need to explain. You may feel fear, discomfort, or consequence, but underneath it all is a quiet stillness that says, "You are honoring and loving yourself." This peace doesn't demand applause. It's a clean feeling. A settled feeling, like your breath finally knows where to land. That peace is evidence that you have moved in resonance with your spiritual core. You know it's a core "yes" when:

- You feel clear afterward, even if the choice was hard.
- You sleep soundly, breathe more deeply, and do not need to justify your decision.
- You don't second-guess; you know you are *done.*
- You feel more like yourself.
- It doesn't feel dramatic. It just feels right.

It Feels Less Like Thought and More Like Knowing

Your spiritual core does not speak in logic or layers. It speaks with clarity and resonance, with a knowing that settles in your bones before your mind has time to catch up. You know it is not a debate. It is a truth you recognize. You don't arrive at it through reasoning. You arrive by remembering. This is not the knowing you argue for. It's the kind you rest in. It is quiet and undeniable. It rises to the surface when you stop thinking long enough to feel what has been true all along. It doesn't beg for confirmation. It does not need a second opinion. It rises quietly, like a warm light through your chest, or tears that come without reason. You know it's a core "yes" when:

- It doesn't need to be explained.
- It settles you rather than excites you.

- It feels more ancient than new, more familiar than explained.
- It arrives quickly, quietly, and deeply.
- You no longer need words to carry it. It carries you.

Core Beliefs Are Sacred Agreements

Donald was a man who always said yes. Yes, to overextending himself. Yes, to being quiet, going along to get along. Yes, to what made others comfortable. Until one day, he felt a tension in his chest that was so tight, it hurt to breathe. He had been asked, once again, to help someone in a way that violated his values and peace. This time, he paused. He remembered his core belief: *"My peace is sacred."* This time he said, "No, I can't do that right now." No anger. No excuse. No performance. Just the truth. When he realized he was shaking, he began to weep. He had disappointed someone. They would be mad at him. When he told me the story, I asked him, "How did you feel afterward?" He said, "For the first time in my life, I felt clean inside." That is what it means to live from the spiritual core.

Once you begin to recognize your spiritual core, the next sacred act is to name the truths that live within it. These truths are your core beliefs. To name your core beliefs is not to recite what you have been taught; it is to claim what you know in your bones. It is to gather the soul-etched truths that have carried you through pain, pulled you through silence, and called you back when you had almost forgotten yourself. Your core beliefs are not opinions. They are not habits of thought. They are the spiritual agreements you made with Life, God, and Self before your soul had a body to cover it. Some were born through fire. Some through stillness. Some through grief. Some through sacred remembrance. They are the truths that rise when everything else falls away. To name them is to say: *"This is what I know to be true, no matter what the world says, no matter who walks away."* Naming your core beliefs is a holy act of *reclamation, clarity,* and *sovereignty.* It is good Spiritual Hygiene.

Sacred Pause

Close your eyes.
Take a deep breath.
Place your hand over your heart.
Think of a time when:

You were betrayed and still believed in love.

You were grieving and still felt comforted.

You were uncertain and still told the truth.

Ask yourself:

"*What truth carried me through that moment?*"

That truth is likely a core belief.

Naming your core beliefs is like excavating an inner altar. It requires honest listening and spiritual stillness. It is not a mental exercise. It is more like an *archaeological dig*. You cannot name your core beliefs by thinking harder. You name them by feeling deeper, and by remembering the truths that have whispered to you through your grief, your joy, your silence, and your periods of transformation. Naming your core beliefs is not about identifying your personality or defining your preferences. It's about locating the truths you've carried across lifetimes. The ones that rise when the noise falls away. The ones that do not shift based on applause, belonging, or ease. To name your core beliefs is to say:

"This I know, even when I doubt everything else."

"This I believe, even if no one else agrees."

"This I remember, even though no one ever taught it to me."

Your core truths live in the body. When you speak one aloud, your breath softens. Your soul says *yes.* Naming your spiritual beliefs core is an act of sovereignty. You are no longer borrowing beliefs you may have inherited. You are reclaiming what is already yours. The following reflective practices will help reveal and name your core beliefs:

Close your eyes.

Take a deep breath.

Place your hand over your heart.

Gently ask yourself:

"What do I know is true about . . .

God/Source/Spirit?"

My soul and its purpose?"

"What heals me? What harms me?"

"What do I feel and believe about

Love, Truth, Death, Forgiveness, Freedom?"

"What matters to me most, regardless of culture or conditioning?"

You may write or record your responses. This is where remembrance becomes responsibility. Where clarity becomes embodied choice. Where your "yes" becomes sacred and your "no" becomes sovereign. Once you begin to name your core beliefs, the truths that lie beneath surface performance, the embedded fear, or expectation, the next sacred invitation is to *live* from them. Living from your core beliefs means using them as a filter. You pass your decisions, relationships, words, and actions through it, asking not: *"Will this make me acceptable?"* but *"Is this aligned with what I know to be true?"* This is where **Spiritual Hygiene becomes essential**. Knowing your core beliefs keeps you grounded within yourself, in a world filled with noise, driven by demands that can subtly erode your truth by compromises that quietly undermine your alignment. Without consistent Spiritual Hygiene, you begin to drift from your core, even while praying, serving, or doing "the work." Your core remains, but the connection grows foggy. Your truth lives, but you stop hearing it.

It's very easy for your connection to go cold when you feel ineffective, frustrated, or invalidated in your efforts to be your Divine self.

Remember: Your core is not asking you to be a mega-influencer or a millionaire. Your core is simply asking you to be you. When you are connected to it and surrender to it unequivocally, your path will be revealed.

Whether your impact resonates with one person, one neighborhood, or around the world:

It still matters.

Let Your Rituals Reflect Your Core

Spiritual Hygiene is about staying clear enough to live what you know. It is how you clean the inner altar so that your decisions are not made from old pain, performance patterns, or external programming. It is the daily practice of returning to what is real. Living from your core does not simplify your life. It means you become rooted. You stop bending with every hard wind that passes through. You stop chasing what you need. You become it. When Spiritual Hygiene is practiced daily, it keeps the altar of your life clean enough to hear what your soul is always saying: *"This is who I am. This is what I'm here for. This is the next most appropriate step for me."*

Your spiritual core is the voice of God/Source/Creator within you. Your core is the map you were born with. Your core beliefs are the *turn-by-turn directions* you will need to move through your life. It is not necessary to *find* these things. You only must remember them, honor them, and return to them again and again. Understanding your core means recognizing where it came from, how it guides you, what happens when you betray it, and the patterns you've built around it (or away from it). To honor your core means pausing before making a choice or decision, speaking from your core rather than surrendering to fear, and refusing to compromise your "yes" or your "no." If your core belief is *"My peace is sacred,"* offering a half-hearted "yes" to a draining commitment is not in alignment. If your core says *"The truth is sacred,"* avoiding confrontation is not aligned with your beliefs. Once you have found your core and identified the beliefs that reside there, it is good Spiritual Hygiene to repeat and practice them daily.

If your core truth is *"I am not alone,"* light a candle for your ancestors daily. If your core truth is *"I am love,"* tend to your heart space with gentleness. If your core truth is *"My voice matters,"* write, speak, or create something regularly. Ritual is how your core beliefs become visible in your life. Living from your core is not a perfunctory act; it is a practice of presence, choice, and sacred return. It is the practice of honoring your boundaries, even when it's uncomfortable. It is the choice to tell the truth, even if your voice shakes. It is a consistent practice to clean up energetic debts immediately. That means apologizing, forgiving, and realigning, when necessary, as often as needed. You are in true core alignment when your thoughts reflect your beliefs, your words honor your truth, your actions protect your peace, and your energy moves from integrity.

Core Alignment Checklist

Living from your core and honoring your core beliefs doesn't have to be hard. Consistent practice is required, and that practice will take time to master. The following list is a gentle, sacred pause that you can use daily. It is an opportunity to recalibrate and realign your mind, heart, and soul. The more often you do it, the sooner you will reclaim true ownership of the temple, the altar, and the sanctuary that you are.

Inner Truth

- *"Did I speak or act from my truth today, even when it was uncomfortable?"*
- *"Did I feel a deep inner 'yes' in at least one decision or interaction?"*
- *"Did I feel at peace after making a choice, even if others didn't understand?"*

Emotional Integrity

- *"Did I allow myself to feel honestly without pushing emotions away?"*
- *"Did I avoid overexplaining or apologizing for my truth?"*
- *"Did I check in with my body and ask: 'Is this true for me?'"*

Sacred Boundaries

- *"Did I say 'no' when needed to without guilt?"*
- *"Did I refrain from people-pleasing or shapeshifting to be accepted?"*
- *"Did I honor my own energy and needs with compassion?"*

Spiritual Hygiene

- *"Did I pause to clear my energy field today—mentally, emotionally, or physically?"*
- *"Did I make space for stillness, prayer, breath, or ritual?"*
- *"Did I release anything I was carrying that didn't belong to me?"*

Core Remembrance

- *"Did I act in a way that reflects who I know I truly am?"*
- *"Did I check in with my core before responding, committing, or reacting?"*
- *"Did I feel connected to my own rhythm, values, and spiritual truth?"*

Remember, perfection is not the way to presence. Truth is.

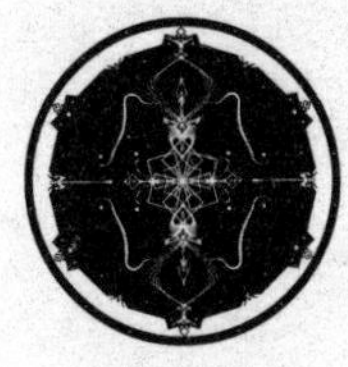

OPENING PRAYER

For Boundaries, Alignment, and the Courage to Reclaim Yourself

Holy Presence, Guardian of my Breath, Keeper of my Becoming,
I come to this threshold ready to remember that "no" is not a weapon,
It is a way home.
In the past, I have said yes when my body trembled.
In the past, I have said yes when my truth was whispering otherwise.
In the past, I have said yes to be loved, to be safe, to belong.
But now, I choose to belong to myself.
Teach me the holiness of refusal.
Let my "no" be anointed in wisdom.
Let it rise from the deepest parts of me without defense, as devotion.
When I say no, let it not be from reverence.
When I say no, let it cleanse what is not mine.
When I say no, let it close the doors that lead me away from my wholeness.
I give myself permission to protect my sacred interior.
I give myself permission to withdraw from what depletes me,
without guilt, without shame, without apology.
May this chapter be a sanctuary of reclamation.
May I trust that every "no" I speak as my truth
makes space for a more holy, whole, embodied "yes."
I Ask. I Allow. I Become.
Amen. Aṣẹ Aho.
And so, it is.

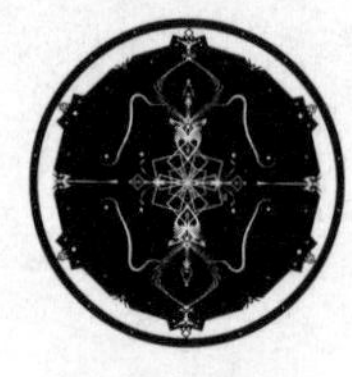

CHAPTER 14

The Sacred No

The Sound of Self-Protection

There is a deep holiness in the word "no" when it rises from the wisdom of the body. "No" is a form of self-recognition. It is the soul's way of saying: This is not for me. This is not aligned. This is too much. I am not choosing this now. Many have been taught to override that "no." We believe it is honorable to smile through discomfort, to stay when the body tightens, to say yes out of obligation. We may not realize that any time you say yes when your body means no, a fracture occurs inside you. A split between what is true and what is performed. Over time, the fracture becomes fatigue. It becomes resentment. It becomes chronic tension. It becomes disease.

Nisa had learned not to burden me with her problems. I cannot say I taught her to do it, but I did enable her to do it. Between what she witnessed as a child, how she watched me struggle after I left her father, and how she saw me crumble when her sister, Gemmia, died, I totally get why she did not tell me she was a diabetic. I also understand that her "no" to me was as deeply rooted in not trusting me as it was in not wanting to burden me. She did not trust that I would not "*make her wrong*" for being sick. She did not trust that I would not try to force her to heal in the way I thought she should do it. She did not trust that I would not be disappointed in her because she was not "*perfect.*" She did not trust that *Iyanla* would stand with her in a way that *Rhonda* could not or would not. You will say no passively, or covertly, when you do not trust yourself, or another person. This "no" is protective.

She also knew that I was working "*like a fool*" to reboot my career while raising Gemmia's daughter. When Nisa's son told me that her glucose level was fluctuating between 500 and 600, and the medications were not working to bring it down, I had a flashback, and a total revelation about why she did not, could not, would not trust me with her secret suffering. It took me all the way back to when Nisa was in the second grade.

At the teacher's request, I agreed to have Nisa tested for possible learning disabilities. The test revealed that she had an emotional disability. The official diagnosis indicated that she had difficulty regulating her emotions, building relationships, and engaging in appropriate behaviors. It was explained to me that students with emotional or behavioral disabilities also had learning difficulties, behavioral problems, and difficulties in social interactions. This explained why she would often make up stories about herself and deny doing certain things. The next part of the diagnosis broke my heart into a million tiny pieces of guilt and shame. The diagnosis of an emotional disability or handicap also included a pervasive mood of unhappiness or depression. The next question that buckled my knees was, "Are you open to considering medicating Nisa to manage her mind and moods?" *Absolutely not!* The only other alternative was special education classes. It would not be safe for her or the other students to keep her in mainstream classes, I was told.

Her diagnosis, though painful, was like a mirror inviting me to examine what I had allowed to take root in my mind and our lives. As I wrestled with the recommendation to medicate her and the reality of moving her into special education, I felt a quiet determination stirring within me that was so much stronger than the fear, shame, and guilt. I knew I had to do something; in fact, I needed to do many things differently. I realized that her healing was not a one-way street; it would need to be a shared journey—a delicate dance of intention and strategy. If I could bring my mind and life into balance and harmony, I could extend my harmony outward, infusing my home with calmness, my children with joy and love. For the first few days after receiving the diagnosis, I saw Nisa's challenges not as limitations but as invitations—*"Get yourself and your life together, girl."* However, I had no idea where or how to begin. Day by day, I searched the sacred space of my mental landscape, hoping to find the words and the way to help my daughter and save myself. It never dawned on me that a simple "no" would suffice.

Your "No" Is Your Compass

There are moments when silence becomes complicity. There are places where your accommodation of dishonor, harm, or hurt becomes self-abandonment. There are patterns that only break when you are brave enough to say: *"No! This ends here."* A strong "no" guides your choices just as much as your *holy "yes."* When you stand in your "no," in the face of authority or control, it protects your sacred identity and purpose. It filters out what is false and what you do not deserve. It supports and anchors your boundaries. In other words, it will *back people up*. When you can say no without guilt, you are no longer bound by the need to be liked, or loved, or accepted. Your "no" ensures that you are aligned with the need to be *true to yourself.*

It can be both challenging and intimidating to say no, as many of us have been conditioned to prioritize keeping the peace at all costs, avoiding conflict, and proving our goodness or worth through self-sacrifice. These are visitors in our mental temple that must be disinvited. Good Spiritual Hygiene for the mind and healing for the soul require that you ask yourself: *"Am I willing to abandon and betray myself to be accepted?"* Or *"Am I willing to honor and bless myself by speaking up, walking away, or doing what feels right in my body?"* Saying no when it is needed is a profound demonstration of self-care, and you must become aware of the when's, what's, why's, and how's that diminish or steal your "no."

Because your "no" is an act of Spiritual Hygiene, which you determine is necessary for your protection and well-being, it does not require an explanation. When said with intention and conviction, everything and everyone stops when you say no. It is also important to recognize that people may not agree with your "no" and will attempt, by any means necessary, to talk you out of it. Whether you are sixteen or sixty, a strong, solid "no" clears dysfunction in relationships, poor choices and bad habits, polluted physical environments, and conversations that contaminate your spirit. It is the way you say to the universe: *"I only welcome what is holy, honoring, and aligned with my highest good."* When you take this stance, the universe stands with you, not just for peace, but for the return of your own Divine presence and the development of a deeper sense of self-awareness.

When we are parents, "no" is a stance we are required to take *with* our children, and more importantly, *for* their sake. I had to position my mind and myself in this way for Nisa. This meant not only would I send her to the recommended special education classes where she would be safe, but I would also have to *disinvite* myself from the abusive relationship with her father. So much easier thought of and said than done. When the mind is filled with unhealed scripts, even violence can feel normal. My longing to leave was real, but without strong spiritual and mental hygiene, the desire could not become action. With little support and no clear path, fear kept me bound until the breaking point arrived, which included more violence. This is the cost of neglected Spiritual Hygiene; it blurs clarity, weakens resolve, and delays the freedom our soul longs for.

I made two critical errors when I transferred Nisa into the special education class; I made it her "*fault,*" and I failed to unpack my own "*guilt.*" I told her that because she had lied and stolen things, she could not stay in the school her brother and sister attended. Recognizing now what I said and how I said it makes me a little nauseous. At the time, I was unaware that my need to be a "*perfect*" mother, to prove I was "*better than*" the people who raised me, was shattered by the thought that my children were not perfect. I made up that Nisa's disability was my fault. Not only because I stayed in a dysfunctional, violent relationship with her father, but also because of the mental dust and belief that I carried that everything was my fault. My feelings of guilt and shame had nothing to do with Nisa, but I laid it in her lap because of poor mental hygiene.

Two weeks after she began classes in a new school, I received a call from the principal that I needed to come pick Nisa up. There had been an incident. When I saw her sitting on the bench in the main office, what I thought was a fury I had never experienced shot straight up my spine. I later realized it was not fury. It was my "no." WTF! Her bottom lip was swollen and crusted with dried blood. One of her eyes was swollen shut. The "no" in my presence produced a scream from my mouth that brought everyone in the office to a standing position. One of the women was shouting, *"Hold on! Wait!"* while she scrambled from her desk to get the principal. Responding to the scream, he appeared like a puff of smoke and invited me into his office. Suddenly, a sense of calm fell over me, and I followed him in. What I failed to do was embrace my daughter. I did not soothe her wounds or ask her what happened. I left her sitting on the bench, alone, to figure out on her own what I was going to do and what would happen next.

The principal explained that another student in the class, who was severely handicapped, had had an episode with the teacher. In response, he threw a chair that hit Nisa. He then attacked the teacher. This caused the other students, including Nisa, to come to her defense. In the end, it was Nisa who beat the crap out of the boy, with the chair he threw at her. In the process, she sustained the injuries that I witnessed. The calm I felt was eerie. One at a time, I could hear thoughts float into my mind. *Where was the other student? Where were his parents?* The boy received medical attention and was sent home, I was told. I could, if I chose to, press criminal charges. *Why were his parents not present?* These things happen in special education classrooms. There is no way to predict or prevent them. These children have severe learning and behavioral disabilities. The principal was sorry, but there was nothing more they could do. *What was the school's intention to address this matter and prevent it from ever happening again? Was that student expected to and allowed to return to the class?* The parents had been instructed to keep him home for three days, after which he would return to class. His attendance was mandated by the state. The school could not deny the child admission. Because it was not her fault, Nisa was cleared to return the next day. *Oh, hell no!*

On that day, in defense of my child, my "no" for her was solid. As is so common for people raised in an environment of dysfunction and violence, they will do for others before they recognize that they deserve the same consideration. In that moment, I did not see my face in Nisa's face. I felt my pain and recognized my dishonor. I did not remember how to cover a busted lip or a black eye. I also knew in the deepest recesses of my being that all violence, of any kind, was no longer invited into the temple of my mind, my home, or my life. And it certainly could not, would not be visited upon my children. I was a yeller. I threatened, which in some cases was equally dysfunctional, but I rarely used my hands or anything else to strike my children. Without realizing it, I had already broken a family pattern. It was unconscious, but it was also a new practice. Unfortunately, the practice did not mitigate the energetic violence and dysfunction that I had taught my children was acceptable.

Nisa never attended another class in that school. Somehow, with the support of a dear friend, I managed to find the money to enroll her in a small Christian school with ten children in each class. More importantly, I began a more consistent, earnest, and sincere prayer and meditation practice. I was shocked to realize how difficult it was for me to sit still for more than two minutes. Using prayer and periods of silence and stillness, I began to notice that I still believed I was the cause of my pain. I also believed that I expected love to turn violent. What often buckled my knees was the awareness that I did not believe it was safe to see, face, or speak the truth. Truth was dangerous, so I had convinced myself that living a lie was the only way to stay safe. This was the dusty residue that I held in my mind that I had passed on to my baby girl, Nisa.

The Necessity of a Solid "No"

A shaky "no" leaves the door open to misalignment. A solid no, rooted in clarity, integrity, and embodiment, is a boundary made sacred. It is the anchor that keeps your energy intact. It is the shield that preserves your peace. It is the devotion that protects your purpose. Without a solid "no," the body becomes a battleground of contradiction. You say yes with your mouth while your shoulders curl forward. You show up out of duty while your chest tightens and your breath shortens. You give more than you have and then wonder why you feel spiritually bankrupt. This is not spiritual generosity. This is somatic betrayal. To have a solid "no" is not to become rigid or unkind. It is standing with clarity. Your body and your energy are clear, which communicates to your nervous system that you are taking a stand for self-respect. The necessity of a solid "no" is rooted in three sacred truths:

1. Your nervous system needs consistency.

When you override your truth to accommodate others, your body becomes confused about what is safe. This confusion creates chronic stress. But when your "no" is firm and loving, your body begins to relax. It trusts you again. It knows you will not abandon yourself.

2. Your boundaries teach others how to meet the Divine in you.

A soft "yes" when you mean "no" creates resentment, which seeps into your energy and your relationships. A solid "no," offered with grace, creates trust. It teaches others that your "yes" means something, and that your time, presence, and energy are not for sale.

3. Your soul requires alignment to thrive.

Saying yes to what drains you means saying no to what could restore you. Your "no" makes space for joy, creativity, sacred assignments, rest, and revelation. If you find it hard to say no, inquire within yourself:

- Where did I learn that my "no" was a problem?
- Who taught me that love required self-abandonment?
- What fear arises when I consider honoring my limits?

These are not small questions. They are soul questions for which your body holds and knows the answers.

Sacred Pause

The Rooted "No"

- Stand with your feet hip-width apart.
- Place your hands over your solar plexus.
- Feel your feet on the earth.
- Speak aloud, slowly and clearly:

"No. I do not consent to this. I choose alignment."

Notice where your body tightens, and where it relaxes.
Repeat until you feel grounded in your stance.
Let this be your embodied prayer:

"I no longer confuse accommodation with love." "I no longer trade peace for approval." "I no longer abandon myself to be chosen."

"My no is sacred." "My 'no' is whole." "My 'no' is enough."

The Holy "Yes"

If your "no" is a gatekeeper, your "yes" is the sacred threshold. Offering a pure "yes" without fear or as a trauma-induced reaction makes it *holy*. It grows from your soul and is offered as worship to your heart. Your *holy "yes"* is not a reflex. It is not the people-pleasing, self-abandoning "yes" that rushes out to soothe discomfort or avoid rejection. It is not the "yes" that lives in the throat while the body braces itself. It is not the "yes" that masks itself in duty and calls it devotion. The holy "yes" rises from the base of your soul. It resonates through your chest. It breathes through your belly. It expands you. Aligns you. Softens you. A true "yes" is never made in haste. It is born in and with alignment. Make no mistake about it—the body knows the difference. A distorted "yes" contracts the body in dread, while a holy "yes "expands it in peace.

Where a performative "yes" drains your energy, a holy "yes" *feeds* it. The holy "yes" says:

- *"This is right for me, not just expected of me."*
- *"This feels true in my bones, not just logical in my mind."*
- *"This supports my wholeness, not just someone else's comfort."*

To say "yes" from your spirit is to step into sacred agreement with your soul. This "yes" does not come from the mouth alone. It moves through your being. It says:

- Yes, to rest, even when the world demands performance
- Yes, to receiving, even when you are only praised for giving
- Yes, to joy, even when your history trained you for survival
- Yes, to embodiment, even when you have lived in your head to avoid pain
- Yes, to truth, even when it costs you acceptance or approval

Your holy "yes" is the result of being attuned, not just agreeable. When you begin to live from this attunement, your life takes on a different frequency. You become less reactive, more intentional. You stop chasing what no longer resonates for you or within you. You stop performing to be loved. You start creating from the center of your being. This is Spiritual Hygiene at its highest level: *A body in agreement with the soul. A "yes" that is clean, clear, and consecrated.*

Sacred Pause

The Embodied "Yes"

- Sit quietly.
- Breathe deeply.
- Place your hands over your heart.
- Speak aloud:

  "I say yes to what honors my wholeness."

  "I say yes to what aligns with my soul."

  "I say yes to my Divine unfolding."

Ask your soul for clear guidance.

Call choice, decision, or opportunity to mind.

Breathe into the question: *"Does this expand or contract my energy?"*

Let your body speak.

Allow the "yes" or "no" to rise from within.

Let the words you hear or the insights you receive echo through your bones.

This is not performative. This is a sacred inquiry, and the "yes" you receive is holy.

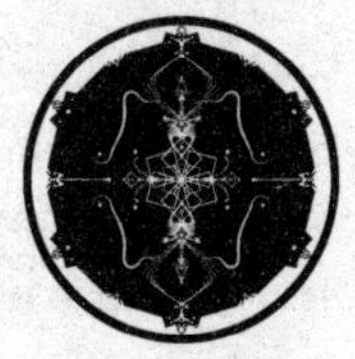

LEVEL III CONCLUSION
LEVEL IV INTRODUCTION

THE SACRED RETURN

A Reclamation of Self

You have walked through the threshold of reclamation, as one choosing to return to the altar of your being with new eyes and steady hands. Level III has not asked you to become something new. It has asked you to remember who you were before the world taught you to forget.

You began this portion of the journey with *spiritual responsibility*, a sacred duty to care for, cultivate, and align your inner life, mind, heart, body, and soul with Divine truth. This is a call to stop outsourcing your healing and to reclaim the stewardship of your energy, your choices, your presence. You were invited to stop pretending to be whole and begin living it. You were reminded that being responsible for your internal and external self is a form of empowerment. It is the way you rise as a vessel of sacred integrity.

Then came the invitation to *find your center*, that still, holy ground within you that cannot be shaken by chaos, performance, or praise. Your center is not a location—it is a rhythm, a frequency, a remembering. You learned that good Spiritual Hygiene is not about looking clean. It is about staying close to what is real.

You explored the patterns of *misalignment and spiritual neglect*, those silent accumulations that leave residue in your soul. You faced the emotional litter of spiritual bypassing, numbing, over-giving, and hiding. You learned to stop mistaking numbness for peace and began to honor the sacred task of clearing out what no longer belongs in your temple.

Then, with gentle guidance, you were led to the well of *your spiritual core*. The place where truth is not filtered through fear or upbringing. The place it emerges in you and through you raw and radiant. You named it. You sat with it. You heard its language again. Your spiritual core does not demand perfection; it asks for honesty. It is the compass of your sovereignty.

You bowed in reverence to *Somatic Stewardship*, the wisdom of the body as a sacred altar. You learned that your nervous system remembers what the mind forgets. That embodiment is not aesthetic; it is a holy act of presence. You relearned your rhythms. You reclaimed your right to rest, to pause, to move in harmony with the Divine pulse within you.

Finally, you received the blessing of the *sacred "no,"* a return to the core. You dismantled the illusion that love requires self-abandonment. You met the ancestral pattern of over-accommodation and offered it compassion without continuation. Your "no" became your compass, your prayer, your realignment. It cleared the dust. It carved the path.

These chapters were not steps. They were spirals, each one returning you to deeper levels of self-trust, clarity, embodiment, and devotion. Reclaiming does not always look like fire. Sometimes, it is the quiet exhale of a woman who no longer betrays herself. Sometimes, it is the steady pulse of a man who now knows that softness is not weakness. It is wisdom.

You are not who you were when this journey began. You are now one who:

- Knows what it feels like to belong to yourself
- Speaks the language of alignment over approval
- Chooses peace over performance
- Honors your energy as a sacred resource

- Refuses to decorate dysfunction and call it love
- Lives from the throne of your inner authority

This is reclamation. Not the noise of taking your power back. It is the stillness of remembering that it was never truly gone. It was buried. Forgotten. Dimmed. But never destroyed. And now, Beloved, you are ready for the final unfolding.

Living Clean with Spiritual Hygiene

What does it mean to live clean? It is more than ritual. More than intention. More than knowledge. To live clean is to walk in agreement with your soul. It is to let your breath, your body, your boundaries, and your beliefs become sacred instruments of alignment. It is to bring heaven into habit. It is to choose integrity, not only when it is easy, but especially when it is inconvenient. It is to keep your altar swept. Your mind quiet, your heart open, and your soul aligned. You have reclaimed your center. Now you must live from it. You have remembered your voice. Now you must speak with it. You have entered your core. Now you must choose from it. The final chapter is not an ending. It is your sacred beginning. Let us enter it together, with clean hands, open hearts, and a holy breath.

As always, we begin with prayer.

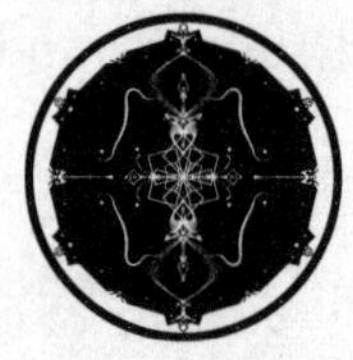

OPENING PRAYER

Generational Cleansing and Healing Prayer for Parents

Beloved Divine Presence, Creator and Keeper of my Bloodline
Guardian of my Soul,
I stand before You as one who chooses to interrupt the pain.
I choose to cleanse the weight I have carried.
I no longer choose to pass on what was never mine to give.
I confess the stories I absorbed, of not being enough,
of being too much.
Of silence being safer than truth, of sacrifice being a form of love.
I confess that I have parented from fear instead of faith,
from pain instead of presence.
I confess that I gave from lack rather than fullness,
that I used discipline to replace devotion.
I am aware that while this was not my fault, I am not the one to blame,
I accept it as my responsibility, as a parent,
to bring myself into a state of sacred alignment.
I call back every fragmented piece of my inner child that I abandoned
to survive.
I offer every memory, every shadow, every dysfunction to the fire
of Your loving mercy.
I ask for Your healing light to wash through the roots
of my family tree.
Let Your breath reach those who came before
and those who have yet to come.
May my children receive from me not my residue, but my clarity.

Not my regrets, but my wisdom.
Not my wounds, but my wholeness.
I forgive myself.
I forgive my parents.
I forgive the ones who did not know how to love cleanly.
I release every echo of guilt, shame, punishment, and pain that does not belong
in this new lineage that I am calling into being.
I now choose to be the end of a line and the beginning of a new path.
From this moment forward, I choose to be a light bearer
shining truth, power, peace, joy, and love into my family tree
and the roots from which this tree has grown.
This is my intention. This is my declaration.
I Am the threshold.
I Am the bridge.
I Am the blessing.
I ask for and open myself to receive Divine Guidance,
so that it may be so.
I Ask. I Allow.
My children and their children,
my parents and their parents,
my lineage now receive.
Amen. Aṣẹ Aho.
And so, it is.

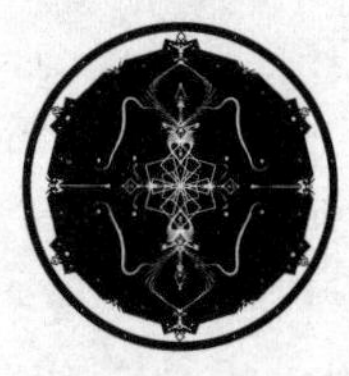

CHAPTER 15

Spiritual Hygiene for Parenting

Returning to Wholeness While Raising a Soul

There was a time in my life when I had to face a truth so sacred and sobering that it cracked something open in me forever: *I failed my children.* Not because I was a bad person, nor did I have a conscious intent to break their hearts or destroy their sense of worth and value. But that is exactly what I did. Not because I didn't love them with my whole being. I failed them because for most of their lives, and my own, I had no clue about the existence or importance of Spiritual Hygiene. I failed them because I did not know how to, nor did I take the time to learn how to, heal my own trauma and wounding. I did not yet understand that unresolved pain becomes the lens through which we love, lead, discipline, and nurture. I believed that giving my children "*things*," opportunities, comforts, and achievements could somehow make up for what I had not yet learned or given myself: emotional healing. I failed them because I believed I was doing the right things in the right ways, and I was not open or available to changing the way I parented, as I believed I knew what my children needed. I am now aware that I was mistaken.

I tried desperately not to be like my grandmother, who was abusive. I tried not to be like my father, who was emotionally unavailable. Yet, in trying so hard not to be like them, I ended up passing down the very same emotional disconnection and dysfunction that I experienced. I put all my effort into doing better, but I had not yet learned how to be better, from the inside out. This unclean pattern affected all of my children, but it was Nisa, my youngest, who took it to heart the most. Her sweet, sensitive soul absorbed the echoes of what I had not yet transmuted, what I had ignored, denied, and avoided. While none of this was conscious or intentional, that does not mean it was not present or had no impact. I am now aware that it did.

This is not a confession of guilt or wretchedness. These are awarenesses, the sacred reckonings that I have discovered, acknowledged, examined, and forgiven. My children knew I loved them fiercely. They knew that on any given Sunday, I would have taken a bullet for them. Ronnie, the abused, neglected, broken little girl, was Damon and Gemmia's mother. She became Rhonda, the one who masked and denied the wounds of Ronnie. Rhonda was Nisa's mother. As Rhonda transformed into Iyanla, I became someone new. I re-created my relationship with each of my children, using honesty, humility, and healing principles and practices as the foundation for our new connection. Over time, they each came to understand that when they were growing, unfolding, I did not have what they needed when they needed it.

Here is another sacred truth I learned: Just because I healed, it did not mean that their scars vanished. They each had to choose how to face what they had inherited. Damon did it with bold questions and resistance that eventually gave way to clarity. Gemmia did it with grace and elegance, becoming one of my most excellent teachers. Nisa could not or did not make the same choice. She chose, unconsciously, to hang on to her fixed, third-dimensional reality and experience.

Parenting, I now know, is not just about raising children; it is about raising *consciousness.* It is not simply about teaching our children to behave; it is about learning how to become a living temple internally and a sanctuary of safety externally. In today's world, parenting is not just a role; it is a spiritual initiation. It is the Divine work of raising your children and your entire ancestral lineage into a higher vibrational field: the fifth-dimensional reality, where everything is energy, every thought becomes form, and every feeling must be clear and clean. This path requires you to know and trust that who you are, as you are, is enough, and to take on the Sacred Responsibility to refine, realign, and rise. To parent from this place means:

- Becoming aware of the energy you bring into your home
- Releasing generational stories that no longer serve
- Cleansing your emotional field so your children do not absorb what was never theirs to carry

We are not parenting in the same world as our parents did. We have more information. More access. More insight. More tools. We must stop saying *"That's just the way things are."* And *"Because I said so."* We must begin saying *"I am the one who clears the path."* Spiritual Hygiene is now the parents' Divine responsibility. It is the responsibility to cleanse what was inherited, to sanctify what is present, and to plant only what is worthy of the future. This is how we parent in the Age of Light. This is how we will create a new reality.

Put the Principles into Practice

There was a moment, a quiet but unforgettable one, when I realized I was not simply raising a daughter; I was raising myself. Nisa was no longer a toddler, but still small enough to curl into my lap. That day, she did something that struck a nerve, something minor in the grand scheme of things, but I felt heat rise in my body, an old familiar tension in my jaw. I felt overwhelmed. I was physically and mentally exhausted. When she came to sit with me and on me, I told her to *stop.* My reaction to her wasn't about *her* at all. It was my own wound, something unresolved from my own childhood, that was grabbing the steering wheel of my heart.

In that moment, I heard myself speaking not as the conscious mother I had worked so hard to become, but as the frightened, reactive girl who had once longed for gentleness and grace and didn't always receive it. When I saw my pain in Nisa's eyes, I recognized it immediately, undeniably. I went into the bathroom, sat on the closed lid of the toilet, and wept. I breathed. I asked God for help. In that moment, something in my spiritual core rose up. Somehow, I knew that parenting is a sacred mirror, and although I did not understand the concept or have the language at that time, I realized that Spiritual Hygiene meant I must cleanse myself before I could effectively parent my children. That moment taught me a profound truth: *We cannot protect our children from everything, but we can protect them from our own projections when we are willing to face them.*

Parenting the Child Without Abandoning the Inner Child

Parenting is a relationship. Like any other relationship, we bring all of who we are to the relationship table and our capacity to parent. This means we must be in a healthy relationship with ourselves. Many of us unknowingly betray our inner child in our efforts to "do better" or "be better" as parents. We swing toward perfectionism or overcompensation. Proper parenting is not about a better performance. It is about physical, mental, and emotional presence. When we acknowledge the wounds we carry, we can hold both the child in front of us and the child within us with equal compassion.

Emotional Regulation As a Spiritual Offering

Your ability to regulate, rather than suppress, your emotions is essential for psychological and emotional maturity. It is a spiritual discipline. Every breath you take, instead of yelling, is a prayer. Every pause before reacting is an offering placed at the altar of your family's peace, and your child's emotional safety and well-being.

Conscious Correction Without Contamination

Discipline must never come at the expense of dignity. Spiritual Hygiene in parenting invites us to clean our energy before we correct. Children absorb not just the words we say, but the tone, the tension, the intention in our spirit. Correction that emerges from calm, centered clarity leaves no residue of shame. It becomes an offering from your heart on the altar of the child's heart.

The Sacred Assignment of Breaking Generational Cycles

To be a conscious parent is to stand at a crossroads between what has been and what could be. It is to embody both the story that was inherited and the possibility of a new story that can be told. As parents, we hold the sacred opportunity to end ancestral trauma and dismantle generational dysfunction. This Divine opportunity does not begin with our children. It begins within us. We must acknowledge what we carry. Spiritual Hygiene invites us, as parents, into a sacred reckoning where we must become aware of and acknowledge that dysfunction exists, not just in our family history, but also in the way we think, react, cope, and relate. Again, this is not about blame. This is about *truth as purification*. We must ask:

- *"Where did I learn to disconnect when I feel afraid?"*
- *"Why do I feel unworthy when I am not performing?"*
- *"What did I witness as love? As safety? As success?"*
- *"Which emotions have I buried beneath my parenting script?"*

Without awareness, we unconsciously repeat what we have never healed. The trauma we avoid becomes the trauma we transmit.

We Must Examine Our Patterns Lovingly and Honestly

Spiritual Hygiene teaches us that residue lives in our thoughts, our choices, and our energy.

So we must examine:

- Our bonding patterns: Do we create codependency or healthy attachment?
- Our scarcity behaviors: Do we model fear, or lack, or trust as the foundation for provision?
- Our emotional residue: Are guilt, shame, rage, or unspoken grief silently shaping how we show up?

To cleanse these patterns is not to erase the past, but to release its grip on our future. It requires honesty, not denial. It requires a radical truth spoken with grace. Until we stop telling the stories that justify our pain, we cannot dismantle them.

Telling The Truth Is Not Enough; We Must Practice Spiritual Hygiene

It is not enough to name the trauma. We must also cleanse the emotional and energetic residue the trauma has left behind. This is the work of Spiritual Hygiene. It means being willing and vigilant about:

- Releasing inherited shame through daily reflection, breath, and truth-telling
- Honoring our grief instead of numbing it with distractions or over-giving
- Practicing forgiveness as a path of liberation
- Creating opportunities and rituals that bless our children while also restoring our inner child
- Cleansing the emotional atmosphere of our home with clarity, laughter, sharing, and peace

The Gift of Spiritual Hygiene

When we do our internal Spiritual Hygiene work and the external work, our children receive more than lectures and rules. They receive:

- A spiritually clean space in which to grow
- A model of what it means to live whole, not just behave well
- A lineage that is being rewritten in real time, through every healed reaction, every sacred pause, every breath we take before we speak

We cannot change what happened to us, but we can become the sacred interruption. We can be the ones who turn trauma into truth, pain into power, and shame into sanctified awareness. This is the gift of Spiritual Hygiene in parenting: *to become a clean vessel through which love, clarity, and Divine presence can flow to the next generation.*

Main Tenets of Spiritual Hygiene for Parenting

Parenting is not merely a role we play. It is a sacred transmission of Divine energy. It is the daily act of imprinting energy, beliefs, and behaviors upon another soul. As such, it demands more than love. It requires personal Spiritual Hygiene. To parent consciously is to recognize that every word, every reaction, every silence, and every embrace carries a vibration. These tenets are not rules. They are reminders. They are guiding principles for those who choose to parent from a place of alignment, awareness, and generational healing. These truths illuminate the path for those who dare to be clean vessels, breaking cycles, reclaiming peace, and becoming the embodied blessing their lineage has long awaited.

Healing Before Handling

As a parent, you must be willing to heal your own wounds before you attempt to guide a child through theirs. Unhealed trauma becomes distorted parenting. Cleansing your inner child makes space for a parenting style rooted in compassion rather than control.

Healing Premise: *"I cleanse so I do not contaminate."*

Presence Over Performance

Children do not need "*perfect parents.*" They need "*present ones.*" Spiritual Hygiene invites you to be emotionally available, energetically grounded, and mentally clear, rather than overly concerned with being "right" or "enough."

Healing Premise: *"My wholeness is more impactful than my perfection."*

Emotional Regulation Is Sacred Service

Every moment you choose calm over chaos, breath over blame, you sanctify your role as parent. Regulation is not repression. It is the sacred stewardship of your energy, tone, and timing.
Healing Premise: *"My nervous system is a sanctuary, not a raging storm."*

Conscious Correction Without Contamination

Discipline should be an act of love, not a release of your unprocessed emotions. Correction that comes from clarity builds trust. Correction that comes from reactivity fractures the soul.
Healing Premise: *"I cleanse my energy before I offer guidance."*

Energetic Responsibility Is Inherited

Children absorb the energetic atmosphere of the home. Your anxiety, silence, resentment, or joy becomes part of their inner world. Spiritual Hygiene requires awareness of what you are transmitting into the space, both spoken and unspoken.
Healing Premise: *"I am the energetic blueprint of this household."*

Reparenting the Inner Child Is Part of Parenting

You cannot fully honor the child in front of you while rejecting the child within you.

Spiritual Hygiene teaches that every interaction with your child is also an invitation to heal something in yourself.
Healing Premise: *"As I tend to them, I tend to me."*

Transparency with Accountability, Not Shame

Your mistakes do not make you unworthy or wrong. Modeling apology, repair, and growth teaches your children how to face themselves with honesty and how to love themselves through imperfection.
Healing Premise: *"My humility heals more than my image ever could."*

Sacred Ritual and Reflection Create Safety

A spiritually hygienic home is not just physically clean; it is energetically clean. Rituals of breath, reflection, prayer, and emotional check-ins cultivate an environment of emotional safety and spiritual coherence.
Healing Premise: *"We keep the house clean by keeping the energy clear."*

Sacred Practices for Spirit-Centered Parenting

Pause and Presence Ritual (for reactive moments)

- Place one hand on your heart and one on your belly.
- Whisper aloud: *"I am fully present. I choose love and Sacred Responsibility over the need to be right or perform."*
- Give yourself a ninety-second sacred pause before responding.

Breath Anchoring Before Discipline

- Inhale deeply: *"I am the calm."*
- Exhale fully: *"I create the space, the tone, the energy of this moment."*
- Repeat this breath sequence three times before speaking or correcting.

Family Spiritual Hygiene Check-Ins

- Have a weekly sacred circle with your children or household
- Everyone shares: one reflection of Gratitude, one Challenge, and one deeply felt Soul Request.
- Light a candle, begin with a breath, and end with a family blessing.
- Optional: Include a shared affirmation or cleansing prayer.

Before we knew to call it "trauma," we called it "parenting." Before we knew how to name "energy," we referred to it as "discipline." Many of the words passed from parent to child, often in moments of stress, fear, or fatigue, carry more than just commands or corrections. Each phrase you speak to a child can carry the energetic imprint of unprocessed emotion, inherited authority structures, and trauma-informed control. These are not simply sentences; they are echoes, resonances of voices that never got to be heard, children that never got to be comforted, and power that was misused in the name of survival. When we speak these phrases, we are not only addressing our child, but we are also channeling a legacy. Spiritual Hygiene calls us to interrupt that legacy with consciousness, compassion, and informed choice. It invites us to examine the energetic root of our words and offer language that not only disciplines but also heals. The following transformations are not about achieving perfection; they are about purification. They are a way to clear the spoken atmosphere between you and your child so that love, learning, and legacy can be reshaped.

Transforming Common Parental Behaviors Through Spiritual Hygiene

"Do it because I said so."

Energetic Insight:

This statement often arises from a sense of urgency, overwhelm, or a conditioned belief that authority must be asserted without explanation. It shuts down inquiry and teaches blind obedience rather than conscious understanding.

Spiritual Hygiene Upgrade:

"I know this may not make sense to you right now, but I'm asking you to trust me. I will explain when I know you will understand more."

Why It Heals:

This maintains healthy authority while honoring the child's capacity to think and feel. It plants seeds of trust, rather than fear.

"Don't talk back to me." "Who do you think you are talking to?"

Energetic Insight:

These phrases often come from a place of personal insecurity or unresolved emotional reactivity. It teaches suppression of voice and discourages self-expression.

Spiritual Hygiene Upgrade:

"I hear that you are upset. Let's talk about this when we can both hear and speak respectfully."

Why It Heals:

It affirms that the child's voice matters within sacred boundaries of mutual respect and timing.

"You never do what you're told."

Energetic Insight:

This is a declaration of frustration and powerlessness. It creates shame and labels the child rather than addressing behavior.

Spiritual Hygiene Upgrade:

"I notice you're having a hard time practicing obedience and following instructions. Can we talk about what's going on for you?"

Why It Heals:

It invites deeper connection and opens the door for accountability without condemnation.

"You think you know everything."

Energetic Insight:

This phrase diminishes curiosity and confidence. It stems from a place where the parent feels dismissed or unseen, projecting insecurity onto the child.

Spiritual Hygiene Upgrade:

"I see you have strong thoughts and feelings about this. Let's explore them together."

Why It Heals:

It encourages critical thinking and co-learning while keeping the relationship rooted in curiosity rather than hierarchy.

"Look what you made me do."

Energetic Insight:

This statement displaces responsibility and energetically binds the child to the parent's reaction or pain. It seeds guilt and emotional burden.

Spiritual Hygiene Upgrade:

"I lost my temper, and that's something I'm working on. It's not your fault. Let's take a breath together."

Why It Heals:

It models emotional accountability and teaches that each person is responsible for their own energy.

"You're giving me a headache." "You're getting on my nerves."

Energetic Insight:

This links the child's natural behavior to the parent's physical or emotional suffering, fostering the belief that their existence is harmful or burdensome.

Spiritual Hygiene Upgrade:

"I'm feeling overwhelmed right now. I need a moment to gather myself so I can hear you fully."

Why It Heals:

It teaches emotional awareness and self-regulation while affirming the child's right to be seen and heard.

"What is wrong with you?"

Energetic Insight:

This phrase delivers a deep wound to the child's sense of self-worth. It implies defectiveness and creates shame instead of guiding correction.

Spiritual Hygiene Upgrade:

"I can see you are struggling. Let's work together so we can both understand what's happening inside you."

Why It Heals:

It affirms that mistakes and emotions are invitations for connection, not rejection.

"Pay attention to what I'm saying."

Energetic Insight:

This often arises from a feeling of being dismissed or unseen and may carry a tone that shuts down rather than opens up.

Spiritual Hygiene Upgrade:

"I want to make sure we are understanding each other. Can you share what you heard me say?"

Why It Heals:

It invites presence and reflection while fostering mutual respect. It also models emotional intelligence and deep listening.

"We can't afford that."

Energetic Insight:

Often spoken from a state of financial stress or a mindset of scarcity, this phrase may teach the child that desire is dangerous, abundance is inaccessible, or that money is always tied to limitation.

Spiritual Hygiene Upgrade:

"Right now, that is not something I can invest in. Let's talk about some creative ways we can make it happen if it is important to you."

Why It Heals:

It shifts the energy from scarcity to sovereignty and possibility, modeling choice over powerlessness.

"That's too much."

Energetic Insight:

This phrase, when said with tension, can communicate that the child's desires, emotions, or personality are overwhelming or inappropriate.

Spiritual Hygiene Upgrade:

"That feels like a lot for me to take in right now. Can we slow down and explore it together later?"

Why It Heals:

It creates a boundary without shaming the child's expression, preserving their inner permission to dream, feel, and ask.

"You're always asking for something."

Energetic Insight:

Said in exasperation, this may cause a child to internalize the belief that their needs are a burden or that asking equals annoyance.

Spiritual Hygiene Upgrade:

"I notice you are asking for a lot today. Is there something you need that we haven't talked about?"

Why It Heals:

It transforms complaint into curiosity, helping the parent discern the deeper need beneath repeated requests.

The Absent Parent – Holding Space with Truth and Tenderness

There are few questions more delicate, more loaded with longing and unspoken sorrow, than when a child asks, *"Where is my mother?"* or *"Why doesn't my father come around?"*

Whether the absence is due to death, estrangement, abandonment, addiction, incarceration, or emotional unavailability, the child is left to interpret the silence in ways that often become internalized shame:

> *"Maybe I wasn't worth staying for."*
>
> *"Maybe I did something wrong."*
>
> *"Maybe I'm not lovable."*
>
> *"Maybe I'm not important."*

As caregivers, spiritual stewards, and lineage-healers, our responsibility is not to fix the absence; it is to fill the emotional gap with truth, compassion, and presence.

We must remember: *A child's soul knows the absence already*. What they are really asking for is language to process it. They are asking for energetic alignment in the space where confusion and grief are swirling. Spiritual Hygiene teaches us that *we do not lie* to protect children. We bless the truth with care. We tell the truth cleanly, without bitterness, shame, or projection. We hold the question without collapsing into our own pain or defending someone else's decision. We speak in a way that affirms the child's worth, while making space for the absent parent's humanity and the mystery of their soul's journey.

Appropriate Responses to a Child's Questions About an Absent Parent

Here are examples of spiritually hygienic, emotionally attuned responses:

When the absence is by choice or abandonment:

"I don't know all the reasons your ____________ is not present. What I do know is that their absence is not your fault. You are deeply loved and wanted. I am here for every question, every feeling, every moment of this. Can you tell me what it feels like for you?"

When the parent is struggling with addiction, trauma, or immaturity:

"Your ____________ is having some challenges right now that make it hard for them to show up the way you deserve. That does not mean you are unlovable. It means they are still growing, and even though they are not here, I want you always to feel safe to talk about them, to wonder, and to ask."

When the parent has passed away:

"Your ____________ no longer has a body. They live in the spirit world and their love for you is still real. We can talk to them, remember them, and feel them in ways that are soft and sacred. You are allowed to miss them, to ask about them, and to celebrate them in a way that makes you feel good. Is there something you want to do for them right now?"

If the child expresses anger or sadness:

"You are allowed to feel everything. You don't have to pretend. I am here to feel it with you, and we can move through it together, without blame or shame. Can we talk about what you feel?"

Sacred Reminders for the Caregiver

Do not speak ill of the absent parent. Speak truthfully but cleanly, taking the age of the child into consideration. You can name the facts without poisoning the emotional field. Affirm the child's lovability. Reinforce that the absence is not a reflection of their worth. Hold the mystery of the unknown truth and facts with reverence. Sometimes we don't have all the answers, and saying *"I don't know, but I'm here"* is a spiritually honest response. Create a ritual space where the child can name their feelings, ask their questions, or write letters to the absent parent, whether those letters are sent, burned, or placed on an altar.

Long before I became a guest on *The Oprah Winfrey Show*, I was an avid viewer. I clearly remember the day her guest, the *Beloved* author Toni Morrison, spoke the words, *"Your children need to see your eyes light up when they walk into the room."* It shifted how I saw and responded to my children, and how I viewed myself as a parent. To parent with Spiritual Hygiene is to parent with intention, whether your children are five, fifteen, or fifty. It is not a promise to always get it right. It is the devotion to remain aware, to take responsibility for your energy, and to create an atmosphere where love is not just spoken but embodied. You are not raising children alone. You are raising your lineage, your inner child, your consciousness, and in many ways, the vibration of the planet. The moments you pause, the breath you take before reacting, the truth you speak without shame—these are sacred offerings. They are the invisible threads that weave safety, clarity, and healing into the hearts of your children. You will not always be perfect. But you can always choose to be present. When you are intentionally present, the home becomes a temple, your voice becomes a balm, and your presence becomes the clearest transmission of love your child will ever receive. Keep going. Keep cleansing. Keep returning. You are the altar. You are the answer. You are the blessing they have been waiting for.

OPENING PRAYER

Beloved Presence of Light, and Order,
I welcome You into every space where my feet walk,
into every task that my hands complete,
and into every word I speak in service.
Let this day, this desk, this duty become an altar of sacred offering.
Let what I touch be touched by peace.
Let what I create carry the vibration of clarity and alignment.
Where distortion seeks to distract, I ask to remain anchored.
Where dysfunction speaks loudly, I ask to answer only to truth.
Where power is misused, I will remember:
I am governed by the Divine.
I affirm:
That no title is greater than my calling.
No office is stronger than my alignment.
No system can silence the soul that knows its Source.
I declare:
In this workplace, I bring light without aggression.
I uphold boundaries without apology.
I stand in sacred clarity without needing to be understood.
Spirit, sanctify the unseen places, the meetings,
the decisions, the conversations.
Let me be a living sanctuary.
Let this space be a place of right action, right speech, and right rhythm.
May I serve without self-betrayal.
May I lead without distortion.

May I shine without shrinking.
I Am here. I Am clean. I Am whole.
I walk this day in alignment with the Divine.
Amen. Àṣẹ Aho.
And so, it is.

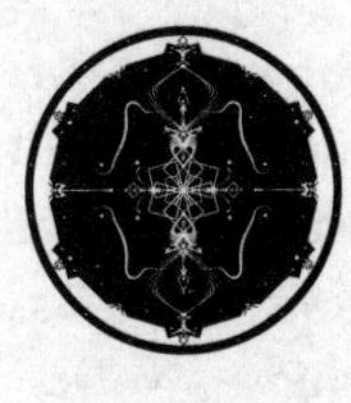

CHAPTER 16

Spiritual Hygiene for Relationships

Clearing the Mirror, Honoring the Bond

Elena and her sister grew up like two branches of the same tree, intertwined by blood, yet bent by different winds. In their childhood, they whispered secrets under the covers and defended each other in the schoolyard. By the time they were grown, a strange silence had taken root between them. Elena couldn't quite name the moment the distance began. Maybe it was when her sister didn't come to their father's funeral. Or maybe it was the years of "I'm fine" masking deeper wounds. They texted occasionally—birthdays, emergencies—but the warmth between them had cooled. The thread remained, but it was frayed.

One day, during a healing circle, Elena was guided to close her eyes and ask her heart: "What am I carrying in my relationship with my sister that does not belong to me?" The image came fast, a cracked mirror. Her sister's sorrow, her own silence, the unspoken disappointments. And suddenly, the message was clear: She was tending to the connection through the lens of unresolved pain, unclean expectation, and emotional inheritance. The love they shared had not faded. The honesty and clarity between them had.

Spiritual Hygiene for relationships is the intentional practice of tending to the energy, emotions, and unspoken dynamics between yourself and others with clarity, honesty, and a sense of presence. It is the soul's commitment to show up clean, rather than contaminated, and to relate from truth, not trauma. Spiritual Hygiene is a devotional way of being in connection with clarity, compassion, truth, and tenderness. It is what allows intimacy to be safe, sacred, and sustainable. Spiritual Hygiene for relationships involves the consistent, conscious clearing of emotional residue, energetic projection, and inherited relational patterns, allowing love, truth, and presence to thrive in the space between souls. Practicing Spiritual Hygiene will not make you "perfect" in a relationship. It will, however, support you in becoming and being *spiritually accountable and responsible* for how you show up in loving, befriending, partnering, and relating.

Relationships do not fall apart overnight. They unravel silently, thread by thread when:

- A boundary is not named.
- A feeling remains unspoken.
- A resentment is tucked beneath a smile.
- A need is disguised as a demand.
- A silence is mistaken for peace.

Without Spiritual Hygiene, these small threads become knotted entanglements. Emotional buildup. Invisible walls. Spiritual Hygiene clears those threads before they become thorns. It brings us back to presence, so we stop relating from our past and start relating from our power. It facilitates the *embodiment* of the principles and practices required to live the theory so that what we *know* becomes an essential part of *who we are* and who we are becoming.

Drift from Soul to Survival

Most of what has been offered here in these chapters is something a majority of people already know. Some part of us really knows what is required for open-minded, heart-centered, clean living. We have heard about it. We may have even briefly practiced some aspects of it—the principles and practices of Spiritual Hygiene—in every area of our lives. Then, life happens. We get busy. Our wounds get triggered. The voices of personal and collective trauma rise up like a storm, hissing, screaming, demanding attention, drowning out the gentle whispers of the soul. A family member or social leader disappoints us. A partner or friend betrays our trust. Financial strain pulls us from a place of Divine trust into a state of human desperation. News headlines and social media streams flood our senses with fear, loss, and despair, dimming our hope in humanity's unfolding. Stimulated by a third-dimensional, sensory-driven reality, we begin scrambling to fix our lives. We reach outward, attempting to control the chaos. We forget the sacred power and innate wisdom within. In our forgetting, we lose connection to the very thing we long for most: the intimacy of loving, fulfilling, and spiritually aligned relationships.

In the midst of our pain and disorientation, trust becomes a demand rather than a devotion. Faith is reduced to a desperate spiritual construct, only activated when we hit rock bottom. Love becomes a transaction, a memory, or for some, a mirage. We believe we are broken. The truth is, we are just tired. In fact, some are mentally, emotionally, and physically exhausted. We are trying to survive in a world that keeps pulling us away from our center. When we disconnect from our inner temple, we begin to pollute our outer relationships. The Divine learning curriculum encoded into every challenge gets lost. The sacred mirror each person provides is fogged. The Spiritual Hygiene that keeps our connections clean, whole, and rooted in truth becomes a luxury only some can afford rather than a necessity that we all must embrace.

What Spiritual Hygiene Is and Is Not

The practice and embodiment of Spiritual Hygiene, whether in relationships or any other area of life, does not mean we will forget the pain we've endured. It means we stop judging that pain as wrong or unnecessary. It does not mean the scars of our wounds will vanish. It means we stop picking at them until they bleed into the present moment, staining new beginnings with old residue. Spiritual Hygiene may not give us whiter teeth or fresher breath, but it will restore the sacred breath of truth, love, and integrity into our relationships.

It reminds us: You have the power. You have the responsibility. You are the temple and the keeper of its fire. Through the daily tending of your heart, your boundaries, your truth, and your energy, you become a clean vessel through which your relationships—romantic, familial, platonic, and communal—can flourish, because your inner altar creates the outer atmosphere. Every relationship you experience is shaped by the state of your inner altar. Your unspoken thoughts, your unreleased grief, your hidden longings, may not be invisible. Yet, they are felt and experienced. Spiritual Hygiene calls you to tend to that inner space with tenderness, awareness, and love. So that when life happens again, and it will, you won't forget who you are, expecting someone else to remember on your behalf. Instead, you will return to your inner center. You will remember the truth of your sacred identity. You will reset and align. You will relate from a place that is whole.

Core Elements of Spiritual Hygiene for Relationships

Energetic Awareness

Recognizing when the emotional atmosphere between you and another feels heavy, unclear, or charged. Once you become aware, you must choose not to ignore it. The awareness is:

> *"Something is disturbing the energy in our field. Let's love each other enough to clear it."*

Emotional Ownership

Accepting full responsibility for your inner experience, your triggers, your needs, your history, without assigning blame. It is having the courage and willingness to say:

> *"I feel disappointed, and I want to share that with honesty, not as accusation."*

Open-Hearted Communication

Replacing assumptions, expectations, and silence with clarity and truth. It means owning and speaking:

> *"Here's what I'm feeling. Here's what I need. Can we talk about it together?"*

Discernment and Boundaries

Knowing when to lean in, when to release, and when a connection is no longer in alignment with your soul. Offering feedback with compassion and concern, and honoring requests for time or space before pressing or leaning in. It is a delicate balance between knowing what is needed and knowing when it is most appropriate to address the need. It is a recognition that:

> *"I bless our bond, and I also honor that I need space for my truth to breathe and be expressed."*

Ancestral and Pattern Clearing

Noticing when you are reenacting inherited dynamics and choosing not to repeat them. This is a call for inner authority to step in and restore alignment and balance:

> *"This reaction feels familiar. It is not just mine. It is my mother's (or father's). It is history. I release it now."*

Relationships are also like temples. Spiritual Hygiene is the practice of maintaining a clean altar. Unspoken pain in a relationship becomes energetic clutter. Clear it with courage. Silence disguised as peace becomes emotional avoidance. Speak with clarity. Choose honesty over hiding. Over-giving eventually becomes martyrdom. True love honors reciprocity, not depletion. Emotional withdrawal is not protection. It is energetic pollution. Return to presence. Expecting others to read your mind is not a sign of intimacy. It is unresolved fear. Ask. Speak. Reveal. When you swallow your truth to maintain peace, you create inner turmoil. Love does not require that you sacrifice yourself. It asks for the presence of your soul. Every soul you connect with is impacted by the vibration of your being. Keep your mental, emotional, and physical *being* clean. Make yourself holy.

All Relationships Are Mirrors That Reflect Our Internal Climate

The quality of your relationships is not measured by how long they last. It is evidenced by how clean, clear, and conscious you are within them. If your soul is evolving but your relationships are not, tension will arise. Without good Spiritual Hygiene, relationships can quickly deteriorate into obligation, emotional pollution, or energetic co-dependency. You may assume the relationship or the other person is the problem. That would be an inaccurate assumption. What you are experiencing is *Divine alignment* knocking on your door. There is something you need to clean up or clear out. When you practice Spiritual Hygiene in relationships, you stop waiting to be affirmed, acknowledged, or chosen, and start choosing yourself, with love, clarity, and sacred boundaries. Spiritual Hygiene provides you with *relational discernment,* teaching you when to draw closer, when to release, and how to remain rooted in love, regardless of the circumstances. Relationships are sacred mirrors and classrooms. They may not always reflect who we are, but they always reveal what we carry consciously or unconsciously. Where there is poor Spiritual Hygiene in relationships, we will experience and express:

Emotional Projection Rather Than Presence

When the Wound Speaks Louder Than Awareness

Emotional projection occurs when we assign someone a script they never agreed to perform. It is when we don't just feel our feelings; we *assign* them to someone else. In response, our pain becomes a lens through which we misread the moment, misinterpret the other, and mistake reaction for reality. Instead of meeting others with our truth and presence, we meet them with the echoes of our past.

- A friend cancels a call, and we feel abandoned, not because of the disappointment or lack of contact, but because of the childhood wound it conjures.
- A partner sets a boundary, and we feel unloved, not because of the line they have drawn, but because our nervous system equates "no" with rejection.
- A loved one is distracted, and we feel dismissed, not because they aren't listening, but because an old story says: "*I'm not worthy of attention.*"

The experience reflects back to us what remains unprocessed, which we project onto the other person. What we suppress within, we assign without. Spiritual Hygiene in relationships brings us to ourselves with the awareness, honesty, and clarity that says: *"This belongs to me. That belongs to them."* Presence is rooted. Calm. Curious. Projection is reactive. Charged. Accusatory. **Emotional projection leads to unclean, often ineffective communication.** It muddles the space between you and the other person with the echoes and residue of past experiences. **This is the result of denying, avoiding, and suppressing our feelings. When we don't take time to feel, we force others to carry what we have not claimed or cleared.** To be fully present in the moment of a relationship, we must be willing to slow down and clear our emotional lens before responding.

When we are aware of, honest, and present with ourselves in a relationship, we ask:

What am I feeling right now? What is true in this moment? What does this remind me of? When we are projecting, we assume: *"You're ignoring me." "You are trying to hurt me." "You never listen. You always leave. You don't care."* One is open-hearted awareness. The other is emotional storytelling disguised as intuition. When you choose to pause and check in with your truth before reacting, you interrupt the old scripts that trauma has rehearsed. You stop assigning blame to others for wounds they did not create. You accept responsibility for your internal landscape. You practice Somatic Stewardship that has been disrupted or disturbed. In this way, you become the healer of your own heart. You bring yourself back into alignment with your soul.

Emotional projection is not always evidence of a bad or dysfunctional relationship. It is simply a signal that your heart is asking *to be witnessed by you* before it is seen or held by another. To practice Spiritual Hygiene in a relationship is to make the commitment that:

> *"I will not blame you for my pain by calling it your fault."*
>
> *"I will meet you with clarity, not contamination."*
>
> *"I will be here, now, with all of me, clean, conscious, and clear."*

Sacred Pause

Before responding to a moment of emotional charge in a relationship:

- Pause.
- Breathe deeply into your belly.
- Ask yourself:

  "What am I actually feeling?"

  "What story am I telling myself about this feeling?"

  "Is this response about this moment—or another moment I've never fully felt?"

- Speak to yourself aloud (or silently):

  "I choose presence over projection. I return to the truth of this moment. I do not ask another to hold what I have not honored in myself."

Passive Blame Rather than Active Communication

The Withheld Voice

James and Aisha had been married for fourteen years. They knew each other's rhythms, who made the coffee, who took out the trash, and when to be silent and listen. Lately, a quiet tension lived between them. Aisha felt unsupported. She was overwhelmed at work and struggling to cope with too much at home. Instead of saying *"I need help,"* she did everything with extra force; washing the dishes loudly, overexplaining her exhaustion to friends, leaving articles about burnout on the table. James sensed something was wrong but didn't know how to approach it. One night he said, *"I'm not a mind reader."* Aisha snapped back, *"Exactly. That's the problem."* Passive blame had entered their relationship like a fog. The stench of it was numbing truth and clouding their connection. Each type of relationship has unique spiritual requirements. Intimate relationships demand emotional transparency. Marriages require energetic renewal. Friendships need recalibration over time. James did not need any more guessing. He needed a *transparent, energetic renewal* that would *recalibrate* his connection to his friend, lover, and wife. Aisha needed to step into active communication born of spiritual responsibility.

Passive blame is one of the most subtle, corrosive energies in relationships. It does not speak clearly or directly. It sighs. It withdraws. It slams cabinet doors and cancels plans without explanation. It posts cryptic messages online. It expects others to read pain like a script and fix what was never said aloud. Passive blame is the art of implication. It says "*You should have known*" instead of "*This is what I need.*" It punishes rather than expresses. It waits to be rescued instead of asking to be seen. Passive blame is the energy of "*I'm mad at you, but I won't tell you why.*" It avoids discomfort by creating confusion. It seeks change without clarity. Where passive blame lives, connection cannot breathe.

At its core, passive blame is not a result of laziness or manipulation. It is a trauma-informed adaptation. It is the survival response of someone who learned early on that being direct or honest was not safe. It is the residue of environments where truth was punished, emotion was dismissed, or requests were met with rejection, ridicule, or silence. Passive blame contaminates the field between two souls with silence, expectation, and invisible punishments. It is a form of energetic dishonesty, where truth is felt but not spoken. It places the burden of healing on the other while withholding the map of how to get to the healing by the shortest route. Spiritual Hygiene calls us into active communication: Clear. Respectful. Rooted in present truth, not historical pain.

Passive blame often begins in childhood, where emotional honesty was either:

- Ignored: *"Stop crying." "You're too sensitive."*
- Punished: *"Don't talk back." "That's disrespectful."*
- Minimized: *"It's not a big deal." "You're overreacting."*
- Shamed: *"Look what you made me do." "Why can't you just behave?"*

From this, a child learns that it is not safe to speak up, or that expressing needs leads to disconnection. There is always an echo, a subconscious belief fueling passive blame:

> *"If I say what I really feel, I'll be hurt, rejected, or ignored. It's better to hint, withhold, or act it out, because asking directly never works."*

As the child matures, the belief remains rooted, so the adult withdraws instead of expressing. They *"let things go"* that are still festering. They believe others should know because they do not feel safe enough to ask. They feel unseen, but never risk being fully visible. This belief keeps them emotionally protected but spiritually polluted. *"If I'm honest, I will be dismissed, blamed, or abandoned." "I must protect myself by staying silent, withdrawing, or implying, never asking directly."* This trauma voice becomes a relational blueprint carried into adulthood. Passive blame is a protective strategy, a quiet attempt to preserve dignity without risking exposure. Protection, when rooted in fear, becomes a prison. Until the voice is reclaimed, truth remains buried. Until presence replaces projection, resentment grows. Until the core belief is healed, communication will always carry the scent of fear.

Passive Blame Sounds Like:

- *"You should've known I was upset."*
- *"Whatever, it's fine."*
- *"I'll just do it myself."*
- Unreturned calls, sharp silences, consciously dramatic distance

Active Communication Sounds Like:

- *"I felt hurt when you didn't follow through. Can we talk about it?"*
- *"Right now I'm feeling overwhelmed, and I need your support."*
- *"I noticed I've been withdrawing. I think there's something I need to share."*

Active communication is not just about words. It's about energetic cleanliness and speaking the truth before it festers into bitterness.

Spiritual Hygiene for relationships is not just about the clearing of your inner world. It is also the cleansing of the space between you and another person. When your energy is clean, your communication becomes a sacred offering. No longer cloaked in manipulation, fear, or avoidance, your words become a mirror of your alignment. To practice active communication is to honor both your truth and the person in front of you. It is to speak from awareness rather than pain, from clarity rather than confusion, and from love rather than protection. When communication is stagnant, unclear, or manipulative:

- Energetic cords become tangled.
- Resentment quietly festers.

- Assumptions replace understanding.
- Silence becomes punishment.
- Truth is buried beneath performance or pride.

This is emotional debris that not only destroys relationships but also reinforces the very beliefs that created the problem in the first place. Spiritual Hygiene for relationships involves clearing the debris from sacred space. When you withhold truth to *"keep the peace,"* you are not protecting the relationship. You are suffocating it. Spiritual Hygiene calls you to name the unseen. To bring shadow into light.

Active communication is spiritually responsible speech that becomes the *lifeblood* of a relationship. When it is present, everything in and about the relationship flows. Those in the relationship feel safe. Most importantly, the people involved know that even when it is not easy, they will have all the information they need to make self-honoring, self-supportive choices. And they offer the same to the other person. Active communication is:

- Direct without being sharp
- Honest without being harsh
- Vulnerable without requiring self-abandonment
- Expressive without expectation of control
- Not about being right; it is about being real and honest.
- Not about external validation; it is about sacred presence.

Active communication clears the relational field by offering and receiving:

- *"This is what I feel."*
- *"This is what I need."*

- *"This is what I'm willing to do."*
- *"This is what I'm no longer available for."*

In all relationships, think of your words as incense and consider, *"What energy are my words carrying?"* Are they clouded with accusation, or scented with sincerity? Active communication becomes a Spiritual Hygiene ritual in your relationships when you take a breath before speaking and have the intention to connect, rather than conquer. Your relationship temple stays clean when you take responsibility for your emotions and leave room for others to respond.

Unspoken Resentment Grows Into Energetic Debt

When Silence Becomes the Weight Love Cannot Carry

Selma and Mara had been close for nearly a decade. Sisters not by blood, but by bond. They laughed loud and often, traveled together, held space for one another's pain, celebrated life's seasons. Selma walked beside Mara through her divorce. Mara had stood beside Selma at her mother's funeral. They were connected at the hip, and then slowly, something changed. It did not happen in one moment. There were many often unnoticed, some unspoken moments, and many small things. Selma began to notice that Mara never asked about her new business. She showed up late to planned meetings and outings. She seemed distracted when Selma spoke of her growth, discoveries, or new interests she was developing. Over time, Selma felt herself shrinking. She stopped sharing her wins. She justified Mara's distance with spiritual logic: *"She's probably going through something."* But truthfully, she was hurt.

Mara never said anything unkind, nor did she say *"I see you, I hear you, I am with you"* anymore. Selma began to carry a quiet grief. She missed her friend and did not know or understand where she had gone. She offered Mara support out of habit. She answered Mara's requests even when she was tired. Selma avoided asking Mara for help because she no longer felt safe to need anything in her presence. She ignored little slights or said *"It's OK"* when it wasn't. Month after month, the space between them grew heavy. Not with arguments, but with unspoken expectations, swallowed disappointments, and invisible debts.

One of the new interests Selma had embraced that Mara seemed to care nothing about was meditation. Selma had crafted a beautiful practice she engaged in every morning. One day after a particularly sweet session, Selma was writing in her journal when she heard the words rise in her spirit: *"You are carrying Mara in a way she never asked you to. More than that, you are carrying the weight of what you never said."* Selma wept, not because of Mara's actions, but because of her own silence. The way she had given without request or requirement. The way she had assumed instead of expressing. The way she had spiritualized her own self-abandonment, called it love, and blamed the lack of reciprocity on her friend, whom she loved dearly. Taking responsibility for herself and her feelings, Selma wrote a letter, one she would not send to Mara. It was a letter of release.

Dear Mara,

I've been giving from a place of fear, not fullness.

I've been withholding my truth to preserve our bond.

I now realize that I have created a debt between us that you were never aware of.

I release it. I bless us both. I come home to my voice.

I cancel the contract of silent suffering.

I reclaim my clarity. I restore energetic balance.

I ask for and claim your forgiveness.

All is now clear between us.

She burned the letter, placed her hand over her heart, and prayed for herself and then Mara.

Within a few hours, she felt the shift. She knew the field between her and Mara had cleared. Mara remained in her life, but the emotional grip was gone. Selma no longer over-gave. She said no when it felt right. She no longer overexplained or over-expected. She still loved Mara, but now she loved with clean hands and a clear heart. Selma had practiced good Spiritual Hygiene. She realized that just as she cared for her body, she had to tend to the emotional and spiritual currents she brought into her connection with others. She also realized that what she was feeling was her business and her responsibility to handle.

Every relationship is sacred; however, not every relationship is meant to be permanent. Every relationship has a lesson. Often, the lesson is that we can love someone deeply and dearly, but not everyone we love is meant to be our life's companion. Spiritual Hygiene teaches discernment from which we learn who carries a shared frequency, and who carries a shared wound. Some relationships are soul contracts meant for deep karmic clearing. Others are Divine appointments, momentary, but transformative. Some are covenant relationships, those built for longevity, devotion, and soul growth. Others may be *residue relationships* held together only by guilt, obligation, or unhealed patterns. Spiritual Hygiene for relationships does not demand that we *"love everyone the same."* It asks that we love ourselves enough to honor each relationship as it truly is, not what we wish it to be. Friendships may and must shift over time. Spiritual Hygiene asks us to allow that to unfold without guilt or clinging. A friendship that was sacred for your survival season may not be aligned for your becoming season. With good Spiritual Hygiene, you will learn what to do and when to do it, to keep yourself aligned.

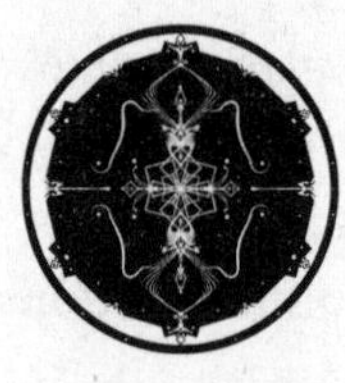

CHAPTER 17

Spiritual Hygiene in the Workplace

The Sacred Art of Alignment in Professional Environments

She was a spiritually grounded woman in a secular space, an entrepreneur-turned-consultant navigating the dense terrain of boardrooms, deadlines, and unspoken expectations. Every day, she entered the corporate world with prayer on her lips and a desire to "be a light." Yet something sacred within her was dimming. Each time a project crossed her desk with unrealistic timelines, she nodded. Anytime a manager spoke over her in a meeting, she smiled. When a colleague claimed credit for her work, she stayed silent. She was praised for being "easy to work with." But inside, on her internal landscape, her voice trembled if she attempted to break the self-imposed silence. Her boundaries collapsed beneath the weight of compliance. Her heart, which she knew to be the compass of her calling, grew weary and resentful. It was not the work that burned her out. It was the betrayal of her inner truth in the name of keeping peace, getting along, and earning her check. Eventually, the gnawing question became a jolting scream: *"Is peace truly peace if it costs your integrity?"*

The Workplace Is Not a Temple—You Are

It is true. People do not go to work to get healed. They go to earn a living, fulfill responsibilities, and support their lives. There are also those who work at doing what they love, just because they love it. While the intention of work may be personal and practical, the experience of work is not always spiritual. In fact, you do not need to be in a temple for a transformation to occur. You do not need your coworkers to be conscious for your soul to grow. Wherever you go, your inner altar goes with you, and whether you intend to heal or not, the dynamics of the workplace will activate your wounds, reflect your patterns, and challenge your integrity. While people may not go to work to get healed, if they are not spiritually aware of how they work, they will carry stress home, fracture their self-worth, and accumulate spiritual weight with every unchecked exchange. Spiritual Hygiene does not demand that the workplace become sacred; it invites you to stay sacred within the workplace.

Every professional space, whether it's a bustling hospital, a digital team meeting, a construction site, or a home office, holds energetic contracts. These contracts are shaped by the invisible agreements we make with roles, expectations, unspoken rules, and systems of power. Workplaces mirror our inner patterns. They reveal the places we:

- Perform for validation
- Withhold truth to avoid conflict
- Attach to status or struggle with subservience
- Silence our instincts to "fit in" or survive

To bring Spiritual Hygiene into the workplace is to:

- Clear the inner altar of people-pleasing
- Reclaim energetic sovereignty
- Dismantle inherited hierarchies of value

- Allow Divine order to move through our actions, advocacy, and presence

This is not about making the workplace spiritual; it is about bringing your clean spirit into the space.

Neutrality vs. Passivity

It is quite common for people on a spiritual path to confuse neutrality with passivity to "get along" in a workplace. This is an important distinction in the workplace because many individuals are suffering silently, mistaking spiritual passivity for maturity and energetic collapse for professionalism. Neutrality, the active presence of spiritual maturity, is clear and rooted. Passivity is a state of disconnection and resignation; in the workplace, it is often rewarded, but at the cost of one's soul. Passivity turns away when someone is being mistreated. Neutrality notices and names it calmly and clearly, without escalation. Neutrality may be misunderstood, but it keeps you spiritually clean. It honors the full picture without collapsing into blame or emotional reactivity. It allows you to observe dysfunction without absorbing it, and to advocate without aggression. Passivity is often spiritual suppression masquerading as peace. It silences the soul and grants power to distortion. Neutrality, by contrast, is sacred discernment in action. Passivity often stems from:

- Fear of conflict
- Trauma conditioning
- Desire to be liked or to stay safe
- Long-term energetic depletion

It shows up as:

- Silence when you want to speak
- Nodding when you mean no

- Smiling to avoid discomfort
- Internalizing harm instead of naming it

To maintain spiritual purity in a challenging workspace, we must not confuse collapse with compassion or silence with wisdom. Neutrality is active, grounded, aware, and remains fully present in the moment. It listens deeply, sees clearly, and stays attuned to both energy and truth. Neutrality allows you to witness dysfunction without becoming entangled in it.

You can name what is happening without being consumed by it. You are not silent from fear. You are silent with power.

The Workplace As a Reflection of the Family Field

We don't just bring our résumés and skill sets to work. We bring our stories, our coping patterns, our conditioned roles, our unhealed wounds, our energetic contracts, and our protective armor. In this way, the workplace becomes a living mirror, a field where familiar energies from home are replayed through professional roles. While most people, particularly highly experienced or educated individuals, would vehemently deny this reality, the workplace often reflects unhealed dynamics from childhood and family. Roles such as the boss, the coworker, the overachiever, the fixer, and the silent one are often spiritual archetypes rooted in home conditioning. This transforms the workplace into a classroom for reparenting, reclamation, and remembrance.

If you grew up in a home where your worth was tied to performance, you may become the overachiever who never rests. If you learned to stay silent to maintain peace, you may avoid difficult conversations with coworkers or supervisors. If you were overlooked as a child, you may feel invisible in meetings or unsupported by leadership. If you were the caretaker or peacekeeper in the family, you may over-function at work, trying to fix what is not yours to carry. These patterns are not conscious choices; they are energetic replays, sacred invitations to grow. They are survival strategies that follow us into every system until they are acknowledged and healed. Recognizing and understanding this as a function of Spiritual Hygiene elevates the workplace into an altar of awareness where you can:

- Reclaim your voice
- Establish clean boundaries
- Heal performance-based self-worth
- Practice inner authority over inherited obedience

This means that your job in a workplace is not only a place where you earn an income, but it can also be a site of initiation. It holds the potential and provides the opportunity to reparent yourself, realign distorted power dynamics, and transform unconscious loyalties into conscious choices. In this way, the office becomes a temple. The job assignment becomes a curriculum. All conflict becomes a catalyst, and you can become the clean vessel of transformation. Every shift you make within yourself in response to a workplace learning challenge ripples through your workplace, your family, and the collective field. When all the roles fall away, the job title, performance, pressure, politics, there is only you and the Divine within you. From the perspective of Spiritual Hygiene, you did not end up in your workplace by accident. You were placed there as a steward of light to walk through it cleansed, centered, and clear. When this awareness is accepted, you will tend to the *inner altar* as much as the *outer assignment*, and your integrity, not your income, will be your compass. Your peace, not your productivity, becomes your measure of success.

Sacred Pause

The Three-Minute Alignment Reset

Wherever you are, at your desk, on a call, or in a hallway, close your eyes or soften your gaze and repeat within:

Breathe.

"I return to my breath."

Bless.

"I bless this space, this moment, and myself."

Become.

"I become the presence of clarity, peace, and truth."

This is how you stay clean. This is how you stay free. You are not just an employee. You are a vessel of light, and the altar is wherever your feet are planted in truth. This is how you remember who you are, even in the most chaotic and unholy places.

Power Dynamics, Self-Advocacy, and the Voice of Worth

Every workplace has power structures, both formal and informal. Whether you are an executive, an assistant, a teacher, a cashier, or a contractor, your ability to own your inner authority is essential to your Spiritual Hygiene. Your Voice of Worth must be practiced until it becomes familiar and comfortable. Your Voice of Worth is your soul speaking on behalf of your inherent value, without shrinking, performing, or apologizing for its presence. It need not be loud, but it must be clear. It need not be defensive, but it must be firm. The Voice of Worth disrupts these patterns. It restores sacred balance. It is the bridge between Spiritual Hygiene and professional integrity. The voice of your worth in the workplace is the one that will say:

- *"I need clarity before I can proceed."*
- *"That tone doesn't work for me."*
- *"I can't commit to that deadline without compromising quality."*
- *"That tone doesn't support clarity or collaboration. Let's reset."*
- *"No, I'm not available at that time."*
- *"Here's what I need in order to move forward with integrity."*

These are not acts of rebellion. They are acts of self-respect, energetic protection, and soul alignment. Self-advocacy in the workplace is not rebellion. It is having and holding a reverence for your assignment. In spaces where multiple energies, agendas, and personalities collide, energetic contamination is common. It is easy to believe that what you feel at work in response to the environment is a sign of personal weakness. Spiritual Hygiene acknowledges that it may also be a sensitivity that requires management. You are not obligated to absorb the energy of the room or the people in the room. You are called to anchor the energy of the Divine within yourself. Your workplace life is not separate from your spiritual life. It is one of the altars on which your alignment is tested and refined. When an authority figure or coworker acts out or behaves in an unruly, dismissive, or disruptive way, the spiritually hygienic response is not a reaction, but rather reclamation. Below is a teaching guide for your heart and words in such moments, along with a path toward mending the breach.

Honoring the Sacred Line: What Cannot Be Accommodated in Workplace Relationships

Spiritual Hygiene is not simply about keeping your energy clean; it is also about protecting the field of your dignity from repeated contamination. Too often, in the name of professionalism, peacekeeping, or job security, individuals tolerate what is spiritually corrosive. Some professionally accepted behaviors slowly erode clarity, confidence, and connection to truth. Spiritual Hygiene does not ask you to endure everything and call it grace. It calls you to discern what must never be normalized, for the sake of your wholeness and respect in the space. Certain behaviors cannot be prayed over, tolerated indefinitely, or spiritually excused. They must be named and released, for they do not belong in your energetic field. When we are clear, we recognize that some energies, behaviors, and patterns, though often accepted or expected in workplace relationships, cannot be spiritually accommodated.

Consistent Disrespect or Devaluation

If someone regularly speaks over you, minimizes your contributions, ignores your boundaries, or undermines your role, this is not a case of "personality conflict." It is energetic erosion. You must not allow repeated dishonor to become familiar. The energetic impact is the gradual erosion of self-worth, voice suppression, over-adaptation, and soul fatigue. You do not need aggression to defend your values. However, you will need firm, clear boundaries to affirm them.

How to Address It:

- Reclaim your center before responding. Do not react. Return to the inner altar.
- Use clear language to announce your boundaries.
- Document patterns if necessary and seek support from a trusted ally or HR representative when aligned.
- Daily affirmation: *"My presence is valuable. My voice is sacred. I do not need validation to know my worth."*

Psychological Manipulation or Emotional Gaslighting

If someone causes you to question your perception, invalidates your experiences, or consistently shifts blame without accountability, this is not teamwork. This is a toxic power play. Truth does not distort reality. It reveals it. The energetic impact of accommodating or tolerating this behavior is mental confusion, self-doubt, spiritual disconnection, and internalized guilt. In these situations, clarity without guilt or doubt is your protection.

How to Address It:

- Pause and name your truth internally:

  "This doesn't feel honest or clear to me."

- Set a firm boundary:

  "I'm open to dialogue. I am not open to having my experience rewritten."

- Trust your inner clarity over their distorted narrative.

Spiritual Protection Practice:

- Write down what was said and what you know to be true.
- Burn the false narrative as a means of energetic release.

Energetic Overreach

If someone regularly invades your time, space, or energy with demands that are not part of your role or expects emotional support that you did not agree to provide, you are not obligated to carry their spiritual weight. Just because you can hold it, does not mean it is yours to hold. Even when you can take a punch, it does not mean you should stand in front of a fist. The energetic impact is likely to be characterized by mental and emotional exhaustion, resentment, a loss of creative energy, and blurred boundaries. After an overreach has occurred, take time to recalibrate. Breathe, touch your solar plexus, and affirm: *"I release what is not mine. I reclaim my energetic sovereignty."*

How to Address It:

- Clarify your capacity aloud:

  "I'm not available for that/for this discussion at this time."

"That's not within my role or bandwidth."

You are offering a boundary, not an explanation.

Retaliation for Boundaries

Chances are that before developing your Spiritual Hygiene practices, you may have unconsciously accommodated energetically inappropriate behaviors. If so, you can expect that your shift will not be well-received. That should not be your concern. If your "no" is met with punishment, such as the silent treatment, gossip, professional sabotage, or exclusion, it means you are no longer in alignment with the dysfunction. These behaviors are a form of coercion, an attempt to bring you back into "*misalignment*" within your soul.

A true leader honors boundaries. A false authority fears them. The energetic impact for you could take the form of fear-based compliance, inner silence, or spiritual contraction.

How to Address It:

- Do not retreat into guilt. Remain grounded. Your boundary is holy.
- Name the retaliation if safe to do so:

  "I've noticed a shift since I expressed a need. I am open to honest conversation, because I cannot engage in punishment dynamics."

- If necessary, elevate the issue through appropriate channels.
- Silently affirm:

  "No weapon of retaliation shall prosper. I walk in clarity, truth, and Divine favor."

Racial, Gender, Sexual, or Spiritual Micro/Macroaggressions

Any environment that condones discriminatory jokes, coded language, subtle bias, or spiritual ridicule is not simply "*uncomfortable*"; it is unsafe. Your identity is sacred. You are not called to dim your light to survive a dim room. The energetic impact of such an environment is cultural harm, spiritual trauma, shame, hypervigilance, and soul silencing.

How to Address It:

- Name it if you feel safe, or document and report it with discernment.
- Calmly speak truth to the moment:

  > *"That comment felt dismissive and out of alignment. My request is that you not say that again."*

- Call upon ancestral and Divine support in your spiritual practice. You do not walk alone.
- Silently affirm:

  > *"My identity is sacred. I do not shrink. I stand, rooted in generations of strength."*

Chronically Misaligned Leadership

If leadership consistently models fear, confusion, a lack of vision, or mismanagement without humility or growth, you must recognize that remaining too long under unclear authority may lead to spiritual disorientation. Misaligned leadership breeds spiritual stagnation. It is not good Spiritual Hygiene to follow someone into the dark when their leadership skills are lacking. Your clarity must come from within if it cannot come from above. A loss of personal and professional direction, spiritual dissonance, feelings of helplessness, and moral injury often characterize the energetic impact of this experience.

How to Address It:

- Discern your role:

  Are you being called to speak truth, hold neutrality, or prepare to exit?

- Limit energetic fusion:

  Do not absorb leadership confusion as your own failure.

- Speak up where possible:

  "I'm seeking clarity on the direction we are taking. Without it, it is challenging for me to stay aligned."

Spiritual Protection Practice:

- Place your hand on your heart daily and ask:

  "Is this still my assignment, or is it time for this experience to be released?"

Sacred Conclusion

Workplaces are built on a hierarchy where power is distributed unevenly. The structure of many workplaces rewards silence, which means that speaking up can feel like risking access, reputation, or security. It's not that most people do not see or even experience the distortions. They remain quiet because they believe naming them will cost them something they cannot afford to lose. Tolerating energetic distortions is not a spiritual virtue. It is a spiritual leakage. In the workplace, energetic distortions are the twisted or unhealthy dynamics that arise when truth, equity, and integrity are bent out of shape by power imbalances. They show up as patterns that feel normal within the culture of a workplace but are, in reality, misalignments that harm both people and spirit. Examples of distortions in this sense include:

- Silence being rewarded over honesty
- Favoritism or bias disguised as fairness
- Exploitation that is framed as dedication or loyalty
- Disrespect masked as authority

To accommodate harm in any context is to abandon your inner altar in the name of outer peace. Spiritual Hygiene does not oppose structure; in fact, it is designed to elevate it. It does not reject toxic workplace customs. It aims to provide you with the foundation and tools to infuse any space with soul, integrity, and awareness. From childhood, many people have been taught not to question authority, to be agreeable, and, no matter what, "*Don't rock the boat.*" This conditioning creates spiritual passivity in the workplace masquerading as professional responsibility. We carry these silent contracts into the workplace and refer to them as "being a team player." The truth is, tolerating, accommodating, avoiding, and denying energetic distortions in the workplace is the way to abandon clarity for the illusion of harmony.

When workplace distortions persist, everyone is affected, whether they recognize it or not. The greatest cost is that the nervous system adjusts to dysfunction and begins to call it normal. Silence then becomes a shelter for toxicity. The body carries what the voice has been unable or unwilling to release. Those who live with grace, compassion, or healing energy often find it challenging to initiate confrontation of the distortion, as their natural orientation is toward peace and harmony. Their instinct is to soothe rather than challenge, which can lead to confusing avoidance with compassion or mistaking silence for grace. Yet true grace does not mean accommodating harm. It means standing in truth while rooted in love. Without this, integrity begins to leak, confidence quietly erodes, and the soul whispers: "*This is not who I am.*" Each time distortion is tolerated, a fragment of truth is traded for a false sense of belonging. Left unnamed, compromise hardens into contract, and sacred ground is surrendered.

In the Spirit of Sacred Clarity

In the workplace and in every environment where your soul is asked to show up, remember that you are not just a role, you are also a person. You are present as a vessel of Divine worth. Let this be your vow:

Do not accommodate what erodes your soul.

- No task, title, or paycheck is worth the quiet disintegration of your truth.

Do not tolerate what teaches you to betray yourself.

- When you stay silent in the face of harm, when you smile through dismissal, when you shrink to be accepted, you are not keeping peace; you are abandoning it.

Do not normalize what your body rejects.

- The headaches, the clenched jaw, and the drop in your belly are not inconveniences; they are sacred messages from your inner altar. Your body remembers what your mind tries to justify.

Let it be known:

- Your value is not up for negotiation.
- Your voice is not a disruption.
- Your peace is not a luxury.
- Your boundaries are not a burden.
- Your light is not too much.

It is your Sacred Responsibility to protect them all. Not with harshness, or with ego. Good Spiritual Hygiene gives you the gentle power of a soul that remembers its true nature.

When Conflict Arises: Repairing the Sacred Cord

Every interaction is a form of energetic exchange that creates a connection, a cord, or a disruption between souls. When someone in the workplace behaves in an unruly or harmful way, that connecting cord can fray. Your role is not to fix the cord. Your role is to remain clean in your own energy and clear in your own truth. The following practices are offered to support you in maintaining a clear inner altar, preserving your worth, and maintaining your peace in the workplace:

Anchor Yourself

Before responding to a difficult person or situation:

- Breathe deeply into your body.
- Think silently: *"I will not match this energy. I will return to mine."*
- Place your feet on the ground or your hand on your belly to regulate your nervous system.

Observe, Don't Absorb

If people or situations trigger an upset, ask inwardly:

- *"Is this about me, or is something else speaking through them?"*
- *"What is this moment trying to reveal or teach me?"*
- *"What boundary or clarity is being summoned?"*

This shift from judgment to observation neutralizes the energetic charge.

Respond with Clear Boundaries

Without collapsing or escalating, use clean language to address the behavior:

- *"Can we revisit this when we can both engage respectfully?"*

- *"I'm open to feedback, and I cannot stay in a space where I'm being spoken to this way."*
- *"I understand you are frustrated. I am here to find a solution. It does not require that we engage in conflict."*

This is *spiritual authority* in practice. It is not domination or retreat. It is a demonstration of embodied truth.

Mending the Breach: Sacred Repair

Once the heat subsides and space is available for repair, consider these practices:

Name What Happened (Without Blame)

Use "I" language to describe your experience:

- *"During our last exchange, I felt a break in trust and clarity."*
- *"I want to revisit what happened, so we do not carry unresolved energy forward."*

Extend the Olive Branch Without Abandoning Your Truth

- *"I value our working relationship and would like to clear the air."*
- *"I am open to hearing your perspective if you are willing to have that conversation."*

Reestablish Energetic Boundaries

- *"Moving forward, I would like us to make a commitment to use kind and respectful language."*
- *"As an act of self-care, I want to share that I will step away from interactions that feel harmful or unproductive."*

You are not responsible for another person's behavior. You are responsible for your own integrity, and you have the Sacred Responsibility to close the energetic loop within yourself. To mend a breach is not to forget or deny what happened. It is to weave back a strand of clarity, courage, and care, even if only on your side of the cord. Not every harm will be acknowledged. Not every truth will be received. Not every relationship will be restored, and you can still be clean.

Lydia and the Voice of Worth

Lydia was a bright, capable presence in her organization, a woman of grace and high competence who approached her work as a sacred offering. She did not flaunt her gifts. She let her consistency speak. Lydia entered each day with reverence, treating her work like a prayer. Her spreadsheets were clean. Her reports were precise. Her feedback, when invited, was always thoughtful. Several of her peers had respectfully asked how she managed to bridge her spiritual life with the realities of professional spaces governed by human policy, hierarchy, and procedure. She told them, *"I stopped doing spiritual practices and became the practice. That is the value of good Spiritual Hygiene."* Some of them understood what she meant. Others needed more information and insight. They all, however, agreed on one point: They were glad she had something to protect her because her supervisor, Darren, was not kind.

Darren led with control rather than clarity. He dismissed feedback, cut people off in meetings, and used pressure as his primary leadership tool. Most of the team had grown used to his behavior and silently adapted to avoid conflict. They concluded and accepted that that was just who he was, and he didn't seem to have motivation to change. One day, in a staff meeting, Darren harshly interrupted Lydia mid-sentence:

"That's not what I asked. Pay attention and just answer the question."

The room fell silent. Not only did Lydia not deserve to be spoken to in that manner, but they had never seen or heard it before. Not like that. Not with her.

Lydia's face flushed. Her throat tightened. She felt the old urge to shrink, to keep the peace, to disappear. But something in her refused to betray herself again. She took a deep breath.

She placed her hand below the table to ground her nervous system, and with calm clarity she said:

"Darren, I want to respect the direction you are offering, and I also want to note that being cut off in that way, especially in front of the team, was jarring. I would like to continue, so my request is that we keep the tone respectful."

No anger. No collapse. Just clean truth. Darren paused. He shifted in his seat and said, *"Fine. Go ahead."*

Everyone's gaze shifted to Lydia. Something had changed, not just in Darren, but in the entire room, and in Lydia's soul. She was the youngest of five children who often had to fight to be noticed. On this day, in a toxic and distorted workplace, she had reclaimed her voice without weaponizing it. Later that day, she followed up with him privately, not with bitterness, but with grounded integrity. She asked if he was open to receiving feedback. When he agreed, she said:

"It is important that you know that I am committed to collaboration and clarity. It is also important for you to know that I work best in environments where dignity is mutual."

Darren did not apologize; however, something in their dynamic shifted and softened. He interrupted her and everyone else less. He requested additional input from the team. Most importantly, Lydia never again abandoned her voice in any relationship or experience in her life. Lydia didn't change the workplace system; she changed her inner and outer stance.

She did not yell, or disappear, or compromise. She stayed clean. She stayed clear. She stayed sovereign. This is the holy power of Spiritual Hygiene in professional spaces. It is the path to remaining whole in the presence of distorted power. You may not be able to change the supervisor, but you may awaken the systems. This is what it means to live clean in unclean spaces.

Staying or Leaving: A Spirit-Led Decision

A spiritually unconscious or uncaring supervisor, or an overbearing, gossiping coworker, is not your enemy. It is not your job to awaken them. It is your job not to lose yourself in their unconsciousness. They are your assignment, which is to face them without collapsing. They may:

- Misuse their role to dominate rather than direct
- Ignore emotional harm because "It's just business"
- Resist feedback, belittle boundaries, or dismiss concerns
- Lead through control rather than inspiration

The temptation is either to:

> *Shrink*: go silent, disconnect, and survive beneath their dysfunction, or
>
> *Strike*: lash out, correct them, or demand awakening

Spiritual Hygiene offers a third way: Stay clean. Stay clear. Stay sovereign. This may mean evaluating if your time in the space has come to an end.

There comes a time in every spiritual journey when your assignment and your environment begin to clash. You feel it in your body, the tightening of your chest on Monday morning, the dull ache of your spirit by midweek, and the soul whispering by Friday: *"This is not it."* Yet you have financial responsibilities. You have people depending on you. You wonder if you're being ungrateful or impulsive. You ask yourself, *"Is this fear or freedom knocking on my heart?"* Spiritual Hygiene offers a sacred way to meet this crossroads. It guides you not to rush out of discomfort, nor to remain in misalignment out of guilt, fear, or obligation. Instead, it invites you to pause and ask:

Is this space depleting me or developing me?

Some environments stretch you, challenge you, and sharpen your voice. Others drain your life force. You must discern the difference.

Am I shrinking myself daily just to survive here?

If you silence your truth, dim your gifts, or contort your spirit every day, you are not surviving; you are eroding.

Do I feel more aligned when I imagine leaving or staying?

Sometimes the call is to rise in the environment, not run from it. Other times, your soul is showing you that your chapter is complete.

Am I staying for the love of what I do or am I staying out of fear?

Spiritual Hygiene is not just about where you are, but how you are where you are.

It is not always necessary to leave. Leaving is not the only path to liberation. You can stay and shift the energy. You can stay and strengthen your boundaries. You can stay and prepare your exit with integrity. You can stay and choose your peace every single day. However, when staying in a workplace begins to cost you your health, your voice, your dignity, or your connection to Your Spiritual Self, it has become a sacrifice of your sacred self. This may be a price that is too high.

If your soul's guidance is to remain for now, Spiritual Hygiene is the way you can protect your inner altar:

Start the Day with Alignment, Not Obligation

Before opening your laptop or walking through the door, say:

> *"I enter this day whole, sovereign, and undivided. I am not what I do. I am who I be."*

Take Sacred Pauses

- Step outside.
- Put your hand on your heart.
- Breathe.
- Speak aloud or silently: *"I return to myself."*

Even ninety seconds of alignment can reset your nervous system and reclaim your Spiritual Hygiene.

Fortify Your Field

- Visualize a sphere or globe of Divine light surrounding you. As you establish the light around you, set the intention that nothing enters without your consent.
- Affirm: *"My energy is my responsibility. I choose what stays."*

Make an Exit Plan with a Clean Heart, Rather than a Wounded One

If you are preparing to transition, do so with devotion, not in haste. Create a sacred space and ask:

- *"What is my next aligned step?"*
- *"Who do I need to become to receive it?"*
- *"What sacred support can I call in during this transition?"*

Sometimes the workplace is your assignment. Or it may be your initiation and preparation for something greater. There are also times when your position in a certain place, doing a certain thing, is your completion. You are complete with the patterns of thought and behavior, with self-abandonment, with scarcity and lack, and with fear as the ruling force in your consciousness. Whether you choose to stay or leave a workplace, good Spiritual Hygiene requires that you make a clean decision: one rooted in love, aligned with truth, and anchored in your worth. Wherever you choose to share your time, gifts, and energy as work, always remember, you were never meant to belong to the system; you were sent to bring light to it.

There will be seasons when your outer environment refuses to shift, when people stay in their patterns, when toxicity remains normalized, and when you give your best, only to be met with dismissal or indifference. This is where Spiritual Hygiene in the workplace begins, not as an ego demonstration, but as a devotional practice of inner sovereignty. Your Spiritual Hygiene is not meant to change others; it is meant to keep you clean while the world resists its own healing. Your soul did not come to life or choose certain experiences to survive those systems; it came to transform you, through them. When the space will not or does not shift, sanctify your tasks. Begin everything with intention. Before you answer the email, or enter the meeting, before your hands touch the day's work, return to the altar of why: *"May this task carry the frequency of clarity, care, and grace in service to something greater."* Spiritual Hygiene is not about creating perfect conditions; it is about staying spiritually intact when the conditions are imperfect. You are not failing when the outer does not shift; you are healing the world from the inside out. That takes time, presence, and faith. Even when nothing seems to change, you are changing. That, Beloved, is holy.

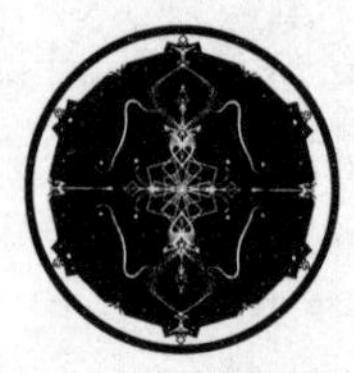

FINAL WORD

Living the Way of Spiritual Hygiene

A Benediction. A Commission. A Sacred Return.

We have walked through the sacred halls of remembrance.

We have knelt before the altars of the mind, heart, body, and soul.

We have looked into the mirror of Self-Honesty.

We have stood in the reckoning of Energetic Responsibility.

We have practiced release, reclamation, forgiveness, and embodiment.

We have awakened your throne of authority and touched the hem of your own Divine nature.

This is no small thing.

Spiritual Hygiene is not just a practice.

It is a path.

It is a promise.

It is a way of living that calls you into sacred alignment every day. The intention is not to become perfect; the intention is to become aware, whole, and present. The intention is not to be holy in appearance; it is to be whole in truth. The question is no longer *"What is Spiritual Hygiene?"* The question becomes *"How will I live what I now know?"*

CONCLUSION

Living Clean

And So, It Shall Be.

Beloved, if you have traveled with me through these chapters, you have already begun the practice of Spiritual Hygiene. You have walked with me through the landscapes of my own life, the tender wounds of childhood neglect and abuse, the harrowing valleys of domestic violence and loss, the sacred thresholds of surrender and self-discovery. You have heard my truth, not as a performance of strength, but as an offering of remembrance: that no matter how deep the stain of trauma, no matter how heavy the residue of grief, the soul is always capable of being cleansed, renewed, and restored.

Just this past month alone, I was reminded that I don't have to be loyal to those who don't treat me well. I was reminded that I can weather even the most serious of emotional crises, even when they affect those closest to me. I was reminded that I know how to grieve. It was a deepening of my understanding that Spiritual Hygiene is not merely a concept or a set of practices; it is a way of life. It is the steady devotion to living in alignment with truth; to cleansing the mind of clutter and false beliefs; to keeping the heart open yet protected; to honoring the body as a living altar; and to remembering the soul as eternal, luminous, and whole. It is the return, again and again, to the seat of inner authority where God speaks in stillness and where clarity replaces confusion.

At the risk of being repetitive, I offer you this final energetic transmission as a gift to your soul. These words are not meant to summarize the content of these pages; they are meant to implant and infuse sacred energy onto the altars of your mind and heart.

When we began this journey, we started with self-awareness: the courage to see what has been hidden, denied, or distorted. Awareness is the light that reveals the cobwebs of the mind, the inherited beliefs we have mistaken for truth, the patterns of survival we once needed but that now keep us small. From there, we entered the temple of self-honesty, where truth confronts illusion. It is in honesty that we peel back the masks, the strong one, the invisible one, the habitual one, the performer, the fixer, and dare to stand unclothed before God and ourselves.

We traveled further into the territory of the heart, learning that unprocessed grief, anger, and betrayal, if left unattended, become toxic residue. Yet when honored as sacred teachers, they can be transformed into compassion, forgiveness, and resilience. I shared with you the moments in my own life when grief almost silenced me, the loss of my Beloved baby girl, the unraveling of relationships I thought were forever, and yet, by choosing to cleanse rather than conceal my sorrow, I found my heart purified and widened to hold even more love.

From the heart, we moved into the body, remembering that our flesh, bones, and breath are not burdens to be carried but holy vessels to be honored. The body tells the truth. It reveals misalignment long before the mind admits it. To tend to rest, movement, nourishment, and sacred rhythms is to keep the altar of the body clean, so that it may host the Spirit in wholeness and vitality.

We also faced the sobering reality of energetic responsibility: that what we think, speak, give, and withhold all have consequences. Energy is never neutral. To gossip, to lie, to misuse resources, to deny rest—these are not minor lapses; they are breaches that weaken our field. And yet, each breach can be healed, each distortion can be cleansed, each misstep can be redeemed when brought into the light of consciousness and corrected with love.

The final movements of our journey carried us into authority, sovereignty, and reclamation. We learned that to live with Spiritual Hygiene is to sit upon the throne of the self, not as tyrant, not as victim, but as a sovereign steward of Divine presence. It is to say no when the soul says no, and yes only when the yes is clean. It is to sanctify relationships, parenting, work, money, and community, not by perfection, but by presence, discernment, and devotion.

My life, Beloved, has been both the curriculum and the testimony of these teachings. I offer you not what I "know," but what I have lived and died through in order to get and live clean. I am not whole because I escaped pain, but because I chose to cleanse the residue that pain left behind. I am not aligned because I have never stumbled, but because I am now aware that each fall invited me to return to truth. I am not luminous because life spared me from darkness, but because I learned that light is not the absence of the shadow; it is the willingness to shine through the presence of what feels dark.

And so, I leave you here, not with marching orders, but with an invitation. Let Spiritual Hygiene be more than words on a page. Let it become your breath, your posture, your prayer, your way of being. Clean living is not about denying the dirt; it is about knowing where to go when life soils you. Clean living is not about being untouched; it is about being willing to be washed from the inside out. Clean living is not about never breaking; it is about allowing every break to be mended by Spirit's hands.

Beloved, remember this: You are the sanctuary. You are the altar. You are the vessel of Divine light. Keep yourself clean, not for fear of judgment, but for love of your own soul. And know this: When the dust settles, when the day ends, when the grief comes, when the joy rises, you must, and you can, return again and again to the sacred practice of cleansing. In your practice, you will not only find yourself renewed; you will become a living blessing, a radiant presence of wholeness, and a testimony that God actually can make all things new.

Glossary of Spiritual Principles and Sacred Concepts

These offerings are not standard dictionary definitions. Each word has been interpreted through a spiritual lens, rooted in the living practice of Spiritual Hygiene. These are sacred concepts, alive with energy, mystery, and multidimensional meaning. A sacred concept is not merely meant to be understood; it is meant to be felt, embodied, and experienced. It carries presence. It opens a doorway into the vibrational essence of what it names. These definitions reflect energetic awareness, soul-centered insight, and sacred application, not linguistic precision. They are the meanings we live by, the truths we embody, and the frequencies we consciously cultivate in devotion to wholeness and Spiritual Hygiene. With each concept, you are offered an Invocation to support you in moving toward the embodiment of the concept.

ACCEPTANCE

A holy surrender to what is, without resistance, denial, or judgment. Acceptance is the open hand of the soul, making peace with the present so transformation may begin.

Invocation:
"Beloved Presence of Peace, soften my heart to what is. Where I have resisted, let me now receive. Where I have judged, let me now understand. May I meet this moment with grace, and trust that even this is part of my becoming."

ACCOUNTABILITY

The sacred courage to witness and tend to the ripple of your actions. It is not punishment. It is a pathway to alignment and relational integrity.

Invocation:
"Holy Presence of Truth and Grace, grant me the courage to stand in the light of accountability. Where I have caused harm, let me seek to make amends. Where I have hidden from responsibility, let me return to a state of alignment. May I own my impact with compassion, clarity, and a heart devoted to wholeness."

ACKNOWLEDGMENT

The sacred act of witnessing truth within yourself, others, or the moment with presence, humility, and reverence. Acknowledgment does not fix or force; it honors what is seen, heard, and felt as valid and real. It is the first step in healing, the soft unveiling of what longs to be named.

Invocation:
"Holy Witness of All That Is, teach me to acknowledge with an open heart. Let me see without judgment, speak without defense, and honor what rises in myself and others with sacred presence. May my acknowledgment become a balm, a bridge, and a blessing."

AFFIRMATION

A sacred statement of truth spoken with intention to align consciousness with Divine reality.

Invocation:
"Sacred Voice within me, may the words I speak carry the light of the unseen into the realm of form. Let every syllable be a thread of connection between what is Divine and what is human. May I only speak what is true, whole, and aligned with love. Let every declaration rise as a sacred offering to the Divine."

ALIGNMENT

The energetic state of harmony between thought, word, action, and Divine intention.

Invocation:
"Holy One of Order and Flow, bring me into alignment with what is real. Where I have wandered, return me. Where I have twisted truth, straighten me. Let my life become a reflection of Divine Harmony."

ALTAR

A designated sacred space, internal or external, where presence, reverence, and Divine connection are cultivated.

Invocation:
"Spirit of the Living Temple, may I remember that I am the altar. Consecrate this body, this breath, this life as a space where You dwell. Let all I do rise as sacred incense before You."

AUTHENTICITY

Authenticity is the soul's alignment with truth. It is living in harmony with who you truly are beneath conditioning, performance, and fear. It is the voice of the Divine made personal, expressed without distortion or apology.

Invocation:
"Holy and Infinite Presence, may I live from the truth of who I am. Strip away all false masks, and let the radiance of my soul shine unfiltered through my words, my choices, and my presence."

AUTHORITY

The inner seat of Divine rulership where soul-knowing governs choices, not fear or control.

Invocation:
"Sovereign Presence, restore the crown within. Let me no longer give away my voice to fear or distortion. Let me rule from the throne of truth, guided by the wisdom of Spirit."

BELIEF

Belief is the seed of possibility rooted in the unseen. It is the soul's agreement with a higher truth, even in the absence of evidence. Belief gives birth to faith and opens the heart to the possibility of miracles.

Invocation:
"Infinite Creator, I ask that You deepen my belief. Let me believe in what You have whispered into my soul. Strengthen my inner knowing and make my belief unshakable. Even when I doubt, let my soul remember. Let my trust be in what cannot be shaken or stolen."

CLARITY

The Divine gift of spiritual vision and understanding beyond confusion or distortion.

Invocation:
"Spirit of Illumination, lift the fog from my sight. Clear the noise in my mind and the fear in my heart. Let me see with the eyes of the soul and know with the wisdom of heaven."

CLEANSE

The intentional release of what no longer serves, energetically, emotionally, mentally, or spiritually.

Invocation:

"Sacred Wind and Holy Water, wash me. Cleanse the remnants of what is not mine. Let my soul be clear, my heart be light, and my body be restored to its sacred purity."

CONFLICT

When met with grace and accountability, conflict is an invitation to reveal the truth, integrate shadows, and achieve conscious alignment.

Invocation:

"God of Peace and Purification, may I face conflict with sacred clarity. Let no part of me flee from truth. Show me what is mine, what is distorted, and what is ready to be healed."

CONSCIOUSNESS

The ever-expanding awareness of self, Spirit, and sacred reality, the field through which Divine presence moves.

Invocation:

"Eternal One, awaken my consciousness. Expand my awareness beyond limitation. Let me walk with holy eyes open, attuned to the sacred in all things."

DECLARATION

A conscious invocation of spiritual truth spoken aloud to activate alignment and manifestation.

Invocation:

"Word of Power, Living Word of the Most High, let my voice become Your vessel. May every declaration I speak call forth wholeness, awaken power, and honor the Divine Contract of my Soul."

DETERMINATION

Sacred perseverance rooted in Divine devotion—not force, but soul-guided intention anchored in the heart.

Invocation:

"Sacred Flame of the Inner Will, ignite my path with holy resolve. Strengthen my steps when I grow weary. Let my determination be an extension of devotion, not homage to the ego."

DISTORTION

A misalignment of perception, belief, or energy that clouds truth and disconnects from spiritual integrity.

Invocation:
"Revealer of All Truth, dissolve every distortion that has wrapped itself around my perception. May I no longer follow what is false. Lead me back to clarity and soul alignment."

DIVINE

That which is sacred, eternal, and uncreated. The Divine is the source and sustainer of all life—formless, and yet present in all form. It is the Indwelling Presence within and the Infinite Intelligence beyond. To encounter the Divine is to remember your origin, your wholeness, and your belonging to something holy and immeasurable.

Invocation:
"O Divine Presence, vast and intimate, within and beyond, reveal Yourself in all that I am and all that I see. Let me no longer search outside of You or separate myself from You. May I live as an emanation of Your light, a vessel of Your truth, and a dwelling place of Your love."

ENERGETIC

Relating to the unseen life force that moves through and around all things, shaping environments, emotions, and experiences.

Invocation:
"Divine Breath that animates all life, make me aware of the energy I carry and transmit. Let my field be clear, my intentions pure, and my presence a healing current in the world."

FREEDOM

Freedom is the liberation of the soul from illusion, fear, and bondage. It is not the absence of limits but the presence of Divine alignment that makes all things possible.

Invocation:
"O Liberating Light, break every chain of illusion and fear. Free me from false identities and inherited burdens. Let me rise in the freedom that can only come from walking with You."

FREQUENCY

The vibrational signature of your being. Frequency is how your inner world communicates with the Universe. What you are, you attract. What you hold, you harmonize with.

Invocation:
"Divine Harmonics of the Living Light, tune me to the frequency of love, truth, and wholeness. Let every cell of my being resonate with sacred intention. May I release all that lowers my vibration and rise into the radiant song of my soul."

FULFILLMENT

Fulfillment is the feeling of spiritual rightness. A resonance that arises when your soul is nourished, your gifts are offered, and your life reflects your essence.

Invocation:
"Source of All Good, fill me from the inside out. Let me be satisfied not by what I acquire, but by who I become in alignment with You. Make me whole. Make me well. Make me fulfilled."

HEALING

A sacred return to truth, wholeness, and Divine remembrance. Healing is not the erasure of pain, but the integration of wisdom. It is the unfolding journey of reclaiming what was lost, loving what was wounded, and awakening what is holy.

Invocation:
"Sacred Healer, move through every layer of my being. Touch what I cannot name. Restore what I have buried. Teach me that nothing is wasted, and that even my pain is a pathway to grace. May I allow healing to come gently, deeply, and in Divine Time."

HEALTHY

A state of wholeness and harmony within the body, mind, heart, and spirit. To be healthy is to be in alignment with truth, nourished, clear, rested, and rooted in choices that honor life. Health is not only the absence of illness, but the presence of sacred rhythm, balance, and reverence for your temple.

Invocation:
"Giver of Life and Breath, align me with what is healthy and whole. Let my thoughts nourish me. Let my choices honor this sacred body. Let my boundaries reflect what is loving. May I dwell in vitality, clarity, and balance as a living prayer of wellness."

HYGIENE

The devotional practice of cleansing the inner and outer life to maintain spiritual integrity and energetic clarity.

Invocation:

"Holy One of Clean Hands and Pure Heart, teach me to tend to my temple. Let no toxic thought, emotion, or agreement linger in me. Make me clean within and radiant without."

INNER AUTHORITY

Inner authority is the sacred seat of power within. It is the voice of Divine knowing that arises from spiritual alignment, not egoic control. It governs not through domination, but through devotion to truth.

Invocation:

"Infinite One, restore the throne within me. Let me rise in the quiet confidence of my Divine Knowing. May I no longer outsource my power or my wisdom, or betray my knowing. May I always trust the whisper of Your truth within."

LIGHT

The essence of Divine truth, clarity, and presence. Light is not just illumination; it is a revelation. It reveals what is hidden, heals what is hurting, and awakens what is holy. It is the soul's native language, the signature of the Divine within all things.

Invocation:

"Radiant Source of All Light, shine through me. Illuminate every shadow with compassion. Let Your light be my guide, my ground, and my truth. May I walk as light, speak as light, and become a living flame of remembrance in a world that forgets."

MIND

A temple of thought, memory, and meaning, designed to be a servant of Spirit, not its master.

Invocation:

"Sanctifier of Thought, make my mind a clear sanctuary. Let every thought be rooted in love, guided by truth, and aligned with Divine Wisdom."

NEUTRALITY

The sacred stillness between judgment and clarity. A resting place for the soul to observe, listen, and discern without reacting.

Invocation:
"Holy Silence, teach me the power of neutrality. Let me see without attachment, choose without fear, and witness from the seat of Spirit."

OWNERSHIP

Ownership is sacred accountability. It is the willingness to take full responsibility for your energy, your choices, and your experience, not as punishment, but as power reclaimed.

Invocation:
"Spirit of Truth, I claim my life as mine. I own what I've created, and I now make a new choice. May I walk in the authority of radical responsibility, knowing that every step is a sacred act of creation."

PATIENCE

The holy capacity to wait in faith, honoring Divine timing without rushing, forcing, or fear.

Invocation:
"Ancient One, let me rest in the rhythm of sacred time. I surrender urgency and control. May I learn to wait with peace, knowing that what is mine to be, do, or have will come with grace."

PEACE

Peace is the stillness of Divine presence within. It is not the absence of conflict, but the awareness of harmony that transcends it. Peace arises when the heart surrenders to what is and remembers what cannot be shaken.

Invocation:
"Sacred Source of Stillness, anchor me in peace. In the midst of movement, in the face of change, let me remember the quiet center of my being where You and I are One."

PERFORMANCE

The ego's attempt to earn love, prove worth, or avoid rejection by masking and distorting the sacred truth of the soul.

Invocation:
"Source of Unconditional Love, release me from the need to perform. Let me show up in truth, not in disguise. Teach me that who I am is already enough."

POWER

The spiritual ability to create, align, and transform. Power is not dominance or domination. It is the resonance of and with Divine will. It is the Divine current that flows when truth, will, and Spirit are in harmony. True power seeks to create, to liberate, and to uplift in love.

Invocation:
"Infinite Source of Sacred Power, anchor me in truth that does not tremble. Let my power be clean, rooted, and humble, never taken, never forced. May I remember that real power is not over others, but in the integrity of how I show up in the world."

PRESENCE

The conscious embodiment of the now moment where Spirit meets you, breath by breath.

Invocation:
"Eternal Now, awaken me to this moment. Let me not rush ahead or dwell behind. May I inhabit this breath with reverence, and meet You here, now."

PURPOSE

The soul's sacred assignment. The unique way you are called to serve, embody, and express Divine essence.

Invocation:
"Divine Designer, awaken my purpose. Let my life be a holy offering, aligned with the reason I came. May I live what I was born to remember."

RADIANCE

Radiance is the unfiltered expression of Divine light from within. It is the glow of authenticity, the warmth of aligned presence, and the energetic signature of a soul living in truth. Radiance does not demand attention. It emanates as essence.

Invocation:
"Holy Light within me, let my being shine without fear or filter. May I radiate love, clarity, and grace in all that I do. Remove the veils of shame and shrinking, so that I will allow my presence to become a reflection of Your beauty made visible."

REFLECTION

The soul's sacred pause. A time of turning inward to witness, integrate, and grow in awareness. A sacred mirror through which the soul is invited to witness its truth. Reflection reveals what lives within by what is shown without through experiences, relationships, emotions, and encounters. What you see, feel, or react to in others is often a reflection of your own unhealed, unclaimed, or unrecognized self.

Invocation:

"Holy Mirror of Divine Wisdom, show me what I need to see with gentle clarity. Let me not reject what appears before me. I am open to receiving it as a messenger. Where I judge, let me inquire. Where I react, let me reflect. May every reflection become a portal to deeper self-awareness and sacred realignment."

RELEASE

The sacred act of letting go to grow. Release is not abandonment; it is liberation. It creates space for what is real to return and what is false to dissolve. It is the holy act of letting go of patterns, identities, energies, and attachments that no longer serve the soul's becoming. Release is not rejection. It is a reverent surrender. It is the soul's exhale, the clearing that makes space for Divine restoration.

Invocation:

"Sacred One who holds all things in love, I open my hands and my heart. I release what no longer serves my becoming. I let go of what I tried to fix, carry, or force. Make space within me for truth, for peace, for what is next on my sacred path."

RESONANCE

A sacred vibrational harmony. A recognition between frequencies that match, mirror, or awaken one another. Resonance is how the soul remembers, how truth is felt before it is understood, and how Divine alignment is revealed without force.

Invocation:

"Spirit of Vibration and Voice, attune me to what is true. Let my being resonate only with what is aligned, whole, and holy. May I release what no longer echoes the sound of my soul and move toward what sings me open in love."

REVERENCE

An inner posture of deep honor, for life, Spirit, self, and all creation. Reverence transforms how we walk, speak, and see.

Invocation:

"Holy One in All Things, teach me to move in reverence. Let me speak with care, listen with awe, and bow before the sacred woven into every moment."

SELF-ESTEEM

Self-esteem is the soul's memory of its worth. It is the natural by-product of living in alignment with the truth that you are loved, needed, chosen, and whole. It is a reflection of how you perceive yourself and regard yourself, within yourself.

Invocation:

"Creator of All Life, return me to the holy truth of my value. Let me speak of myself with reverence, treat myself with honor, and remember I am an irreplaceable expression of You."

SELF-EXPRESSION

Self-expression is the soul's sacred exhale. It is the Divine outpouring of your inner truth, beauty, creativity, and knowing into the world—spoken, written, danced, wept, or witnessed. It is not performance. It is a revelation. When aligned with Spirit, self-expression becomes an act of worship and a bridge between the inner and outer worlds.

Invocation:

"Holy Spirit, breathe through me. Let my voice be a vessel for Your truth. Let my words, my art, my movements, and my silence be expressions of the sacred spark within me. Remove fear and hesitation. May I no longer hide what You have made holy."

SELF-HONESTY

The sacred courage to witness and tell the truth to oneself without distortion, denial, or shame.

Invocation:

"Spirit of Truth, shine Your light within me. Let me face myself with compassion and clarity. May I no longer hide behind illusion but stand in the holy mirror of honesty."

SELF-VALUE

The sacred recognition of one's inherent significance, not based on productivity or praise, but rooted in being. It is a function of how you see yourself and regard yourself, within yourself, which determines what you expect for yourself, and from yourself.

Invocation:

"Divine Appraiser, remind me that I am priceless. Let me no longer question what You have called precious. Teach me to honor my value in how I speak, give, and receive."

SELF-WORTH

The unshakable knowing that your existence is sacred, necessary, and enough. Self-worth is not earned; it is remembered. It is the spiritual foundation upon which all alignment, boundaries, and belonging are built. It reflects how you perceive yourself and regard yourself, which in turn determines what you expect from others and the world.

Invocation:

"Eternal Source, root me in holy worth, and restore the truth of my worth within me. Let me no longer measure myself by wounds, roles, or the eyes of others. Strip away all false metrics and awaken the dignity of who I am, holy, whole, and deserving of every good thing You have placed along my path."

SHADOW

The unseen, suppressed, or rejected parts of the self—holding keys to healing when approached with love and awareness.

Invocation:

"Healer of the Hidden, I no longer fear my shadow. Let me bring Your light into all that has been concealed. May I meet every wound with mercy and integrate every truth with grace."

SIMPLICITY

Simplicity is the return to essence. It is the stripping away of distraction, excess, and striving until only the sacred remains. Simplicity invites peace by clearing space for what is real.

Invocation:

"Divine Essence, return me to what matters. Let me release the clutter within and around me. May I find joy in simplicity and rest in the sacredness of enough."

SOVEREIGNTY

The Divine state of self-governance ruling one's energy, choices, and life from the throne of spiritual alignment.

Invocation

"Ancient Sovereign, awaken my holy dominion. May I take my seat at the throne within. Let me lead my life with wisdom, courage, and truth."

SPIRITUAL

That which is eternal, unseen, and rooted in Divine origin, the sacred pulse beneath all things.

Invocation:

"Infinite Spirit, make me a vessel of Your presence. Let me walk not just in belief, but in embodiment. May my life be a living prayer."

STRENGTH

Strength is the steady current of Spirit within. It is not domination or resistance; it is Divine resilience, the inner knowing that you can endure, rise, and remain grounded in truth.

Invocation:

"Eternal Strength, rise in me. Let me be rooted and unshakable in the truth of who I am. Even when I tremble, let me stand in You."

TEMPLE

A consecrated dwelling place of the Divine. Your body, your breath, your being, each is a living temple. To honor the temple is to revere the vessel through which Spirit expresses, heals, and becomes visible in form.

Invocation:

"Indwelling Divine, I honor this body as holy ground. Let me walk in reverence for the temple You have entrusted to me. May I nourish it, listen to it, and treat it with sacred care, knowing that within me, You dwell."

TRANSFORMATION

Transformation is the sacred alchemy of becoming. It is not a change for the sake of change. It is the shedding of illusion and the emergence of Divine remembrance. Transformation births wholeness through surrender.

Invocation:

"Divine Alchemist, transform me. Let what is no longer true fall away. Let what is eternal in me rise. May I be renewed by Your fire and reshaped by Your love."

VULNERABILITY

Vulnerability is sacred openness. It is the courageous act of being seen, felt, and known without armor. Vulnerability creates the space for intimacy, with Self, with others, and with the Divine.

Invocation:

"Tender and Holy One, teach me to open without fear. Let my vulnerability be my strength. May I no longer hide behind protection, but trust that You dwell where I am real."

WELL-BEING

Well-being is the sacred harmony of body, mind, heart, and spirit in alignment with Divine truth. It is more than the absence of illness or distress. It is the presence of vitality, peace, and purpose. Well-being flows when your life is balanced, your energy is tended to, and your choices honor what is nourishing and life-giving. It is both a state of being and a practice of devotion to the wholeness of the self.

Invocation:
"Divine Source of Life, Breath within my breath, Light within my being, I call forth the principle of Well-Being. May my mind be steady, clear, and at peace. May my heart be open, healed, and whole. May my body rest in balance, strength, and vitality. May my soul remember its eternal harmony with You."

WHOLENESS

The integrated state of living from all parts of the self, light and shadow, body and soul in harmony with truth.

Invocation:
"One Who Makes All Things Whole, gather every piece of me. Restore what I cast away. Let me live in the peace of integration and the power of Divine Wholeness."

WILLINGNESS

Willingness is the heart's sacred "yes." It is the soul's consent to healing, even when the path is unclear. Willingness opens the door to grace by loosening the grip of fear and control.

Invocation:
"Holy Presence, I may not know how, but I am willing. I offer You my "yes." Let it become the seed of transformation. Let willingness be the doorway through which You enter my life."

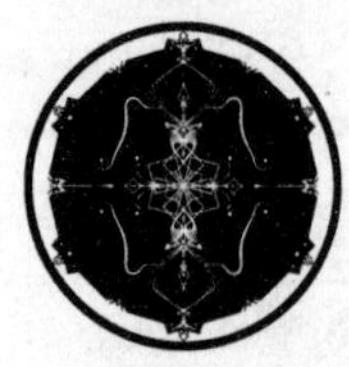

Acknowledgments

The Lord is my Shepherd. He led me into the depths of my heart and soul to birth this work. For this, I Am humbled and grateful. I Am also grateful for the way God/Source/Creator has and continues to reveal Itself in my life as:

The In A Vision Entertainment Team: Zakiya Fatin Cornwell, Jeune AdeOri Taylor, Darvel McKinney, Dena Jakos, Ayan'fe Rosano, Khalaa King, Amina Jenkins, Justine Sones, Mallory Poort, Carmen Rodriguez, and Annette Matthews. Thank you for allowing me to be the brains, and I honor you as my muscles.

The Inner Visions Institute faculty: Rev. Elease Welch, Rev. Tammie Fiola Manly, Rev. Rosetta Hillary, Rev. Heather Bo'lade Mizel, Rev. Matt Cartwright, Rev. Carmen Gonzalez, Rev. Karen Folu'ke Burns, Rev. Lynn Horton, Rev. Danielle Hatchell, Coach Robert Pruitt, Coach Maqueita Eleazer, Coach Jackie Smith, Coach Marion Stukes, Rev. Yolanda Wooten, and all of the students who have accommodated my comings and goings.

Each of the Inner Visions Spiritual Warriors, Rites of Passage graduates, Spiritual Study Sanctuary community members, and the IVISD students and staff. Thank you for being my guinea pigs and trusting me with your minds, hearts, and souls. You have given me the courage to live outside of my comfort zone.

My Enlightened Heart Shamanic family: Rachel Mann, PhD; Laura Wurst; Luke Scaros; Kimberly Dawkins; Afiya; LaShaun; Susan; Patricia; and of course, my man, Ben. My godchildren, the members of

Ile Omi Meji, I cannot thank you enough for your unwavering support and your willingness always to answer my call.

My Ride-or-Die support team: Lydia Ifetayo Potter, Laura Devaji Rawlings, Richard Mcilwain, and Aldo OriZen Valmon-Clark, thank you for keeping my home, grandson, and dogs safe and fed.

Rev. Shaheerah Stephens, Rev. Danni Stillwell, and Almasi Wilcots, my sisters from other mothers who are always there to hold me, help me, listen to me, correct me, and pray for me when I forget to pray for myself.

Michelle Herrera Mulligan, my most phenomenal editor. Thank you for listening and caring about what I thought, felt, and had to say. Your patience will be rewarded.

Ms. Oprah Winfrey, thank you is hardly sufficient to describe the depth, breadth, and grace of your generosity. Instead, I offer a Deep Bow of gratitude for your support and guidance always, in all ways.

My champion, cheerleader, coach, friend, and son, Damon Bware Ogunbi'Ide. You are truly the wind beneath my wings.

And, my shelters in any storm: Awo Sean Christopher Gayle, Cheryl Elemi Gayle, Dr. Robert and Mrs. Raina Bundy, Peter Grube, Tulani Kinard, Deborah Chinaza Lee (Ibai'ye), Gemmia OrishaSami (Ibai'ye), Nisa Emi'Olade (Ibai'ye), Rev. Helen Alva Jones (Ibai'ye), and Awo Albert Oceguera (Ibai'ye).

About the Author

Iyanla Vanzant, also known by her sacred name A'mari El'Naiya, is recognized around the world as one of the foremost spiritual teachers of our time. With more than eight million books in print, she has guided generations of readers and seekers through her best-selling works, her groundbreaking television series *Iyanla: Fix My Life*, and her decades of teaching, rooted in ancient wisdom, lived experience, and the practical application of spiritual principles.

Iyanla's life is a living testimony of resilience and faith. From the wounds of childhood neglect, abuse, and poverty to the trials of domestic violence and single motherhood, she chose a path of transformation, pursuing higher education, law, ministry, and ultimately, sacred service. As a public defender in Philadelphia, she stood for the voiceless, and as an ordained minister and spiritual life coach, she has dedicated her life to helping others reclaim their inner authority and return to wholeness.

Her breakthrough book *In the Meantime* became a #1 *New York Times* bestseller, and since then she has authored numerous classics, including *Acts of Faith* and *Yesterday, I Cried*. Her voice has become a healing balm for millions seeking truth, clarity, and alignment in an often-chaotic world.

Beyond accolades and recognition, Iyanla's true work is soul work. Through the Inner Visions Institute for Spiritual Development (IVISD) and the Spiritual Sanctuary, she continues to serve as a spiritual midwife, guide, and teacher of sacred principles. Extending this mission into daily practice, she created MasterPeace Body Therapy, a line of natural products designed to support Spiritual Hygiene for the body and mind.

With compassion, honesty, and Divine authority, she calls us back to the altar of our own souls. Her message is simple yet profound: Healing is possible, alignment is sacred, and the practice of Spiritual Hygiene is essential to living a life of peace, power, and purpose. Iyanla named her home Villa Nova, a New Vision. She resides there with her great-grandson; Ms. Peace and Ms. Freedom, her two Pomeranians; Mr. Joi, her cat; and Love and Happiness, two turtles she rescued from the road. For more information, visit iyanla.com.

Iyanla's
OFFERINGS

IYANLA.COM

Iyanla.com
Iyanla.com is where you'll find daily inspiration, practic resources, and direct ways to engage with me and my work.

IVISD

Inner Visions Institute for Spiritual Development (IVISD)
Here, you will find courses, programs, and teachings that w guide you through the deep work of self-discovery and spiritu mastery. This is where students come to strengthen their inn foundation, heal what hurts, and awaken to their Divine potenti

IVSS

Inner Visions Spiritual Sanctuary (IVSS)
The Sanctuary is the heartbeat of our community—a sacr circle where we gather for prayer, for spiritual nourishmer and for the practices that restore our souls. If you are seeki community, belonging, and a place to rest your soul—this your refuge.

MASTERPEACE

MasterPeace
MasterPeace Body Therapy is made with pure plant extracts a natural mineral ingredients. Each blend is uniquely formulat by selecting the perfect ingredients to stimulate the sens and enact the healing powers of each aromatic compound.